D1373851

LADIES, START YOUR ENGINES

LADIES, START YOUR ENGINES

❖ ❖ ❖

Women Writers on Cars and the Road

❖ ❖ ❖

EDITED BY ELINOR NAUEN

Faber and Faber
BOSTON • LONDON

Library of Congress Cataloging-in-Publication Data

Ladies, start your engines : women writers on cars and the road / edited by Elinor Nauen.
    p.   cm.
ISBN 0-571-19895-3 (cloth)
1. Automobiles—Fiction. 2. Women automobile drivers—Fiction. 3. Short stories, American—Women authors. 4. Automobile driving—Fiction. 5. Automobile travel—Fiction. 6. Women automobile drivers. 7. Automobile driving. 8. Automobile travel. 9. Automobiles. I. Nauen, Elinor.
PS648.A85L33 1996
813'.0108356—dc20   96-14820
                                                         CIP

Jacket design by Ha Nguyen
Printed in the United States of America

For my mother, my first driver

For some of the women of my road trips: Sherri Clixby,
Maggie Dubris, Deborah (Hansen) Linzer, Sondra McCart,
Janet Mullen, Varda Binglebumpf Nauen, Alexandra Neil,
Kay Spurlock, Rachel Walling, Beth Ward

And for the intrepid and patient Mr. Raymond Shelver,
my driver's ed. teacher

❖

What I like, or one of the things I like, about motoring is the sense it gives one of lighting accidentally . . . upon scenes which would have gone on, have always gone on, will go on, unrecorded, save for this chance glimpse. Then it seems to me I am allowed to see the heart of the world uncovered for a moment.

—VIRGINIA WOOLF

Contents

Part III

Introduction

The story in my family goes that my father was driving to the cemetery after a funeral, when one of his passengers remarked that she hoped this wouldn't be a one-way trip. Dad pulled over, got out of the driver's seat and into the back without a word, and never drove again.

I was born that same year, a kid who somehow grew up thinking that cars and driving are the coolest things in the world. In part that came, for sure, because my dad's case of nerves freed my mother to drive and, eventually, bestow on me a love of driving.

It also came from growing up on the wide prairies of the Dakotas, where cars are a necessity. You got your license on your sixteenth birthday, then drove, you drove, you drove everywhere, anywhere— five hours to see a movie, three hours to go swimming, half a day to tell someone you couldn't make it to their party. You cruised back roads and Main Street, hunting wild asparagus, watching red-winged blackbirds flick off telephone wires, spotting out-of-state plates, revving those big real-steel automobiles up to 120 on the straightaway. Car songs sailing wild and free to the horizon.

Americans, as everyone knows, are famously restless, so it's no surprise that cars are a fundamental part of being an American in this large, well-paved country. (We own 144 million autos and every year drive an average of 11,000-plus miles each on 3.9 million miles of public roads.) A car means getting away, something women have often longed to do. Historically, cars unshackled women from farm and home. Who knew what went on—and if they did, they couldn't stop it. And what went on was anything from an afternoon in town or at a no-tell motel to cross-country drives, singing along to thoughts and not-thoughts. Adrienne Rich's beautiful "Song" sent me on many a continental rave.

The origin of this book lies in the companionship I so often felt, and feel, with others' thoughts on what it means to be on the endless road. So many good trips, so many close encounters in the steamy intimacy of a car, driving through the night, opening up in a way you couldn't anywhere else. Sailing along in that most personal of possessions, we may come to think of the car as a body that encloses us. That's the origin and intention and beauty of *Ladies, Start Your Engines: Women Writers on Cars and the Road.*

In 1896 the first automobile—then known variously as the autowain, self-motor, petrocar, autobat, diamote, autogo, pneumobile, motocycle, or ipsometer—was sold in the United States. Before cars, people got around on horses, which had the disadvantage of dropping forty-five pounds of dung apiece every day, not to mention the tendency to drop dead in the street—15,000 a year died in New York City alone. Horses were the source of air pollution, noise, congestion, flies and disease, and accidents. The automobile, doctors and others confidently predicted, would be a healthy replacement.

For women, advantages piled up. No longer did physical strength, for managing a horse or team of horses, matter so much. A private car was considered more suitable for ladies than the public, and therefore immodest, trolley. In 1899, the first woman received a driver's license. In 1909, six years after it had been done for the first time by a man, Alice Huyler Ramsey undertook a transcontinental drive. Accompanied by three female chaperones and a support vehicle of mechanics and supplies, she became the first woman to drive across America, taking forty-one days to get from New York to San Francisco. She repeated that drive every year until she died in 1983 at the age of ninety-six—still with a valid license. In 1915, by which time a woman was driving a taxi in New York City, Emily Post—yes, *that* Emily Post—made her own cross-country drive. A selection from her amusing *By Motor to the Golden Gate* is included here. Another early adopter was Edith Wharton, from whose *A Motor-Flight Through France* I've drawn a short selection.

With this in mind, "woman driver" as a term of disapprobation can be chucked in a flash. Stats? Men drivers die in accidents at three times the rate of women, according to the National Highway Traffic Safety Administration. (Which has never stopped men from grabbing the wheel—in ancient Rome, they prohibited women from driving chariots.) Women have more stamina on long-distance trips, say other studies.

Women were writing about cars as soon as they were driving. Soon after the turn of the century, they were featured in *Ladies' Home Journal*, *Vanity Fair*, *Harper's Bazaar*, and the new *Motor* magazine with such articles as "A Woman's Viewpoint," "The Frivolous Girl Goes Motoring," and "Woman at the Motor Wheel."

At the start of putting this collection together, I was sure it would turn out to be a book full of Sunday drives, racing, and the joy of the open road. There's a generous dose of that, to be sure, but lots more. Some (Kate Culkin, Maggie Dubris) have written about what it means to be a woman driving, alone or with others, with the clear recognition that the driver, literally and symbolically, has the power. Cars become the subject for some writers (Gail Mazur, Susan Firer) when they collide with car or traffic cop. Love—of, in, around, because of an auto—is a major theme ("This Darknight Speed" by Eloise Klein Healy, "Fast Lanes" by Jayne Anne Phillips), as is the car as house, bedroom, kitchen; it's said that in the Depression, people were more willing to give up their homes than their vehicles (see Deanne Stillman's noirish "You Should Have Been Here an Hour Ago" for a modern *Grapes of Wrath*). Mechanics show up too (Katharine Harer's "Midas Muffler"), with their terrific stories and muscles. According to the Department of Labor, only one-half of one percent of auto mechanics in the U.S. are women. Do we have crushes because they can do what we wish we could?

A note on what's *not* here: As with any anthology, what the editor falls in love with determines how the book comes out. In other words, I have imposed my taste. Given the importance of the automobile, it makes sense that writers have focused on it. The challenge was choosing among the numerous terrific works. Some wonderful stories and poems I decided against because they'd been anthologized to death. Also, novels in general don't stand up to excerpting, and for that reason I urge the reader to Jan Kerouac's *Baby Driver*, Sharlene Baker's spirited *Finding Signs*, and Cynthia Kadohata's *The Floating World*.

I look at *Ladies, Start Your Engines* as a piece of a conversation and not the last word. What's here—this engaging mix of fiction, nonfiction, and poetry with women's view of that most American of icons—rebuts the idea that only guys, only Jack Kerouac's sons, can go on the road.

We're here to stay—and *go*.

New York City
June, 1996

Note: Among the excellent histories I drew upon with interest and thanks are *Automania: Man* [sic] *and the Motor Car* by Julian Pettifer and Nigel Turner, K. T. Berger's *Where the Road and the Sky Collide: America through the Eyes of its Drivers* and especially Virginia Scharff's *Taking the Wheel: Women and the Coming of the Motor Age*. It reassures me to know that women have always driven and owned cars—and always fought with men who thought we shouldn't.

Part One

Everything good is on the highway.
RALPH WALDO EMERSON

EMILY DICKINSON

585

Emily Dickinson was either psychic in writing this—and isn't that just like a poet—or she was talking about a train, since she died the year the car was invented (1886). It's a bit of a joke to include this, I confess—but "docile and omnipotent" nails it, no?—ed.

I like to see it lap the Miles—
And lick the Valleys up—
And stop to feed itself at Tanks—
And then—prodigious step

Around a Pile of Mountains—
And supercilious peer
In Shanties—by the sides of Roads—
And then a Quarry pare

To fit its Ribs
And crawl between
Complaining all the while
In horrid—hooting stanza—
Then chase itself down Hill—

And neigh like Boangeres—
Then—punctual as a Star
Stop—docile and omnipotent
At its own stable door—

ELOISE KLEIN HEALY

This Darknight Speed

Sometimes I feel about love
like driving places at darknight speed
with the radio on,
doing what that saxophone
was barking in the bar:
"better yet, better yet, better get in a car!"

Sometimes I forget
simple words like rapture
for this animal joy,
this sense of being up to speed
and merging from a ramp,
knowing the driver in the mirror
is already adjusting to meet me
and wants it to go smooth,
wants me to have my turn,
not break acceleration
or miss a beat,

wants to meet and make a dance of it
at such a speed,
if you can imagine,
at such a speed that eyes tear from wind
blowing music out the windows.

I always believe
I could start pacing with somebody
on a long highway,
playing all the fast songs
and looking at the truck stops
for that one car

because sometimes I'm lonely
or I need to feel alive
or I just like being on the road in a car,
in a marvelous, monstrous killer-machine
that fills a human body crazy high
on landscape flying by the windows—
just a blur, just a shot of speed.

I always believe
I could get myself in somebody's eyes
wide and interstate-steady,
just flat out speeding along
and scanning the road ahead,
wanting to drive
like that
forever

and if I could keep it up,
god, if I could keep that up

I'd go absolutely right straight crazy to heaven

6.7.79

CAROL MASTERS

hwy 30

three-oh, three-oh,
tires strum
black cracks
base line hum
like the rasp
of cicadas
unending
3–o
should be named
I–I
no curve
no bending

I–illinois
I–indiana

tribes driven
forest to plain
followed streams
could not
have borne
this bald
arrow shot
here to horizon

no
way to go
but straight, follow no dreams
but lines, rules like blue rules
in a school

copybook don't go outside
the lines, no signs beside
dotted lines, no
no-passing zones
here all the way through Indiana.

Horizon
highway, plain
not prairie,
cream of wheat sky, flatiron sky
fat field. On the map,
the names in spider
lines, towns so tiny
they may sink
into the fiber
of the page
you peel open carefully
as an old bible with its fine
onionskin paper (easily torn),
its gaudy gloss of Jesus the boy
lecturing his elders, nowhere
men on crosses bleed, or prophets
like the brother of Tecumseh, driven
across the felled timberland; read
the intricate scoring of the lines
precise, inevitable as music. Straight
roads lace the fields' geometry,
while blue undulations trespass
arithmetic, swell into lake,
reservoir, sea.

On this road, the only undulation
is the corn: Rags torn from the cut dry stalks
race on the highway's crown as snakes of snow

writhe before a winter storm, long leaves gray
as dust ghost dance, caught in fences like wraiths
wrestling to be spirit.

Highway, tick it off, the day's list
of grief, page by page, signs passed
never coming back, hands feet
sinews breaths nerves together,
drive, never arrive, meditate,
monkey mind scale silos, choose fruit
anywhere, could be Paris, Eiffel tower,
how did that ugly iron lattice
get to be a monument? even grain
elevators on the gray sky relief,
but who remembers, carries them on
their hearts like the Eiffel? Golden
grain, though, symbol of goodness
bread of life come to me, mountain
of bread, no, must contain
corn, gold as

gold pools on a map where
mapmakers pour the boldest
names and lordling letters,
those sycophants, suburban,
stand boasting a lineage,
dates etched over earnest
uneasy friezes, flowers
scallops, decorations worn
on their brick chest
like last Sunday's corsage.

I may never see Paris
only grain
elevators, elevators even
in my city, between

Hiawatha and Minnehaha,
streets where Indian children
paint on dying walls
improbable bright
sunflower heat,
crisp north blue
lake, hunter, green, jagged slash:
sudden tree, flash
leap of lightning.

Mileposts tick
by, earth turns
time moving
toward as
fields race
behind us,
something passed
lost,

but not these small towns like opening
a room, going home, places tucked away
across the tracks, in grainshed
shade, pinto pickup racing
off under a kid who doesn't wave,
a town in process, needing repair
porch sagging, laundry on lines,

or your finger tracing
destinations
on the quiet
map, blue veins
my love, thigh,
hairline roads, red,
white, explore
with the lightest
breath, touch, stroke;

we drive, shift
don't stop loving
the roads,

or those incandescent
colors shouting into glory
cinderblocks, cement, grain
elevators all magnificent
plump upended loaves
ascendant, transfigured,
blazing like prophets.

EUDORA WELTY

from One Writer's Beginnings

When we set out in our five-passenger Oakland touring car on our summer trip to Ohio and West Virginia to visit the two families, my mother was the navigator. She sat at the alert all the way at Daddy's side as he drove, correlating the AAA Blue Book and the speedometer, often with the baby on her lap. She'd call out, "All right, Daddy: '86-point-2, crossroads. Jog right, past white church. Gravel ends.'—And there's the church!" she'd say, as though we had scored. Our road always became her adversary. "This doesn't surprise me at all," she'd say as Daddy backed up a mile or so into our own dust on a road that had petered out. "I could've told you a road that looked like that had little intention of going anywhere."

"It was the first one we'd seen all day going in the right direction," he'd say. His sense of direction was unassailable, and every mile of our distance was familiar to my father by rail. But the way we set out to go was popularly known as "through the country."

My mother's hat rode in the back with the children, suspended over our heads in a pillowcase. It rose and fell with us when we hit the bumps, thumped our heads and batted our ears in an authoritative manner when sometimes we bounced as high as the ceiling. This was 1917 or 1918; a lady couldn't expect to travel without a hat.

Edward and I rode with our legs straight out in front of us over some suitcases. The rest of the suitcases rode just outside the doors, strapped on the running boards. Cars weren't made with trunks. The tools were kept under the back seat and were heard from in syncopation with the bumps; we'd jump out of the car so Daddy could get them out and jack up the car to patch and vulcanize a tire, or haul out the tow rope or the tire chains. If it rained so hard we couldn't see the road in front of us, we waited it out, snapped in behind the rain curtains and playing "Twenty Questions."

My mother was not naturally observant, but she could scrutinize; when she gave the surroundings her attention, it was to verify something—the truth or a mistake, hers or another's. My father kept his eyes on the road, with glances toward the horizon and overhead. My brother Edward periodically stood up in the back seat with his eyelids fluttering while he played the harmonica, "Old Macdonald had a farm" and "Abdul the Bulbul Amir," and the baby slept in Mother's lap and only woke up when we crossed some rattling old bridge. "*There's* a river!" he'd crow to us all. "Why, it certainly *is*," my mother would reassure him, patting him back to sleep. I rode as a hypnotic, with my set gaze on the landscape that vibrated past at twenty-five miles an hour. We were all wrapped by the long ride into some cocoon of our own.

The journey took about a week each way, and each day had my parents both in its grip. Riding behind my father I could see that the road had him by the shoulders, by the hair under his driving cap. It took my mother to make him stop. I inherited his nervous energy in the way I can't stop writing on a story. It makes me understand how Ohio had him around the heart, as West Virginia had my mother. Writers and travelers are mesmerized alike by knowing of their destinations.

And all the time that we think we're getting there so fast, how slowly we do move. In the days of our first car trip, Mother proudly entered in her log, "Mileage today: 161!" with an exclamation mark.

"A Detroit car passed us yesterday." She always kept those logs, with times, miles, routes of the day's progress, and expenses totaled up.

That kind of travel made you conscious of borders; you rode ready for them. Crossing a river, crossing a county line, crossing a state line—especially crossing the line you couldn't see but knew was there, between the South and the North—you could draw a breath and feel the difference.

The Blue Book warned you of the times for the ferries to run; sometimes there were waits of an hour between. With rivers and roads alike winding, you had to cross some rivers three times to be done with them. Lying on the water at the foot of a river bank would be a ferry no bigger than somebody's back porch. When our car had been driven on board—often it was down a roadless bank, through sliding stones and runaway gravel, with Daddy simply aiming at the two-plank gangway—father and older children got out of the car to enjoy the trip. My brother and I got barefooted to stand on wet, sun-warm boards that, weighted with your car, seemed exactly on the level with the water; our feet were the same as in the river. Some of these ferries were operated by a single man pulling hand over hand on a rope bleached and frazzled as if made from cornshucks.

I watched the frayed rope running through his hands. I thought it would break before we could reach the other side.

"No, it's not going to break," said my father. "It's never broken before, has it?" he asked the ferry man.

"No sirree."

"You see? If it never broke before, it's not going to break this time."

His general belief in life's well-being worked either way. If you had a pain, it was "Have you ever had it before? You have? It's not going to kill you, then. If you've had the same thing before, you'll be all right in the morning."

My mother couldn't have more profoundly disagreed with that.

"You're such an optimist, dear," she often said with a sigh, as she did now on the ferry.

"You're a good deal of a pessimist, sweetheart."

"I certainly *am.*"

And yet I was well aware as I stood between them with the water running over my toes, he the optimist was the one who was prepared for the worst, and she the pessimist was the daredevil: he the one who on our trip carried chains and a coil of rope and an ax all upstairs to our hotel bedroom every night in case of fire, and she the one—before I was born—when there *was* a fire, had broken loose from all hands and run back—on crutches, too—into the burning house to rescue her set of Dickens which she flung, all twenty-four volumes, from the window before she jumped out after them, all for Daddy to catch.

"I make no secret of my lifelong fear of the water," said my mother, who on ferry boats remained inside the car, clasping the baby to her—my brother Walter, who was destined to prowl the waters of the Pacific Ocean in a minesweeper.

As soon as the sun was beginning to go down, we went more slowly. My father would drive sizing up the towns, inspecting the hotel in each, deciding where we could safely spend the night. Towns little or big had beginnings and ends, they reached to an edge and stopped, where the country began again as though they hadn't happened. They were intact and to themselves. You could see a town lying ahead in its whole, as definitely formed as a plate on a table. And your road entered and ran straight through the heart of it; you could see it all, laid out for your passage through. Towns, like people, had clear identities and your imagination could go out to meet them. You saw houses, yards, fields, and people busy in them, the people that had a life where they were. You could hear their bank clocks striking, you could smell their bakeries. You would know those towns again, recognize the salient detail, seen so close up. Nothing was blurred, and in passing along Main Street, slowed down from twenty-five to twenty miles an hour, you didn't miss anything on either side. Going somewhere "through the country" acquainted you with the whole way there and back.

My mother never fully gave in to her pleasure in our trip—for pleasure every bit of it was to us all—because she knew we were traveling with a loaded pistol in the pocket on the door of the car on Daddy's side. I doubt if my father fired off any kind of gun in his life, but he could not have carried his family from Jackson, Mississippi to West Virginia and Ohio through the country, unprotected.

EMILY POST

from By Motor to the Golden Gate

The famous arbiter of manners wrote an account of her automobile trip from New York to San Francisco, which she took in 1915 (age forty two) with her son and a female relative. The drive took twenty-seven days, with the maximum speed limit being, in most places, twenty or twenty-file miles an hour—often faster than they could average, due to mud, ruts, dust, and breakdowns. Post's notes on the customs of the country most often address food, lodging, and, yes, manners. Her book, published in 1916 by D. Appleton and Company, includes a dozen photos, every one of which includes the car, at various scenic points, but only two or three show any passengers.—ed.

"Of course you are sending your servants ahead by train with your luggage and all that sort of thing," said an Englishman.

A New York banker answered for me: "Not at all! The best thing is to put them in another machine directly behind, with a good mechanic. Then if you break down, the man in the rear and your own chauffeur can get you to rights in no time. How about your chauffeur? You are sure he is a good one?"

"We are not taking one, nor servants, nor mechanic, either."

"Surely you and your son are not thinking of going alone! Probably he could drive, but who is going to take care of the car?"

"Why, he is!"

At that everyone interrupted at once. One thought we were insane to attempt such a trip; another that it was a "corking" thing to do. The majority looked upon our undertaking with typical New York apathy. "Why do anything so dreary?" If we wanted to see the expositions, then let us take the fastest train, with plenty of books so as to read through as much of the way as possible. Only one, Mr. B., was enthusiastic enough to wish he was going with us. Evidently, though, he thought it a daring adventure, for he suggested an equipment for us that sounded like a relief expedition: a block and tackle, a revolver, a pickaxe and shovel, tinned food—he forgot nothing but the pemmican! However, someone else thought of hardtack, after which a chorus of voices proposed that we stay quietly at home!

"They'll never get there!" said the banker, with a successful man's finality of tone. "Unless I am mistaken, they'll be on a Pullman inside of ten days!"

"Oh, you *wouldn't* do that, would you?" exclaimed our one enthusiastic friend, B.

I hoped not, but I was not sure; for, although I had promised an editor to write the story of our experience, if we had any, we were going solely for pleasure, which to us meant a certain degree of comfort, and not to advertise the endurance of a special make of car or tires. Nor had we any intention of trying to prove that motoring in America was delightful if we should find it was not. As for breaking speed records—that was the last thing we wanted to attempt!

"Whatever put it into your head to undertake such a trip?" someone asked in the first pause.

"The advertisements!" I answered promptly. They were all so optimistic, that they went to my head. "New York to San Francisco in an X— car for thirty-eight dollars!" We were not going in an X— car, but the thought of any machine's running such a distance at such a price immediately lowered the expenditure allowance for our own. "Cheapest way to go to the coast!" agreed another folder. "Travel luxuriously in your own car from your own front door over the world's greatest highway to the Pacific Shore." Could any motor enthusiasts resist such suggestions? We couldn't.

We had driven across Europe again and again. In fact I had in 1898 gone from the Baltic to the Adriatic in one of the first few motor-cars ever sold to a private individual. We knew European scenery, roads, stopping-places, by heart. We had been to all the resorts that were famous, and a few that were infamous, but our own land, except for the few chapter headings that might be read from the windows of a Pullman train, was an unopened book—one that we also found difficulty in opening. The idea of going occurred to us on Tuesday and on Saturday we were to start, yet we had no information on the most important question of all—which route was the best to take. And we had no idea how to find out!

The 1914 Blue Book was out of print, and the new one for this year not issued. I went to various information bureaus—some of those whose advertisements had sounded so encouraging—but their personal answers were more optimistic than definite. Then a friend telegraphed for me to the Lincoln Highway Commission asking if road conditions and hotel accommodations were such that a lady who did not want in any sense to "rough it" could motor from New York to California comfortably.

We wasted a whole precious thirty-six hours waiting for this answer. When it came, a slim typewritten enclosure helpfully informed us that a Mrs. Somebody of Brooklyn had gone over the route fourteen months previously and had written them many glowing letters about it. As even the most optimistic prospectus admitted that in 1914 the road was as yet not a road, and hotels along the sparsely settled districts had not been built, it was evident that Mrs. Somebody's idea of a perfect motor trip was independent of roads or stopping-places.

Meanwhile, I had been told that the best information was to be had at the touring department of the Automobile Club. So I went there.

A very polite young man was answering questions with a facility altogether fascinating. He told one man about shipping his car— even the hours at which the freight trains departed. To a second he gave advice about a suit for damages; for a third he reduced New York's traffic complications to simplicities in less than a minute; then it was my turn:

"I would like to know the best route to San Francisco."

"Certainly," he said. "Will you take a seat over here for a moment?"

"This is the simplest thing in the world," I thought, and opened my notebook to write down a list of towns and hotels and road directions. He returned with a stack of folders. But as I eagerly scanned them, I found they were all familiarly Eastern.

"Unfortunately," he said suavely, "we have not all our information yet, and we seem to be out of our Western maps! But I can recommend some very delightful tours through New England and the Berkshires."

"That is very interesting, but I am going to San Francisco."

His attention was fixed upon a map of the "Ideal Tour." "The New England roads are very much better," he said.

"But, you see, San Francisco is where I am going. Do you know which route is, if you prefer it, the least bad?"

"Oh, I see." He looked sorry. "Of course if you *must* cross the continent, there is the Lincoln Highway!"

"Can you tell me how much work has been done on it—how much of it is finished? Might it not be better on account of the early season to take a Southern route? Isn't there a road called the Santa Fé trail?"

"Why, yes, certainly," said the nice young man. "The road goes through Kansas, New Mexico and Arizona. It would be warmer assuredly."

"How about the Arizona desert? Can we get across that?"

"That *is* the question!"

"Perhaps we had better just start out and ask the people living along the road which is the best way farther on?"

The young man brightened at once. "That would have been my suggestion from the beginning."

Once outside, however, the feasibility of asking our road as we came to it did not seem very practical, so I went to Brentano's to buy some maps. They showed me a large one of the United States with four routes crossing it, equally black and straight and inviting. I promptly decided upon the one through the Allegheny Mountains to Pittsburgh and St. Louis when two women I knew came in, one of them Mrs. O., a conspicuous hostess in the New York social world, and a Californian by birth. "The very person I need," I thought. "She knows the country thoroughly and her idea of comfort and mine would be the same."

"Can you tell me," I asked her, "which is the best road to California?"

Without hesitating she answered: "The Union Pacific."

"No, I mean motor road."

Compared with her expression the worst skeptics I had encountered were enthusiasts. "Motor road to California!" She looked at me pityingly. "There isn't any."

"Nonsense! There are four beautiful ones and if you read the accounts of those who have crossed them you will find it impossible to make a choice of the beauties and comforts of each."

She looked steadily into my face as though to force calmness to my poor deluded mind. "You!" she said. "A woman like you to undertake such a trip! Why, you couldn't live through it! I have crossed the continent one hundred and sixty-odd times. I know every stick and stone of the way. You don't know what you are undertaking."

"It can't be difficult; the Lincoln Highway goes straight across."

"In an imaginary line like the equator!" She pointed at the map that was opened on the counter. "Once you get beyond the Mississippi the roads are trails of mud and sand. This district along here by the Platte River is wild and dangerous; full of the most terrible people, outlaws and 'bad men' who would think nothing of killing you if they were drunk and felt like it. There isn't any hotel. Tell me, where do you think you are going to stop? These are not towns; they are only names on a map, or at best two shacks and a saloon! This place North Platte why, you *couldn't* stay in a place like that!"

I began to feel uncertain and let down, but I said, "Hundreds of people have motored across."

"Hundreds and thousands of people have done things that it would kill you to do. I have seen immigrants eating hunks of fat pork and raw onions. Could you? Of course people have gone across, men with all sorts of tackle to push their machines over the high places and pull them out of the deep places; men who themselves can sleep on the roadside or on a barroom floor. You may think 'roughing it' has an attractive sound, because you have never in your life had the slightest experience of what it can be. I was born and brought up out there and I know." She quietly but firmly folded the map and handed it to the clerk. "I am sorry," she said, "if you really wanted to go! By and by maybe if they ever build macadam roads and put up good hotels—but even then it would be deadly dull."

For about five minutes I thought I had better give it up, and I called up my editor. "It looks as though we could not get much farther than the Mississippi."

"All right," he said, cheerfully, "go as far as the Mississippi. After all, your object is merely to find out how far you *can* go pleasurably! When you find it too uncomfortable, come home!"

No sooner had he said that than my path seemed to stretch straight and unencumbered to the Pacific Coast. If we could get no further information, we would start for Philadelphia, Pittsburgh and St. Louis, as we had many friends in these cities, and get new directions from there, but as a last resort I went to the office of a celebrated touring authority and found him at his desk.

"I would like to know whether it will be possible for me to go from here to San Francisco by motor?"

"Sure, it's possible! Why isn't it?"

"I have been told the roads are dreadful and the accommodations worse."

He surveyed me from head to foot with about the same expression that he might have been expected to use if I had asked whether one could safely travel to Brooklyn.

"You won't find Ritz hotels every few miles, and you won't find Central Park roads all of the way. If you can put up with less than that, you can go—easy!" Whereupon he reached up over his head without even looking, took down a map, spread it on the table before him, and unhesitatingly raced his blue pencil up the edge of the Hudson River, exactly as the pencil of Tad draws cartoons at the movies.

"You go here—Albany, Utica, Syracuse."

"No, please!" I said. "I want to go by way of Pittsburgh and St. Louis."

"You asked for the best route to San Francisco!" He looked rather annoyed.

"Yes, but I want to go by way of St. Louis."

"Why do you want to go to St. Louis?"

"Because we have friends there."

"Well, then, you had better take the train and go and see them!" Indifferently he took down another map and made a few casual blue marks on the mountains of Pennsylvania. "They're rebuilding roads that will be fine later in the season, but at the moment [April, 1915] all of these places are detours. You'll get bad grades and mud over your hubs! Of course, if you're set on going that way, if you want to burn any amount of gasoline, cut your tires to pieces, and strain your engine—go along to St. Louis. It's all the same to me; I don't own the roads! But you said you wanted to take a motor trip."

"Then Chicago is much the best way?"

"It is the *only* way!"

He did not wait for my agreement, but throwing aside the second map and turning again to the first, his pencil swooped down upon Buffalo and raced to Cleveland as though it fitted in a groove. He seemed to be in a mental aëroplane looking actually down upon the roads below.

"There is a detour you will have to take here. You turn left at a white church. This stretch is dusty in dry weather, but along here," his pencil had now reached Iowa and Nebraska, "you will have no trouble at all—if it doesn't rain."

"And if it rains?"

"Well, you can get out your solitaire pack!"

"For how long?" The vision of the sort of road it must be if that man thought it impassable was hard to imagine.

"Oh, I don't know; a week or two, even three maybe. But when they are dry there are no faster roads in the country. What kind of car are you going in?"

I told him proudly. Instead of being impressed by its make and power he remarked: "Humph! You'd better go in a Ford! But suit yourself! At any rate, you can open her wide along here, as wide as you like if the weather is right." At the foot of the Rocky Mountains his pencil swerved far south.

"Way down there?" I asked. "That is all desert. Can we cross the desert?"

"Why can't you?" He looked me over from head to foot. I had felt he held small opinion of me from the start.

"I only wondered if the roads were passable," I answered meekly.

"The *roads* are all right." He accented the word "roads."

"I was wondering if there were hotels."

"And what if there aren't? Splendid open dry country; won't hurt anyone to sleep out a night or two. It'd do you good! A doctor'd charge you money for that advice. I'm giving it to you free!"

On the doorstep at home I met my amateur chauffeur.

"Have you found out about routes?" he asked.

"We go by way of Cleveland and Chicago."

He looked far from pleased. "Is that so much the best way?"

"It is the *only* way," and I imitated unconsciously the voice of the oracle of the touring bureau.

One would have thought that we were starting for the Congo or the North Pole! Friends and farewell gifts poured in. It was quite thrilling, although myself in the rôle of a venturesome explorer was a miscast somewhere. Every little while Edwards, our butler, brought in a new package.

One present was a dark blue silk bag about twenty inches square like a pillow-case. At first sight we wondered what to do with it. It turned out afterward to be the most useful thing we had except a tin box, the story of which comes later. The silk bag held two hats without mussing, no matter how they were thrown in, clean gloves, veils, and any odd necessities, even a pair of slippers. The next friend of mine going on a motor trip is going to be sent one exactly like it!

By far the most resplendent of our presents was a marvel of a luncheon basket. Edwards staggered under its massiveness, and we all gathered around its silver-laden contents; bottles and jars, boxes and dishes, flat silver and cutlery, enamelware and glass, food paraphernalia enough to set before all the kings of Europe.

"I could not bear," wrote the giver, "to think of your starving in the desert."

Mr. B. brought us a block and tackle and two queer-looking canvas squares that he explained were African water buckets. All we needed further, he told us, were fur sleeping-bags and we would be quite fixed!

Another thing sent us was an air cushion. Air cushions make me feel seasick, but the lady who traveled with us loved them. By the way, we added a passenger at the last moment. On Friday afternoon, a member of our family announced she was going with us to protect us.

"The only thing is," we said, "there is no place for you to sit except in the back underneath the luggage."

"I adore sitting under luggage; it is my favorite way of traveling," she replied. And as we adore her, our party became three.

We had expected to leave New York about nine o'clock in the morning, but at eleven we were still making selections of what we most needed to take with us, and finally choosing the wrong things with an accuracy that amounted to a talent. Besides our regular luggage, the sidewalk was littered with all the entrancing-looking traveling equipment that had been sent us, and nowhere to stow it. By giving it all the floor space of the tonneau, we managed to get the big lunch basket in. Then we helped in the lady who traveled with us and added a collection of six wraps, two steamer rugs, and three dressing-cases, a typewriter, a best big camera and a little better one—with both of which we managed to take the highest possible percentage of worst pictures that anyone ever brought home—a medicine chest, and various other paraphernalia neatly packed over and around her. Of this collection our passenger was allowed one of the dressing-cases, two wraps and a big bag. As there was not room for three bags on the back, my son and I divided a small motor trunk between us; I took the trays and he the bottom. It seemed at the time a simple enough arrangement.

On our way up Fifth Avenue, two or three times in the traffic stops, we found the motors of friends next to us. Seeing our quantity of luggage, each asked: "Where are you going?"

Very importantly we answered: "To San Francisco!"

"No, really, where are you going?"

"SAN-FRAN-CIS-CO!!!" we called back. But not one of them believed us.

Offering advice on clothes for a motor trip is much like offering advice on what to wear walking up the street. But on the chance that in a perfectly commonplace list there may be an item of use to someone, I have inventoried below a list of things that I personally should duplicate, if I were taking the trip over again:

First: A coat and *pleated skirt* of a material that does not show creases. Maltreat a piece first, to see. With this one suit, half a dozen easily washed blouses and sleeveless overwaist of the material of the skirt, which, worn over a chiffon underblouse, makes a whole dress, instead of an odd shirtwaist and skirt. These underblouses are merely separate chiffon linings with sleeves and collars, and half a dozen can be put in the space of a pound candybox—yet give the same service as six waists to your dress.

On an ordinary motoring trip such as over the various well-worn tours of Northeastern States or of the Pacific Coast or Europe, where you arrive in the early afternoon with plenty of time to rest for a while and dress for dinner, several restaurant or informal evening-dresses may be useful, but crossing the continent, unless you stop over several days in cities where you have friends, in which case you can send a trunk ahead, it is often late when you arrive, and any dressing further than getting clean and tidy does not strongly appeal to you. Besides one suit and blouses, a very serviceable dress to take would be a simple house dress of some sort of uncreasable silk. There is a Chinese crêpe that *nothing* wrinkles—not to be confused with many varieties of crêpes de chine that crease like sensitive plants at a mere touch.

If I expected to go through towns where I might be dining out, I would add an evening dress of black jet or cream lace—two materials that stand uncreasingly any amount of packing. Otherwise my third and last would be a silk skirt and jacket—the skirt of black and white up and down stripes with white chiffon blouses, and the jacket black. The taffeta should be of the heavy soft variety that does not crack and muss. The skirt should be unlined and cut with straight seams gathered on a belt; a dress that folds in a second of time and in a few inches of space. With the coat on, it is a street dress; coat off (with a high girdle to match the skirt), it is whatever the top of the blouse you wear makes it.

A duster is, of course, indispensable. A taffeta one is very nice, especially when you want something better-looking, but on a long journey taffeta cracks, dirt constantly sifts through it and it can't be washed as linen can. In the high altitudes of the Southwest, a day of tropical heat is followed by a penetratingly cold night. The thermometer may not be actually low and the air seem soft and delicious, but it sifts through fabrics in the way a biting wind can, and you are soon thankful if you have brought a heavy wrap. When you need it, nothing is as comfortable as fur. I took an old sealskin coat and I don't know what I should have done without it. On my personal list, a mackintosh has no place. If it rains, the top is up, and to keep wind out, I'd rather have fur.

Nor are shoes under ordinary fortunate circumstances important. But on my list are "velvet slippers." Scarcely your idea of appropriate motoring footwear, but if your seat is the front one over the engine, you will find velvet the coolest material there is— cooler than buckskin, or suède, or kid or canvas—much! And if you want to walk, your luggage, after all, is with you.

Every woman knows the kind of hat she likes to wear. But does every woman realize, which Celia and I did not, that a hat to be worn nine or eleven hours across a wind-swept prairie must offer no more resistance than the helmet of a race driver? A helmet, by the way, made to fit your head and face is ideally comfortable. A hat that the wind catches very little won't bother you in a few hours, but at the end of ten, your head will feel stone-bruised. An untrimmed toque, very small and close, and tied on with a veil is just about as comfortable as a helmet. It has the disadvantage of having no brim, but yellow goggles mitigate the glare, and it is the brim, even though it be of the inverted flower-pot turn-down, that is a pocket for wind that at the end of a few hours pulls uncomfortably.

A real suggestion to the woman who minds getting sunburnt, is an orange-colored chiffon veil. It must be a vivid orange that has a good deal of red in it. Even with the blazing sun of New Mexico and California shining straight in your face, a single thickness of orange-colored chiffon will keep you from burning at all. If you can't see through chiffon, but mind freckling or burning, to say nothing of blistering, sew an orange-colored veil across the lower rims of your goggles and wear orange-colored glasses. Cut a square out of the top so as to leave no sun space on your temples, and put a few gathers over the nose to allow it to fit your face. Fasten sides over hat like any veil. The Southwestern sun will burn your arms through sleeves of heavy crêpe de chine, but the thinnest material of orange—red is next best—protects your skin in the same way that the ruby glass of a lantern in a photographer's developing room protects a sensitive plate.

Wear the thinnest and least amount of underwear that you can feel decently clad in, so as to get as many fresh changes as possible in the least space, because of the difficulty in stopping often to have things laundered. What they put in the clothes in Southern California I don't know, but in any mixture of linen and silk, the silk has been apparently dipped in blue dye. A cream-colored silk-and-linen shirt of E. M.'s that happened to have the buttonholes worked in silk, is now a stippled green with buttonholes of navy blue. It is rather putting your belongings to the test of virtue—as those which are pure silk wash perfectly well. If I were going again I should take everything I could of thin crêpe de chine. It seems to be very easy to launder, and is everywhere returned in a clean and comfortably soft condition, whereas linen often comes back uncertain as to color and feeling like paper.

Although of more service on boats or trains, or in Europe where private baths are not often to be had, a black or dark silk kimono and a black lace bed-cap, if you ever wear bed-caps, are invaluable assets to anyone who dislikes walking through public corridors in obvious undress. My own especial treasures, acquired after many unsuccessful attempts, are a wrapper cut the pattern of an evening wrap, of very soft, black silk brocade. It rolls up as easily as any kimono, and takes scarcely any space. The cap is a very plain "Dutch" one, of thread lace with a velvet ribbon around it. A wrapper that isn't obviously a wrapper, is sometimes very convenient. You could make believe it was an evening wrap, if you were very hard pressed.

And above everything, in traveling you want clothes that are uncomplicated. The ones that you get into most easily are the ones you put on most often. Underblouses, such as I have described above, are a perfect traveler's delight, because there is no basting in, or trying to clean collars, cuffs, etc. A fresh underblouse with lace trimming, rolled like a little bolster, measures one and a half inches by seven.

And remember: Plain skirts crease in half-moons across the back, pleated or very full ones don't. An orange veil prevents sunburn. Western climate is very trying to the skin, so that you need cold cream even if you don't use it at home. A lace veil of a rather striking pattern is at times of ugliness a great beautifier.

Clothes for men are a little out of my province. E. M. had some khaki flannel shirts, breeches and puttees that seemed to be very serviceable. At least he was able to spend any amount of time rolling on the road under the machine, and still brush off fairly well. He had a sweater and an ulster and two regular suits of clothes to change alternately at the end of the day. His evening clothes, tennis flannels, etc., were sent through by express.

To send one hundred and fifty pounds from New York to San Francisco costs fifteen dollars.

Food Equipment

Don't take a big, heavy, elaborate lunch basket. If you want to know what perfect comfort is, get a tin breadbox with a padlock, and let it stay on the floor of the tonneau. In the bottom of it you can keep tins of potted meats, jars of jam, and a box of crackers, some milk chocolate, or if you like better, nuts and raisins. And on top you can put everything you lay your hands on! Books, sweaters, medicine case, and a pack of oiled paper to wrap luncheons in. We had a solidified alcohol lamp, a ten-cent kettle, and thermos bottles, a big thermos food jar, which we filled with ice cream if the day was hot, and one of the bottles with cocoa if it was cool. Coffee (if you put cream in it) has always a corked, musty taste, but cocoa is not affected, neither is soup. Food tastes better if you don't mix your bottles. Keep the jar for ice cream, if you like ice cream, a bottle for cocoa or soup, and two for ice or hot water. On long runs in the Far West, a canvas water bag is convenient. You can buy one at almost any garage, and it keeps water quite wonderfully fresh and cool.

On top of our permanent supplies we put the daily luncheons we took from the hotels: sandwiches, boiled eggs and fruit and the above-mentioned cocoa or ice cream. Cocoa we bought at the hotels, but our favorite place to buy ice cream was at a soda-water fountain.

The tins in our bread box we hoarded as a miser hoards gold—as a surplus that we might need to keep us alive; and, as in the common end of most misers, when we got to San Francisco and our journey was over, the greater part was still left—to give away.

Taking the general average of luck in motoring, no matter how well things have gone for you, the chances are that you have had *some* delays. A day or two of rain that held you up, detours that made you lose your way, a run of tire trouble—something, no matter what it is, that has delayed you more than you expected. And whatever it is, you find yourself thinking this does not matter very much, because when we get to those Nebraska fast roads we can make up lost time easily.

The very sound "Nebraska" correlates "dragged roads" speed! While you are still gently running through the picturesque Sir Joshua Reynolds scenery of the River to River road in Iowa, you find that your mind is developing an anticipatory speed craze. So thoroughly imbued has your mind become with the "fast road" idea that the very ground has a speed gift in its dragged surface. What if your engine is barely capable of forty miles an hour, that miraculously fast stretch magically carries you at the easiest fifty. If you have a big powerful engine, you forget that ordinarily you dislike whizzing across the surface of the earth, and for just this once—even though you think of it more in terror than in joy—you are approaching the race-way of America, and you, too, are going to race!

"We must be sure that everything is in perfect running order," you exclaim excitedly as you picture your car leaping out of Omaha and shooting to Denver while scarcely turning over its engine. "Not many stopping-places," you are told. What matter is that to you? You are not thinking of stopping at all. North Platte, perhaps, yes. Three hundred and thirty miles in a day is just a nice little fast road run.

"A nice little which?" says the head of a garage in Omaha.

"We'll leave early," you continue, unheeding, "and make a dash across the continental speedway——"

"See here, stranger," says the garage man, "what state of fast circuits d'y think y're in? This is Nebraska and the speed limit is twenty miles!"

"Twenty miles a minute?" you gasp, "that certainly *is* speed!"

The garage man half edges away from you. "Fr'm here t' Denver is about thutty-five hours' straight travelin'. You gutta slow down t' eight miles through towns and y' can't go over twenty miles an hour nowheres!"

When you manage to get a little breath into your collapsed lungs you say dazedly, "But we're going over the 'fast dragged' road."

"Road's fast enough! But the law'll have you if you drive over it faster'n twenty miles an hour."

If you can find the joke in all of this, you have a more humorous mental equipment and a sweeter disposition than we had.

Across Nebraska from the last good hotel in Omaha to the first comfortable one in Denver or Cheyenne is over five hundred miles. At the prescribed "speed" of about seventeen miles an hour average, it means literally a pleasant little run of between thirty and forty hours along a road dead level, wide, straight, and where often as far as the eye can see, there is not even a shack in the dimmest distance, and the only settlers to be seen are prairie dogs.

If between Omaha and Cheyenne there were three or four attractive clean little places to stop, or if the Nebraska speed laws were abolished or disregarded *and it didn't rain,* you could motor to the heart of the Rocky Mountains with the utmost ease and comfort.

In May, 1915, the road by way of Sterling to Denver was impassable; all automobiles were bogged between Big Spring and Julesburg, so on the advice of car owners that we met, we went by way of Chappell to Cheyenne. It is quite possible, of course, that we blindly passed comfortable stopping-places, but to us that whole vast distance from Omaha to Cheyenne was one to be crossed with as little stop-over as possible. Aside from questions of accommodations and speed laws, the interminable distance was in itself an unforgettably wonderful experience. It gave us an impression of the lavish immensity of our own country as nothing else could.

KATE CULKIN

The Family Car

Speeding down I-80 in my El Camino I am the most powerful woman in the world. *Look out plastic import*, I think, *take that puny sports car*; if push comes to shove, I'll crush you without a second thought. Eating with one hand, steering with the other, I realize women with big American cars don't need self-assertiveness training—a V-8 engine would empower anyone, male or female. A pop song of a few years ago comes to mind, one in which the lead singer snarls: "I don't know what the world may need, but a V-8 engine is a good start for me; I think I'll drive and find a place to be surly."

The El Camino is half-car, half-truck, the mermaid of the automobile world. Like the mermaid, it transcends categories and allows its owners to do so as well. The car owner values the conservative and the practical, choosing a solid vehicle that won't go too fast or be crushed too easily; my father, in fact, bought me an El Camino so I would be encased in life-protecting steel in case of an accident. The truck owner, however, throws her belongings in the back and takes off at a moment's notice. She crosses the country, flies up mountains and through deserts, sleeps at the side of the road, travels as a solitary pilgrim. My father's plan backfired; what started as an attempt to protect me from the world gave me the confidence to venture into it.

Like I said, any V-8 engine would be empowering, but the eye-catching El Camino may be especially so. Car aficionados describe El Caminos as muscle cars. That's how I feel driving mine; strong, brawny, muscled. Just over five feet tall with a turned up nose, freckles and a whispery voice, I'm often seen as sweet and weak. Men offer to carry my bags and fear I am about to faint, smile benevolently at my opinions. The El Camino, however, screams both *pay attention to me* and *get out of my way*. People stare as it, scurry from its path, notice it from a mile away. Instead of asking if

I know how to pump gas, mechanics come out to admire my car. My attitude behind the wheel affects my demeanor in the pedestrian world. I now expect people to get out of my way, to notice me, to take me seriously; because I expect it, they do.

I am not the first women in my family to love her car. My grandmother once cherished a red Ford convertible. Unlike most females in 1940, she went to college and moved away from home to teach in a one-room schoolhouse; on weekends she cruised to the ski slopes or into Manhattan to see a show. My grandmother purchased the car with money she earned herself, a claim I, with many more opportunities, cannot make. That shiny automobile symbolized her financial, as well as her emotional, independence.

In a picture from that era, my grandmother, turned out in Capri pants and a cardigan, leans against her Ford. She is preparing for one of her weekend excursions; with her ebony hair and slight figure, she could be a Hollywood starlet posing, except for the fierce intelligence radiating from her eyes. Shortly after the photograph was taken, my grandmother met my grandfather. She quit her job, married, had one, then three, then six kids. The convertible gave way to a station wagon, teaching gave way to mothering, financial independence transformed into a household allowance; her world grew even smaller when her only brother died in World War II and the move to a bigger town didn't materialize. Though she has never been anything but loving to her grandchildren, her sons and daughters speak of an angry, frustrated middle age. Through it all, however, she remembered what it felt like to fly down the road in her very own car.

Driving to my grandparents', I pass the landmarks I saw as a child from my car seat, probably the same ones my grandmother passed in her car; the stands selling hot dogs and fried clams, the rocky beach, the Elks' club. The first time I steered the El Camino past them it was to end a solo trip from Denver, Colorado, to their upstate New York home. As I pulled into the driveway, my grandmother ran out to greet me; at dinner that night she proclaimed, "There is nothing like your first car." Her words strike me as significant. She never said anything like, "There is nothing like your first boyfriend," or "There is nothing like your wedding day." To her, the defining moment of a girl's life does not come in attaching herself to another person, but in attaching herself to an automobile. She wishes for her granddaughters the freedom a car brings, the ability to go anywhere at any time; you are never trapped when you have a car. The only other thing my grandmother speaks of with the same reverence as a car is a college education, another venue to independence.

Someone snapped a picture that day I first drove myself to my grandparents'. Like the earlier photograph, my grandmother leans against a solid American car, here in a dark blue windbreaker, her arms dug deep in her pockets to fight the autumn chill. This time she does not stand alone, however; a young woman with much the same face also leans against the car door. They both beam into the camera. The girl rejoices that she completed the cross-country drive alone, without mishap. The grandmother celebrates that her progeny, her flesh, her very genes, are on the move.

PATTI SMITH

ballad of a bad boy

Oh I was bad
didn't do what I should
mama catch me with a lickin'
and tell me to be good
when I was bad twice times
she shoved me in a hole
and cut off all my fingers
and laid them in a finger bowl
my mama killed me
my papa grieved for me
my little sister Annalea
wept under the almond tree

Oh I loved a car
and when I was feelin' sad
I lay down on my daddy's Ford
and I'd feel good
and you know that I got bad
robbed hubcaps from the men
and sold them to the women
and stole them back again
and I got me a car
a Hudson Hornet car
and rolled the pretty ladies
and often went too far
I went to Chicago
I went to Kalamazoo
I went to Nashville
the highways I flew
I went to Salinas
I rode to the sea

and the people all scolded
and pointed to me
they said there's a bad boy
I was so bad boy
they gathered their daughters
I heard what they said
steer away from him, honey
'cause that boy is bad
and tho' he's hung good
and flashes that loot
don't slide by his side
he rides a wrong route
'cause he's a bad boy
I was so bad boy
my mama killed me
my papa grieved for me
my little sister Annalea
wept under the almond tree

And I wept on a stock car
I captured the junkyards
and I sped thru the canyons
though I never went far
from the wreckers mechanics
I worshipped these men
but they laughed at me, man
they called me mama's boy
mama mama mama mama . . .
Monday at midnight
Tuesday at two
drunk on tequila
thinking of you, ma
I drove my car on, ma
wrecking cars was my art

I held a picture of you, ma
close to my heart
I rode closed windows
it was ninety degrees
the crowd it was screaming
it was screaming for me
they said I was nonsense
true diver chicken driver
no sense
but I couldn't hear them
I couldn't see
fenders hot as angels
blazed inside of me
I sped on raged in steam heat
I cracked up and rolled at your feet
I rose in flames and rolled in a pit
where you caught me with a tire iron
and covered me in shit
and I coulda got up
but the crowd it screamed no
that boy is evil
too bad for parole
so bad his ma cut off all his fingers
and laid 'em in a finger bowl
his mama killed him
his papa grieved for him
his little sister Annalea
wept under the almond tree

Oh I was bad
didn't do what I should
mama catch me with a lickin'
and she tell me
You be good

JAYNE ANNE PHILLIPS

Fast Lanes

Colorado, 1975

We walked down a grassy knoll to the lake.

"The truck should be OK there," he said. "Place is deserted."

Behind us the pickup sat squat and red in the sun, a black tarp roped across the boxes and trunks in the bed. Hot and slick, the tarp shimmered like a dark liquid. The rest stop was a small gravel lot marked by a low wooden fence and three large aluminum trash cans chained to posts. Beyond it the access road, unlined and perfectly smooth, glittered in a slant of heat.

"Where are we?" I asked.

"Somewhere in west Georgia."

I could close my eyes and still feel myself across the seat of the moving truck, my head on his sour thigh and my knees tucked up. The steering wheel was a curved black bar close to my face, its dark grooves turning. We hadn't spoken since pulling out of the motel parking lot in New Orleans. Now I stumbled and he drew me up beside him. The weeds were thick and silky. Pollen rose in clouds and settled in the haze. The incline grew steeper and we seemed to slide into the depths of the grass, then the ground leveled and several full elms banded the water. The bank was green to its edge. We entered the shade of the trees and felt the coolness through our shoes. He stepped out of his unlaced sneakers, pulled off his shirt and jeans. The belt buckle clanked on stones. Then he stood, touching the white skin of his stomach. His eyes were blue as blue glass, and bloodshot. He hadn't slept.

"You all right?" he said.

I didn't answer.

"You've got no obligation to me," he said. "I don't tell you who to pick up in a bar. But at eight o'clock this morning I began to wonder if I was going to have to leave you, and dump all that crap of yours in the middle of Bourbon Street."

He turned, moving through the high grass to the water. I saw him step in and push out, sinking to his shoulders. "Thurman," I said, but he was under, weaving long and pale below the surface.

I took off my dress and let it fall into the grass white and wrinkled, smelling of rum. The lake seemed to grow as I got closer, yawning like a cool mouth at the center of the heat. I was in it; I sank to my knees as water closed over me, then felt the settling mud as I lay flat and tried to stay down. I held my knees and swayed, hearing nothing. Their faces were fading, and the lines of white coke across the gleaming desk top. I rolled to my side and the water pushed, darkening, purple. It was Thurman, moving closer, changing the colors, and I felt his hands on my arms. He pulled me up and the air cracked as we surfaced, streaming water.

I wasn't crying but I felt the leaden air move out of my chest. I felt how hard he was holding me and knew I was shaking. My heart beat in my throat and ears, pounding. He held my heavy hair pulled back and bunched in one hand, and with the other he poured water down my neck and shoulders, stroking with the warmth of his palm in the coolness. He said low disconnected words, mother sounds and lullabies. I felt my teeth in my lips and my forehead moving slowly against his chest. Holding to his big shoulders, I could feel him with all my body.

"I drew a map to the motel on that napkin and you lost it, didn't you," he said. "I knew you would. We were both drunk when I gave it to you."

Behind his voice there was a hum of insects and locusts and the faraway sound of the highway. The highway played three chords beyond his reddened arms; a low thrum, a continual median sigh, and a whine so shrill it was gone as it started. The sounds separated and converged, like the sounds of their voices in the room last night and the driftings of music from the club below. There was a discreet jarring of dishes or silver at a long distance, and the sound of the bed, close, under me, but fake, like a sound through a wall that might after all be a recording, someone's joke.

I was talking then, because Thurman said, "No, no joke." As he said it I could feel the water again, around us, between us.

"I lose track of where I am," I said.

"Stand still. You're OK now. No one's trying anything. It's me. Remember me? The driver?"

"Yeah. I remember you. You're the one born in Dallas."

"Right. That's good. Now listen. We're going to walk out of the water and dry off for five minutes. I'm not going to touch you. You'll feel fine in the sun and I'll smoke a joint." He turned in the water, holding my wrist, pulling me gently toward the shore.

"I can't put that dress on again," I said.

"Then leave it for the next refugee. Leave it where it is."

"No one should wear it."

"You can wear my shirt," he said. "You'll look great in blue denim and no pants, like Doris Day in a pajama movie."

Thurman had seen a lot of Doris Day movies in Dallas, in neighborhood theaters that weren't the Ritz. His two older brothers kissed girls in the balcony while he sat in the back row downstairs with the Mexicans. Blue-eyed Doris flickered in a bad print to the tune of bubbly music and wetback jeers. Thurman said he liked Doris in those days because she was so out-of-it she made no sense to anyone, and she kept right on raising her eyebrows, perky, not quite smart, as wads of paper and popcorn boxes bounced off the screen. Afterward he walked home with his brothers across the freeway, up long sidewalks to what was just a few houses then, not yet a suburb. His brothers told tales on the girls and teased him about sitting with the Mexicans. At home they sometimes shook him by his heels over the toilet, flushed it, and threatened to drop him in. That, said Thurman, was a precursor to all of Dallas in the '50s and early '60s: fringed shirts, steaming sidewalk grates globbed with saliva in the summer, first-time gang bangs in a whorehouse with steers' heads on the walls. Not just the horns, he said, the whole fucking head, stuffed, like it was a lion from Africa. And football, always football; Thurman's father was a successful high school coach who took pride in featuring his own sons on his teams. One after another, he'd coached, punished, driven them all to a grueling and temporary stardom.

When I met Thurman he was floating and I was floating home. He drove a Datsun pickup and he lived in the foothills near Denver. He had a small wooden house with a slanted kitchen, a broken water heater, and a new skylight framed in white pine against old ceiling boards and dangling strips of flowered wallpaper. He played music with friends of mine and did carpentry and called me up once to eat with him at a good Indian restaurant. He'd been in the Peace Corps in Ceylon and he said you should eat this food right out of the bowls with your hand, but only one hand. The other stayed in your lap to prove you used separate hands for eating and for cleaning yourself.

He stayed with me that night, mostly because I liked the way he looked from the back as he bought oranges later, threading his way through the panhandlers at an open air market. He had a cloth bag swinging at his hip but none of them asked for change. He was big and broad-shouldered in a blousy white shirt, red-headed and ruddy; he'd gotten slightly dressed up and called me without really knowing me to pretend a good dinner was no big deal. He was probably lonely, but he moved nicely, mannish, not arrogant, tossing the oranges into a bag with the casual finesse of an ex-athlete still in shape at thirty. The sun was going down; it was early summer; the fruit was stacked in green trays like pretty ornaments. I didn't really want Thurman but I liked him and it was time to sleep with someone. I knew he'd be patient and slow and if I got a little high it would be OK, I'd feel better. But we went on too long, he woke me again in the night, and the next morning he wanted to stay around. He'd lived with someone quite a while in San Antonio; it had broken up three years before, but he still dated history from that time: all the towns he'd lived in since, Berkeley, Austin, Jackson, Eugene, Denver, all the western floater's towns. We talked about money—how I'd spent mine having mono I'd caught waitressing and eating off plates, how he was making a lot building houses in the mountains with a crew of dealers from Aspen. Finally he drank his orange juice and left. I didn't think of him much until a month later when I read his notice advertising for riders on a bookstore bulletin board. He was taking off for a while, down through Texas and Louisiana, then up the coast. I went looking and found him installing wooden doors on a cold-storage cabinet at a natural foods store.

"You leaving for good?" he asked. "Going home?"

"Leaving here for good. I won't stay home long."

"Then why go? For the hell of it?"

"It's a long story, Thurman, I'd rather not go into it here by the plum nectar and the juice cartons advertising Enlightenment."

"You're a cynic," he said, measuring the blond frame of the door. "That's why you're leaving. You can't take it here in Paradise where everyone is beautiful and girls aren't allowed to wear makeup."

"You've got it. I want to go back to my hometown and buy mascara."

"You wouldn't be caught dead in mascara." He lifted the piece of glass against the frame, checking the fit, then set it down again. Looking at me through the open door of the cabinet, he held the lock in one hand and rummaged in his apron for screws. "I accept you as my rider."

I looked at the floor, then back up at him. "The thing is, I need to get there pretty quickly. My father is sick."

"How sick?"

"Just sick. He has to have an operation in two or three weeks."

"Well," he said, and ran his hand along the wood, "you'd almost get there in time. Three weeks would be the best I could do. Stopovers on the way. But you won't have to worry about money. Just pay for your food." He looked away from me, leaning back to fit the lock. "Is it a deal?"

"It's the best deal I've got."

"Good. I'm leaving in four days."

"Thurman," I said, "is this a kissy-poo number?"

He tested the hinges and shrugged. "It's no particular number. Whatever works out. Besides, you can handle me. I'm a pushover."

"Fine. I'm going home to pack."

I turned and walked out, and as I hit the street I heard him yelling behind me, "Listen, can you sing with the radio? Can you carry a tune?"

We pulled out of town at dawn. I had the feeling, the floater's only fix: I was free, it didn't matter if I never saw these streets again; even as we passed them they receded and entered a realm of placeless streets. Even the people were gone, the good ones and the bad ones; I owned whatever real had occurred, I took it all. I was vanished, invisible, another apartment left empty behind me, my possessions given away, thrown away, packed away in taped boxes fit into an available vehicle. The vehicle was the light, the early light and later the darkness.

"Hey dreamer," Thurman said, "what are you doing?"

"Praying," I said.

He smiled. "I did some speed, I'm going to just keep going. Sleep when you want to."

"OK," I said.

"New Mexico, tomorrow morning."

"Good. That will be pretty."

Thurman drove straight to an all-night stop in Albuquerque, the apartment of a stewardess he'd known in college. It was the first floor of a complex right off the freeway, motel terraces and a Naugahyde couch. She was gone and it seemed she'd never been there, empty shelves and pebbly white walls with no marks. I sat up in bed while my legs still shook from holding him.

"You could be such a good lover," he said. "I can feel you have been, but you're so busy stepping out."

"This mattress is too soft." I moved away from him. "The sheets feel heavy. I'm going to sleep in the other room on the floor."

"The floor," he said. He lit a cigarette. "It's a shame you can't levitate, so that even the floor couldn't touch you."

I went into the living room and pushed the furniture against the walls. There were only three pieces: the black couch and chair and a Formica table. They all seemed weightless, like cardboard. I lay down in the middle of the carpeted floor with my arms out and my feet together, counting each breath, counting with the hum of the air-conditioner. I went away. I heard nothing until I felt him in the room. He was sitting beside me, cross-legged, in the dark.

"What are you scared of?" he said.

"I don't know. Going back."

"Explain. Tell Thurman."

"I can't. Sometimes it's hard to breathe, like living under blankets."

"Hot?"

"Hot, but cold too. Shaking."

"Then don't go back."

"I have to," I said. "It doesn't help anymore to stay away."

He stood up and went to the bedroom. I heard him pull the sheet off the bed in one motion, the sheet coming clear with a soft snap. He brought a pillow too, stood at my feet, and furled the white sheet out so it settled over me like the rectangular flag of some pure and empty country.

"It's midnight," he said. "Get some sleep. We need to be out of here early."

By nine A.M. we were two hours south of the city on Rte. 25. We didn't talk; the road was a straight two-lane, the light still clear but thickening with heat to come later. Both of us had wanted out of that apartment by dawn; we'd drank a half-carton of orange juice we'd found in the spotless refrigerator, drank it as we pulled out of the parking lot, shrouded in a half-stupor of fatigue. Thurman held the wheel steady with one knee, staring ahead. "Can you drive a standard shift?"

"Maybe," I said, "except I haven't for a while. I'm not sure I still know how."

"What?" His voice was flat. "You're twenty-three and American and you can't drive?"

"I have a license. Just never used it."

"Why not?"

"Because when I was sixteen I pulled into the driveway in my mother's car, sideswiped my father's car, and rear-ended my brother's car."

Thurman shook his head. "Wonderful."

"I was only going ten miles an hour—there wasn't much damage. Scratches and dented chrome. But afterward my driving was a family joke and no one would let me behind the wheel."

"I can imagine."

"Besides, it was a small town. My boyfriends had cars."

"Well," he said, "this is no small town and there's no boyfriend in sight. You're going to learn how to drive."

"Thurman, are you going to liberate me?"

"No, you're going to liberate me. I plan to spend exactly half this trip pleasantly stoned, playing with the radio and reading girlie magazines."

"I didn't know you read girlie magazines."

"Only the really sleazy ones, the ones with no pretensions. And I don't want any shit about it."

He pulled off the road near Cuchillo and took a left off the exit. We could see the town in the distance, brown and white and hunched. Thurman drove in the opposite direction. The land was absolutely flat, wavering with heat, a moony unreal surface even as mirrors. Light glanced off like knife glare. The far mountains were blue and beige, treeless. "Pinos Altos," Thurman said, "or the Mimbres range, I don't know which. We aren't far from Elephant Butte and the reservation." He steered onto the berm of the narrow road, slowed and stopped as yellow dust rose around us. "Good spot for a ceremony." He turned off the ignition and faced me. He seemed amazingly defined in that early, hot light, a film of moisture on his forehead, his big hands opening toward me in even gestures, describing small spheres as he talked.

"Now," he said, "this is going to take twenty minutes. Remember, a standard is always the best transmission—it allows you to feel the machine and the road more efficiently than an automatic. Nobody who knows much about cars drives an automatic."

"Automatics are for cherries, right, Thurman?"

He got out of the truck and stood looking in at me from the road. "Slide over."

"Do we have to be so serious? It was a joke."

"I'm not laughing. In thirty minutes this pleasant eighty-degree interlude will be over and the temperature will be climbing right up to about a hundred and ten. It's early September in Texas. We will need to be moving. So pay attention."

"OK."

"It's easy."

"Nothing mechanical is easy."

He sighed. "Are you ready?" He watched my face as I slid into the driver's seat, then slammed the door of the truck and walked around to the cab. He got in and sat motionless, waiting.

"I'll need a few instructions, if you don't fucking mind."

"Look, it's hot in Texas. Let's both take it easy."

"I'm trying to."

He looked away to where the road disappeared in mirage past a nothingness, and recited, "Right foot, gas and brake. Left foot, clutch. Now, push in the clutch, put the transmission in neutral, and turn the ignition."

The engine turned over and caught. I wanted to get out of the truck and walk into the brown fields, keep walking. Far off, wheeling birds moved like a pattern of circular dashes in the sky. Something was dead out there, yellowed like the dust and lacy with vanishing. Thurman's voice continued, but closer. He had moved over next to me. "Let the clutch out slowly. Give it gas as you let it out, enough gas at the precise moment, or you'll stall. Now try it, that's right, now the gas. . . ." The truck jerked forward, coughed, jerked, stalled. "Try it again," he said, "a little smoother, gauge the release a little more, there you go—now."

He talked, we jerked and moved, rolled cautiously forward, stopped. The fields remained silent. A mongrel dog ambled out of the brush and sat in the middle of the opposite lane, watching and panting. The dog was maybe twenty pounds of rangy canine, immobile, a desert stone with slit eyes. "Do it again," Thurman murmured. "There you go, give it gas, not too much. OK, OK, we're moving, don't watch the dog, watch the road. Good, good, now—if you go too slow in a gear, you force the engine to lug. Hear that? That's lugging. Give it some gas. . . ."

He kept talking in the close room of the truck, both of us sweating, until the words were meaningless. I repeated the same movements; clutch, gas, shift, brake, downshift, up and down the same mile stretch of road. The mongrel sat watching from one side of the pavement or the other, and the last time we came by, got up and ambled back into the field toward nothing. I pulled jerkily onto the entrance ramp of the freeway as Thurman shifted for me, then onto the highway itself as he applauded.

"Do you forgive me?" I asked.

"For what?" He was watching the road, sitting near enough to grab the wheel. "Check your mirrors. Always know what's coming up on you."

I checked. "For last night," I said. "I'm sorry."

"Don't be sorry. What happened was as likely in this scheme as anything else." He reached under the seat for a pack of cigarettes, still watching the road. "I like you."

"You know something? That one time we slept together in Denver was my first time in six weeks."

"I figured."

"What do you mean?"

"Pay attention—stay in your lane." He turned and glanced behind us. "I mean it seemed like you barely remembered how. There are several like you around. Where are all the girls who were smart and feisty and balled everyone all the time?"

"They got older," I said. "I used to ball anyone too, just based on his eyes or his arms. It's easy when you do it a lot. You get stoned and you don't even think about it. Easy. Like saying hello."

"Guess I missed the boat," he said. "You must have been great to say hello to in the old days. I wish I'd known you then."

"Yeah, I bet you do."

He smiled and lit a cigarette. "But don't you ever miss it? Weren't those days *fun* sometimes? Think about it for a minute.

Everyone laughed a lot, didn't they? Group jokes and the old gang. All the dope, everyone with a nickname. Food and big meals and banjos and flutes. People weren't stupid; they just didn't *worry*. The war was over, no one was getting drafted. The girls had birth-control pills and an old man, and once in a while they fucked their best friend's old man, or they all fucked together, and everything was chummy. Right?"

"Sure. That's right."

"Ha," he said.

If I remember right, what we did was this: Rte. 25 from Denver to Albuquerque, 10 to El Paso, 20 to Dallas, 35 to San Antonio, back on 10 to Houston, Beaumont, New Orleans, 65 to Montgomery, 85 to Atlanta and Charlotte, 21 to Wytheville, Virginia, 77 to Charleston and West Virginia; passing through, escaping gravity in a tinny Japanese truck, an imported living quarters. Love in a space capsule, Thurman called it, hate in Houdini's trunk. But there was the windshield and the continual movie past the glass. It was good driving into the movie, good the way the weather changed, the way night and day traded off. Good to camp out for a day or two in a park or a motel, buy a local paper, go to a rummage sale. It was good stopping at the diners and luncheonettes and the daytime bars, or even HoJo's along the interstates: an hour, a few hours, taking off as we'd walked in, as if we had helium in our shoes. Everyone else lived where they stood. They had to live somewhere, and they'd ended up in Tucumcari or Biloxi or Homer, Georgia. All of them, waitresses and bartenders, clerks standing behind motel desks in view of some road, and the signs, place names, streets, houses, were points on a giant connect-the-dots. The truck is what there really was: him and me and the radio, the shell of the space, thin carpet over a floor that reverberated with a hollow *ping* if you stamped down hard. There were the rearview mirrors turning all that receded sideways, holding the light in glints and angles and the pastels in detached, flat pictures so that any reflected object—car, fence, billboard—seemed just a shape, miraculous in motion. There was the steering wheel, the dash with its square illuminations at night, a few red needles registering numbers. The glove compartment: a flashlight, the truck registration, an aspirin bottle full of white crosses, dope and an aluminum foil envelope of crystal meth in the first-aid box, two caramel bars, a deck of cards. Under the seat were some maps and a few paperbacks, magazines, crumpled wrappers of crackers and health-food cookies and Popsicles, Thurman's harmonica. The radio whined and popped and poured out whatever it caught in the air. In the desert there was nothing but rumbling crackles and shrills; we turned the volume way up till the truck was full of crashing static and rode fast with the roar for miles, all the windows open streaming hot air. But mostly the radio was low. He talked. I talked. We told stories. We argued. We argued a lot as we approached Dallas, where we were going to spend a couple of days with his parents.

"Where did you you come from?"

"Thurman, I came from where I'm going."

"I mean in the beginning, like Poland or Scandinavia."

"Wales. But there, in West Virginia, since the 1700s. A land grant. So much land they parceled it out for two hundred years of ten-children families, and only sold the last of it as my father was growing up."

"Sold it to who?"

"The coal companies. Pennsylvania and New York coal companies."

"Uh-huh." He adjusted the rearview mirror. "Why aren't you back there mobilizing against strip mining?"

"Mobilizing? You make it sound like a war." I turned on the radio, and turned it off. "I guess it is a war—New York hippies against New York coal companies." I looked away from him, out the window. "I don't have any excuse, I just wanted to get out."

"You know West Virginia is the only state left where there are no nuclear reactors?" He took a drag on his cigarette and smiled at me across the seat.

"They couldn't put a reactor there," I said. "The land would open like a boil, like an infected Bible, and swallow it." I caught his eye and smiled back. "Impressive. You're up on your eco-lit."

"I'm a good hippie carpenter."

"There are no hippies anymore. There's a fairy tale about working-class visionaries."

"Just a fairy tale? No vision in the working class?"

"Vision everywhere. But in the real working class, vision is half blind. It's romantic to think they really know—"

"You don't think they *know*?" He flicked his cigarette out the window and raised his voice. "They know—they just don't *talk* about it. My grandfather was an Irish Catholic plumber who died of cirrhosis. He used to sit in his chair while the news was on the radio and fold his newspaper into squares. Then he'd unfold it and roll it into a tube, a tight tube the width of a black snake. He'd whack it against the arm of the chair in four-four time, while the announcer kept going and my skinny grandmother grated cabbage in the kitchen by the plates." He checked the mirror and pulled out around a cattle truck. "They knew plenty, sweetheart. You don't know what you're talking about."

"Don't call me sweetheart, and I didn't say they weren't perceptive or frustrated. I said their isolation was real, not an illusion. They stayed in one place and sank with whatever they had. But us—look at us. Roads. Sensation, floating, maps into more of the same. It's a blur, a pattern, a view from an airplane."

"You're a real philosopher, aren't you? What do you want? You want to sink, righteous and returned to your roots? Is that it?"

"I can't."

"Can't what?"

"Sink. I don't know how."

"Oh, Christ. Will you shut up and light that joint before we pull into Dallas?"

I took the joint out of his cigarette pack and looked for matches.

"Here," he said, and threw them at me. "No wonder you live alone and sleep on floors. You're ponderous and depressed. Nothing is any worse than it's ever been."

"No," I said, "only more detached."

"Detachment is an ageless virtue. Try a little Zen."

"I am," I said, and lit the joint. "I'm living in Zen, highway Zen, the wave of the future."

He didn't laugh. We pulled into Dallas and Thurman finished the joint at a roadside park in sight of three Taco Bells, a McDonald's, and a Sleepytime Motel. He squinted behind the smoke, drawing in.

"What does your dad do?" he asked.

"Retired."

"OK. What *did* he do?"

"Roads. He built roads."

"Highways?"

"No. Two-lane roads, in West Virginia. Hairpin turns."

The joint glowed in his fingers. Dusk had fallen, a gray shade. The air was heavy and hot, full of random horns and exhaust. I could see the grit on Thurman's skin and feel the same sweaty pallor on my face.

"What is your father like?" I asked him.

He exhaled, his eyes distanced. "My father is seventy-one. Lately he's gone a little flaky."

We sat in silence until the dope was gone. Thurman turned on the ignition. "You'll have your own bedroom at my parents' house," he said, "and I sure hope your sheets aren't too heavy."

The house was a big old-fashioned saltbox on an acre of lawn, incongruous among the split-levels, badly in need of paint. Drainpipes hung at angles from the roof and the grass was cut in strange swaths, grown tall as field weeds in patches. An old Chevy station wagon sat on blocks in front of the garage. Thurman and I sat in the driveway, in the cab of the Datsun, looking.

"They've gotten worse, or he has. I've hired kids to cut the grass for him and he won't let them on the property."

"Did they know we were coming?"

"Yes."

The front door opened and Thurman's mother appeared. She was small and thin, her arms folded across her chest; and it was obvious from the way she peered into middle distance that she couldn't really see us.

"You go first," I said, "she'll want to see you alone."

He got out of the truck and approached her almost carefully, then lifted her off the ground in an embrace. She didn't seem big enough to ever have been his mother, but a few minutes later, as she looked searchingly into my face, her handshake was surprisingly firm.

The inside rooms smelled of faded potpourri and trapped air despite the air-conditioner. Only the smallest downstairs rooms seemed lived in: the kitchen, a breakfast nook, a small den with a television and fold-out couch made up as a bed. The large living room was empty except for a rocking chair in the middle of the naked floor. The room had been dismantled and holes in the plaster repaired; three large portraits in frames of uniform size were covered with painter's cloths and propped against the wall. Above them were the faded squares of space where they'd hung.

"Oh," I said, "you're painting."

"Well." She surveyed the room. "We were going to paint three years ago, but we never did." She smiled.

Upstairs the hall was dusty. Plaster had fallen off the walls in chunks and exposed the wooden wallboards. Bits of newspaper and chips of paint littered the floor; the master bedroom was clean but unused, and the other bedrooms seemed deserted: furniture pushed to the center of the floor, beds filmed with a fine dust.

"You take this room," Thurman said, "I'll be across the hall." He picked up a broom and began sweeping off the mattress. "I'll get you some sheets."

I said nothing.

He put the broom down. "Look, it was me who got the living room ready for painting—two years ago, not three. I'd hired painters to do that room and the outside; my father called them and told them not to come." Thurman stepped over to the window, looking down at the lawn through streaked glass. "But that grass. . . . Still, he's known I was coming for six weeks, maybe he planned this whole scenario. He won't let me buy him a power mower or do any chores for him. We fight about it every time I come home. This time I'm not fighting."

"Why is he mad at you?"

"Because I bailed out eleven years ago. Eleven years is a lot of mad." Thurman looked up at me. "And don't be surprised if he doesn't talk to you. His hearing isn't really so bad but he pretends to be deaf. He'll act busy the whole time we're here."

We sat at the edge of the concrete patio in deck chairs.

"My father was famous. He was known as the best high school football coach in the history of the state of Texas. Universities offered him jobs, but he wouldn't move his family, he wouldn't leave this house." Thurman shook the ice in his empty glass and looked levelly toward the old wooden garage. His father stood in the open doorway with the push mower, frowned down at the turning blades as he pushed the contraption into the grass of the side lawn. "I knew he was famous from the time I was a kid. And my brothers were famous, six and eight years older than me, both of them drafted to play ball at SMU after starring on his teams. And later I was famous, but not as famous as them. I played on my father's last team and we went to the play-offs; he was sixty years old."

The mower made its high scissoring whirr as the old man shoved it back and forth. The slender wooden handle was as gray and weathered as barn board.

"His kids aren't going to cart him off anywhere, and no one in this posh neighborhood had better try it either," Thurman said. "He was here first. And there are still people around who remember my father. If he wants to let his house fall down, or set it on fire or blow it up, I guess he's entitled."

I watched Thurman's father. He'd barely acknowledged my presence, though he'd discussed the mower with Thurman as they both knelt to wipe the blades clean with a rag. The old man was lean and stooped but he didn't seem fragile.

Thurman picked up the pint bottle between our chairs and colored the ice in his glass with bourbon.

"Did you win?" I asked him.

"What?"

"Win the championships, the last ones."

"By the skin of our teeth. We were behind and tried a long last-resort run as the clock ran out. I played end and blocked for our quarterback, a fast little Mexican named Martinez. I was the last one with him, thought it was over and took two of their backs as Martinez jumped the pile of us. I wanted to knock myself out, too much of a coward to stay conscious if we lost. I came to ten minutes later with a concussion, and we'd won."

"Was your father standing over you?"

"No, he was up there accepting the trophy. Then he came and balanced it on my chest as they lifted me onto the stretcher—big gold monstrosity with three pedestals that multiplied and looked like infinity. I wasn't seeing to clearly. That was 1964; things were just beginning to focus." He looked over at me. "You were about twelve years old then."

I looked back at him. "You didn't go to SMU."

"Not a chance. Football nearly killed me. I couldn't read print for two weeks." He sank lower in the deck chair, stroking the lush grass with his foot. His legs were long and muscular and fair. "If I'd hit an inch more to the right, I'd have bought myself a box. But even without the concussion, I was sick of it. I went to Colorado and ski-bummed and ran dope up from Mexico and went to school, did the Peace Corps trip. Didn't see my father for years."

"Why didn't the war get you? The concussion?"

"No. Knees. Got my brother though, the middle one. Killed him. He didn't even have to go. He was almost twenty-eight years old and enlisted, like a fool. My father thought it was the right thing to do. They shipped him over there and killed him in nine weeks. Nineteen sixty-eight. Saw my father at the funeral. Kept saying to me, 'Barnes was on drugs, wasn't he. They're all on drugs over there. He wouldn't have died otherwise, he was an athlete. Still worked out every day. Drugs killed him.' I said, 'Dad, the war killed him. War doesn't give a shit about athletes.' I did two tours in the Peace Corps after that. I just wanted to stay the fuck out of the country."

"Thurman . . . Thurman?" His mother's voice wavered out across the lawn. I turned and saw her at the kitchen window. "Supper," she called, "come on in now. . . ." Her every phrase was punctuated with a silence.

Thurman didn't move.

"Do you come back here often?" I asked. "How much do you see them?"

"Once a year, maybe twice. He's getting old. There's not much more time to figure it out, any of it."

I couldn't sleep. I crept down the stairs to get a glass of water. Disoriented, I turned the wrong corner into the dim living room and found myself facing the shrouded portraits. I knelt beside the last. If I looked now, no one would know; carefully, silently, I pulled the cloth away. First, a shine of glass, then, in moonlight, the features of a face. I thought it was Barnes, the dead brother, serious and young in his black suit, already marked—but no, the eyes—it was Thurman. I stared, puzzled.

"High school graduation," he said behind me. "We were all eighteen." The rocking chair creaked. "What are you doing up?"

"I couldn't sleep."

"No one sleeps much in this house."

"Who else is awake?"

"My mother. I heard her in the kitchen. When I came downstairs, she went back to bed. That's the way we do it around here." He nodded at the closed door of the little den. "She seems to have had a few drinks."

"Is that usual?"

"Who's to say? Her drinking progresses, like everything." He took a drag off his cigarette, and the glow of the ash lit his face for an instant. "She forgets things when she drinks. Conveniently."

"I doubt it's just convenience."

"What else would it be?"

I shrugged. "Pain?"

Thurman sighed. "You never know when to keep your mouth

shut. Do you think I want to sit here in this house at three in the morning and talk about pain?"

"No." I could see him very clearly in the darkness. I moved closer and touched his forehead. "You talk, Thurman, and let me know when I should speak. I'll say whatever you want."

He stood, and put his arms around my shoulders and held me. We turned to go upstairs, then Thurman paused. We heard broken words, a murmuring. He stepped closer to the den and stood listening, then pushed the door softly open. His mother stood near us in her bathrobe, an empty glass in her hand. She seemed unaware of us and looked up slowly. The dim little room was crowded with furniture and smelled faintly of bourbon. Thurman's sleeping father was in shadow.

"Mom, you should be in bed. You might fall." He walked over to her and took the glass. "I'll put this in the kitchen for you."

She stopped Thurman and grabbed his wrist. "Listen," she said slowly, in a tone of confidence, "Barnes never answers a letter, never calls. Where is he?"

Thurman led her to the bed. "Don't pull that on me."

"She isn't," I whispered, "she really—"

Now she was sitting on the edge of the mattress. Thurman put his hands on her shoulders and shook her once, gently. She looked him in the eye. "Who is that girl?" she said.

"A friend of mine, Mom, you met her earlier today. Here, lie down before you wake Dad."

She said nothing and clutched Thurman's hand; he leaned closer involuntarily. Her eyes widened, her face caught in the light of the one lamp. For a moment I could see how he favored her, how she must have looked at twenty-five: the clear, ruddy complexion, the cast and blue directness of the eyes, the thick auburn hair, maybe worn in a braid to her waist. This close, their faces nearly touched. Her profile was a broken, feminine version of his. I turned away.

"Mom, lie down."

"Don't you be leaving again now."

"Go to sleep, get some rest."

"I don't sleep. Don't you be leaving."

"Thurman," I said. I heard him straighten. Her body shifted in the bed, then he was beside me in the hallway, pulling their door shut. He stood breathing quietly, listening. No sound. The mottled living-room walls lightened as our eyes took in the dark again. Colors of dun and gray, cracked. In one corner, patches of missing plaster were ragged star shapes where the boards showed through. I reached for him.

"I shouldn't come here," he said.

"It's all right."

He stood there, looking at their closed door. "Who saves who?" he said.

I pulled his head down, close to me, touching him, his face. "Let's sleep outside."

I got some blankets and we spread them in the yard. The acacia bushes were a thick bank, bulbous and shadowy, smelling of sweet dust.

Then we hit New Orleans. Checked into a motel. Went to that bar where everyone was dancing.

What happened was scary and stupid, and whirling and sick and drunkenly predictable, and in the cards from the first. Afterward, things were different, and Thurman had no illusions about saving me. He must have worked things out himself after he left the bar alone, while he was waiting for me all night in that motel, the aqua drapes moving over the air vents behind the blue glow of the television. I remember almost all the motel rooms, and I remember that one especially, the big Zenith console TV and those cheap drapes blue as fired gas. In seven hours, Thurman could have watched three movies and twelve sets of commercials. He left me at the bar at two A.M. and I pulled into the motel parking lot in a taxi at nine. He was just drawing tight the ropes of the tarp and the door to the room was standing open. I got in the truck after exchanging one look with him, and nothing else passed between us until Georgia, when we got in the lake.

Then, we kept going.

"Don't drive in the fast lane unless you're passing." Thurman, his voice gravelly with wakefulness.

"Why not? I pass everything anyway, so I might as well stay in the fast lane. I like fast lanes."

"Oh, you do. Well. Someone even faster is going to come roaring up and eat your ass. How will you like that?" He switched off the radio. "God dammit, will you listen to me for a minute?"

I looked at him once, and kept driving.

"Pull the truck off the road," he said.

"Are you going to beat me, Thurman?"

"Pull off, right now."

I pulled off on the berm and shifted into neutral. A cattle truck passed us doing eighty, rocking the cab. There was a bawl and a smell and it was gone. Thurman sat with his back to the passenger door. "Take your hands off the wheel," he said.

"Thurman, what is this?"

"I'll tell you what it is. You're in trouble, and no fast lane is going to help."

"I don't want help. I'll just keep going until I find a way to get off."

"Good for you, sweetheart."

"Screw you."

"Hey, don't worry. You'll get no help from me. Last time I quit fast lanes I made myself a promise—no more Samaritan crap."

"You're all heart."

"You'd better worry about your own heart. You're the one with the racing pulse and the shakes, sleeping on floors and getting picked up by three jokers in a disco."

"OK, Thurman."

"Not OK. I've been there, I know what you're doing. You spend half your time in a full-throttle heat and the other half holding on when you realize how fast you're going. You don't even come up for air. Your insides are blue because you're suffocating. Your guts shake because you scare yourself. You get close enough to see death doesn't give a shit about you."

I turned off the ignition and the truck was silent. Noises of the highway went by, loud vibrations that took on the quality of musical tones. I don't know how long we sat there, maybe only a few minutes.

"Death isn't supposed to give a shit," I said, "is it? Death is a zero. Blue like ice is blue. Perfect. Barnes is perfect. Your father will be perfect, my father. All of us, cold and perfect." Thurman moved close to me across the seat. We were both sweating. He pulled his damp T-shirt away from his body and touched the cloth to my face. I whispered, as if someone were listening to us, "I don't mind the heat. I guess I want the heat."

"I know, I know. And we got heat. We got plenty of heat for you here in the USA."

The cotton of his shirt was soft and worn. "Let's drive," I said. "Who's driving?"

"What the hell. You drive."

"Do you want me to stay in the slow lane?"

"I don't care. Drive on the berm, drive up the median, drive upside down."

I pulled onto the highway with a few jerks but no grinding of gears. Thurman turned the radio back on to a gospel broadcast. There was a choir singing strong and heavy about a land on high in the sunshine; their group vibrato wavered in the dashboard.

"You're something else," came Thurman's voice. "You never did take your fucking hands off the wheel."

"I guess I didn't."

"Jesus. I don't know why I should worry about you. You'll probably come out of this with a new refrigerator and a trip to Mexico."

"Sure I will. A trip to the Gringo Hotel in Juárez, where they eat dog and hand out diseases."

He lit a cigarette and gazed out the window.

Close home, we drove through Virginia mountains in the rain. I had moments of total panic in which I seemed to be falling, spread-eagled, far away from myself, my whole body growing rapidly smaller and smaller. I could feel the spinning, the sensation of dropping. I held tightly to the door handle and concentrated on the moving windshield wiper in front of me, carefully watching its metal rib and rubber blade. I willed myself into the sound, the swish of movement and water, dull *thwack* as the blade landed on either side of its half-rotation. Runnels of rain and the tracks of their descent took me in; I could smell rain through the glass, smell clean water and washed leaves. I sat very still and the spinning of my own body slowed; the aperture of my senses widened, opened in a clear focus. Then I could feel the seat under my hips again and my feet on the floor of the truck, the purr, the vibration of engine. The capsule of the truck's cab existed around me: damp leather, a faint musk of bodies. Close to me, Thurman would be humming tunelessly to himself, staring ahead into the rainy mountains and the twisting road.

The last night, we camped out in a National Forest. Nearly dusk already, and the ground was damp; I raked leaves into a broad pile to make us a softer bed, provide some insulation. The mountains and the air smelled of autumn, soil, rich mulch.

"Sit down here and get warm." Thurman piled more wood on the fire. "Enjoy the wide open spaces. Tomorrow you're safe, if not sound. Remember safe? You'll get used to it again real fast." He blew into the fire, then leaned back and gazed at me through a wavering column of heat. "You scared?"

I touched the border of stones we'd built to surround the campfire. The stones were rough, and warming. "The shakes are coming, right now," I told him. "I can feel them."

"No," he said, "you're OK. I'm sitting right here looking at you."

"You can't always see them. Sometimes they're just in my gut."

He took one of my hands and squeezed it, then kneaded my palm and worked down each finger. He pulled hard on each joint and talked as though neither of us were paying any attention to how hard he was pulling. "You're fine," he said. "We're going to lay down in the leaves and take some deep breaths, then all those jangles will go somewhere else."

I closed my eyes and I could feel the shade creeping across the leaves. Leaves fell slowly at long intervals, dropping with a papery sound. "I think it's better if I sit here and cry," I said.

"You can't. You're not a crier."

"Let me try. Tell me a bad story."

"I got no bad stories." He picked me up in his arms and knelt to put me on the ground. The leaves were thick under us, old leaves smelling of dry mud. "Only one story," Thurman said. "We've been in that truck three weeks. A few more hours, and you're home." I remembered a song that used to play on AM radio when I was gawky and twelve, the tallest girl in the class. *Be my little baby, Won't you be my darling, be my baby now. . . .* I laughed. That's what I was, a baby, a frozen six-year-old baby going back to the start of the cold.

"Funny story, huh?" He kissed my eyes. "Don't get hysterical. I won't force you. Male pride, the Code—"

"You couldn't rape anyone. You might get mad enough to start, but at the crucial moment your equipment would fail you."

"You're right. I was born with a kindly cock." I felt his legs against me, his hard stomach, the buckle of his belt. He unfastened it to keep the metal from hurting me and touched me low on my hips.

"You get turned on when you're paternal," I said. "You're going to be hell on your daughter."

"You're hell on me," he said. "You'll be someone's good lover someday when I'm drinking beer alone in a tavern and hearing the pinball machines."

I opened his shirt and pants and slid down against him. Lake smell, like Georgia, taste of a bruise. He was in my mouth, his hands in my hair, then he moved to stop me and turned my face up. He bent over me, holding my arms, his eyes angry and surprised and wet. "No," he said.

"Thurman." I was crying. "I just want you to drop me off tomorrow. Me and the suitcases and the box of books. I don't want to see you meet my mother, none of that. All right? Please."

The cold was moving up through the ground. He felt me shiver in the dark and pulled me on top of him. I lay there and he held me with one arm. His chest was wider than my shoulders, smelling of the cold tinge of the leaves. He was awake, smoking a cigarette and staring into the trees. He exhaled with a long breath.

"It's all timing," he said. "This whole joke. Timing and the shakes."

"You're better off without me. You don't want any fast lanes."

He moved his warm heavy hand to the back of my head. "I'll tell you this about fast lanes. Don't close your eyes. Keep watching every minute. Watch in your sleep. If you're careful you can make it: the fast shift, the one right move. Sooner or later you'll see your chance."

MARGARET C. SZUMOWSKI

Born Again at the Golden Nozzle

Soon I'll be lifted from this life,
my favorite stew. They'll carry me up
and charge me with light. I'll be the visible woman
in their museum, eyes that blaze, organs that light up,
tape recordings of the heavenly choirs.
I think I'll turn off here

at the Golden Nozzle Car Wash.
All this hot water and rotating action
should do it. Soon I'll be pure, baptised Ruby,
Queen of the Truckstop. Slapping down hands
from my bouncing rear, chunky-calved and lusty,
I drink men up like cups of strong coffee.

I'd rather be Queen of the Semi's
than go to heaven. I'd rather be sponged
at the Golden Nozzle, rise gleaming
as a fresh-furred jaguar, leap
from trees, grow my hair black, catch
falling petals and birds' nests. Be paradise
for all the flagrant.

If heaven is a jungle
where you gobble mangoes and let the juice
drip down your chin . . . if heaven is a carwash
where you come out loving the flesh,
patting it tenderly, calling it Ruby,

then let me go to heaven.

MARGARET C. SZUMOWSKI

Wild Women on Motorcycles

When the wild women on motorcycles ride through the town,
even the trees shake with love.

They are beautiful, these women with hair like bushes of searoses.
They began when all the mermaids

rose from the sea and mounted motorcycles with sidesaddles
and women everywhere

arose from their wigwams delicately painted with leaping deer,
treehouses hidden

in the canopy of rainforests, houseboats and cliff dwellings
to mount red motorcycles.

We want to make a racket louder than dishwashers
and moneychangers,
dictators and garbage trucks,

louder than all the world's crooks outside your window at 5 A.M.—
wild women rousing the world.

MELISSA HOLBROOK PIERSON

On Two Wheels

Going down Route 90 out of Pensacola, making for Mobile. It was a late afternoon in October six years ago, twelve hundred miles from home. The road is straight and flat, heading you right into the declining sun. The map shows only about ten miles to the Alabama border, but it is a clever ten miles, stretching itself out, making it seem one of the most godawful lonely byways ever laid down through nowhere. Or maybe it was just the clear emptiness of that time of day, the dull ache of the temperature. By the time we reached the first stop sign we'd seen in a long piece, just before the state line, my friend and I shot a look at each other. We didn't slow a beat as we pulled a wide U-turn. In another minute we were parking in front of the Country Grill, a white box of a place with an illuminated sign out front and a flag pole displaying the limp stars and stripes, a portable sandwich board saying "open" placed next to the roadway, and neon beer signs casting their glow into the crepuscular vacuum.

The screen door banged open onto the kind of place you could hardly believe still survived in this world. This had been prime bootlegger territory, we were told by the white-haired owner. But we could have guessed as much from the stony countenance of the road just outside, the sort of solitary byway that invites no questions and tells no lies; or at least it was solitary until they built the now parallel Interstate 10.

He gave us a tour through the decades this roadhouse had seen, via the treasures on the walls and in the corners of what I have come to call the Museum of Gulf Coast Memories: oddly shaped gourds wearing painted faces; beer cans shredded and bent into airplanes and windmills; flags and tin advertising signs; a pristine pinball machine from the thirties; suggestive cypress knees polished to a high sheen. Most of this stuff is now called folk or outsider art, titles that in big-city galleries enable it to fetch more money than its creators probably saw in half a lifetime. It wasn't there to give the room an offbeat cozy-fluffy flavor, either, in the appallingly cynical manner of chain restaurants that buy antique memorabilia by the truckload and stick it on the faux fireplace mantel with heavy wax. You think you've wandered into granny's living room until you try to admire the stoneware pitcher by picking it up, at which point you remember you're still in corporate America, all right. The Country Grill and its contents were anomalous for their age: thoroughly organic.

(I got along warmly with the tiny gentleman, thinking him a kindly practitioner of Southern hospitality whom I would have liked to take home in a pocket. Until he reached the cypress knees, sucked for a moment on his top gum, then asked me, "What d'ye think I calls those?" I don't know, what? "I calls 'em my nigger knockers!" Big guffaw.)

I recall precisely that we had coffee and grilled cheese sandwiches made with white cheese and served on paper plates, and that there were bottles of hot sauce on all the checked-cloth-covered tables, and that my friend rushed out in the departing light to get a picture of the place. I look at it every now and then, the neon burning holes in the image since he had to slow down the exposure so much in the twilight.

It seems, to me, a photograph of a marvel. There has to be a reason that we found it, and that I can now return at will. The only thing I can come up with is that we got there on motorcycles.

If I had been in a car I surely would have blown on by. It's easy to do; a car is a warm world unto itself and doesn't prompt one to seek out other warm worlds. It seems so cumbersome to turn, so demanding of a damn good reason to undertake the maneuver. Everything is, anyway, distant on the other side of the glass.

My companion and I had been riding for some time together. Traveling on bikes is much like dancing, in that with some partners you do better than with others. The success is built on those worthy ineffables: the ability to anticipate, similar rhythms, desires that frequently meet exactly halfway as if you planned it like that. We had developed a rudimentary semaphore for communication.

Point at the gas tank if you need a fuel stop; open and close your fingers like a chattering wall shadow if you notice the other one has left a turn signal inadvertently blinking; index finger straight up and wrist rotating for "I screwed up on the directions—we have to turn around."

But our communication at the stop sign, as at countless other points, was signalless. I don't even think our eyes met: we each saw the other's helmet start to turn and knew instantly and with total accuracy what the other wanted. Without words, without air-filling banalities like "Want to stop? You hungry?" "Yeah, sure. How about that place back there?" we remained in solitude and silent until some need required a shortcut right past the prevarication.

I always feel, on my bike, that I have returned to a way of traveling that belongs to another time. It seems more thorough and slower, preindustrial. It is counter to the nineteenth-century excitement of rail travel, the new world of speed meeting distance exemplified by those iron lines across the West. One imagines a passenger pressing her nose against the glass, aghast at the amazement of space. Straining her mind to conceive of how far the destination was from the starting point, she would will the wheels to turn even faster, to see how much of this landscape could get chewed up without it showing a dent. But I on my motorcycle do not wish for more speed to get somewhere; rather I wish for it only to escape the crowds where I've been, which always seem to spread out sequentially to where I am. At this point I crave riding flat-out on my motorcycle to get somewhere finally expansive and lonely, old and not new—at the same time riding on my motorcycle is precisely what gives me the fuel for my periodic hysteria about the closing in of the world.

Sometimes the picture I have arrived at is quite nice, reminiscent of wilderness or what I imagine it must have been like, but I can never shake the knowledge of what is certainly beyond its frame: every inch of land claimed, known, seen, possessed—so easily ruined in potential if not yet in fact that it amounts to the same thing. I suffer, literally and phenomenologically, from claustrophobia, and riding around when I'm in that "godalmighty, isn't there *anyplace* to be alone?" frame of mind makes me feel exactly as I did that day my husband and I got stuck in a dwarf-size elevator in a hostel in Belgium and it suddenly went black and airless; I didn't know whether I wanted to die immediately or whether I was scared to death of dying.

For many years I didn't much like leaving home. Living out of a suitcase gave me the creeps. I also imagined important things must be happening at home that I was missing, which of course was never the case, since nothing much important has ever happened to me, *except* the things that happened out on the road. (I once looked through the trip diary of a German motorcycle trekker, a man who has gotten lost in parts of Africa where they had never seen a white man, much less one on a BMW loaded with luggage. He has devoted himself to befriending other round-the-world bike trippers. One of them, Ted Simon, who wrote in *Jupiter's Travels* of four years and 63,000 miles, had scrawled in the diary, "Remember, the interruptions *are* the trip," and this struck me as the only possible prescription for living a contented life, as well as having a good trip.)

It used to be that whenever I moved anyplace, dorm room or apartment, I was clutched by a need to unpack immediately, order everything to my liking, and rarely rested until I did so; thereafter I would never undertake any repairs or improvements that would cause things to be out of place for more than one day. Sleep was too hard to come by if things in the next room were havoc-struck. Camping—forget it.

Then something changed, and suddenly it seemed that only by being in motion could I truly be at rest. The height of this period lasted just under two years, and during it I put about 25,000 miles on my bike. There was one month I spent on the road, happy to have only the contents of two saddlebags with me, calmed by being temporarily possessionless. I became such an old hand at packing for a bike trip that I can still do it in a five-minute daze.

This epoch naturally coincided with the era of maps, when they exerted a pull on me that was nearly illicit. I would pore over them, unfurled on the living room rug, circling town names I liked the sound of, starring places that appeared in the books *Roadfood* and *Roadside America*, which I consulted as if they were a Magic 8 Ball. I dreamed of riding through the Ozarks, New Mexico, the Pacific Northwest. I used highlighter on small lines I had seen listed in articles like "The Twenty Best Motorcycling Roads in the U.S." Always, I imagined myself finding out there a world that corresponded exactly to what I saw on the maps: towns that were simply dots yielding quickly to the great space beyond them; large green patches that could only be dense woods and vast fields; blue figures that were cool deep water with forested shores betraying no human habitation.

I'd been around enough, of course, to know I was overly investing in fancy, and that for five miles into and out of most of those dot-towns it was four lanes and stoplights every twenty yards and one long Midasmufflerpizzahutmcdonald'skmartspeedylubesearscrackerbarrelcomfortinn. If on the map it was a nice blue lake in the middle of a splotch of green, it would actually take two hours behind a line of heroically struggling RV's to crest the hill and behold below a 500-vehicle parking lot that was almost full and a slight haze from outboard motors hanging over the waters. On rare occasion, though, for some great mystery a beautiful place would be left more or less intact, and the possibility of finding one of these was what kept the wheels spinning.

These discoveries looked different from the seat of a bike, exceeding in joy and sadness anything I'd ever found from a car. It was the simple effect of the way the way of the going affects everything. It changes the land over which you pass; it changes your eyes. The faster, say, or more insulating your vehicle, the less you are able to see, due either to speed blurring or pinholing of the view. When your sight is trained through a window, you are apt to think that since you can't see anything, there isn't anything to see.

The way you go on a motorcycle, however, is marked by two main features: nothing between you and 360 degrees of engagement with your surroundings, and the certainty of enough small hardships doled out by the environment (cold, rain, fog) to keep you humbled in its face. (It took nine years, but once in Germany,

I finally found myself pelted by curtains of hail. It was a sobering half hour.) They are both great gifts.

People travel on bikes for a fabulous variety of reasons, and all of them come down to what it feels like. The truest of the reasons is also the biggest cliché: people do it to feel free. But they also do it to get caught, to feel hopelessly enmeshed in the physical world.

There was a time I used to ride down the New Jersey Turnpike a lot, from exit 14C to exit 4, to be precise. The ride first took me over the Pulaski Skyway, a poetic passage where you are lofted up into the Newarkian air and pulled back down once more to earth. The sky looks huge from there, the scope of the industrially altered world without end. After that I would be duped by the narrow corridor of vegetation through which the turnpike runs, and spend the next two hours of contemplation in blue and green. Then I would find myself racing toward the Betsy Ross Bridge, rarely used and seemingly 16 lanes wide; it prompted the kind of strange loneliness that would make it ripe to reappear in disturbing dreams. The air was totally different now. At that moment I would be dumped into the angry rush of I-95, and then there I would be, in Philadelphia. Another city entirely. After one night there, I would be off to other places, which could all be cataloged and cross-referenced largely by color of sky, smell of air, slant of light, and density of weather.

Pennsylvania coal towns would open out into Amish farm country, then narrow into the old comfort of Main Line overhanging green and flash of sand-color stone house, then flume into Poconos sweeping uphill curves and hard-cloud days, like on a continuous tape loop. There would later be the peculiar closeness hiding just behind the ostensibly wide-open view from Delaware's watery roads. With all those different places, it was as if they had overtaken me, not the other way around. Riding was no power trip, about how much land I could consume or make go away. It was about how much I could be consumed by what surrounded me on all sides and from above, and what impressed me with my own smallness.

Claustrophobia still sometimes comes over me, brought on by

a childish grief that I may have been born in exactly the wrong moment (that point on the population graph that after thousands of years racketing along a horizontal line is suddenly launched like a three-stage rocket straight into the air). I get afraid that all will soon be lost in sameness, and then I will have nothing to feel on my sensation machine.

The cure is generally a ride, accompanied by the thousand scents that can waft past a face shield. There is still the Blue Ridge Parkway and all its many heights, and roads that corkscrew down from them to give you the ride of your life and perhaps some peanut soup at the end. And there is still Route 2 along the West Virginia banks of the Ohio, through Short Creek and Follansbee and New Cumberland and past the World's Largest Teapot. From there you can cross the river to the west and head up to Akron through countryside so gentle you would not think of using the word "beautiful" to describe it. You can still ride, too, all the way down the Georgia border on 27 and in the night be alone on a long stretch except for the whisperous scratching of corn stalks and one police car hidden deep among them. And if you continue south along it you can start to feel the change in the atmosphere before you have a name for it, and start to sense the Spanish moss before you see it.

Going in this way, sitting over a simple twin-cylinder engine and little else—down roads enveloped by their air and under their sun or coated with their drizzle; stopping at the only light in a town and putting your feet down on the very pavement while you wait—ensures that you will truly have been there, and later that you will truly remember. Going in this way also ensures that you will find the kinds of places you are panic-struck might have disappeared, because on a motorcycle you will have seen the abiding fullness of the world and so can say: Not yet.

MARTHA COLLINS

Down the Road

You think Food and you're fed.
You think Sleep and you disappear.
You wake and you're everywhere.

The someone points *You, there,*
and off you go, in your yellow
slicker and red rubber boots,

down the road but do not cross,
do not go past Susan's house, do not
talk to strangers, feed the dog.

Just this morning sun filled
my scrunched nose, snow was good
to eat, I ran ahead.

But *road* is already down
the road, two-car dream, house
machine, on/off is what it knows,

and down the road the road ends
at another road, in a field,
in mid-air, the freeway years

ago in California, or this year,
when the road fell on the road.
Love your country, go to church,

but down the road the road ends
are tied in a knot that only
a child can undo. That's

where you come in, you
of the *everywhere,* but also
you of the here and there,

eating crumbs that lead
to the table, coiling string
on your fingers, keeping time.

I slept over at Susan's house.
I slept over again but now I wake
in the nimble shadow that is

your hands and there we are.
The car starts, we're in it,
but only the road is passing by.

LYNN EMANUEL

A Poem Like an Automobile Can Take You Anywhere,

but you have to wait until Mother gets loaded
on the Greyhound and the bus blotted up
by the black of tobacco at the end of Rook Street
in Bannock, Georgia; until someone's
Aunt Rita, up to her neck again in hot water,
dries the last damp dimple and sweeps away
the constellation of Dier Kiss spilled on her

dressing table, before the plot can come lunging,
purring up to the door of the rental cottage.
It says, We'll go for a spin, and you say, *D'accord!*
thinking of Paris where a vague and soigné sun
rises forever above the seriously drunk, thinking
of Greece where you can fall in love with the sailors.

And suddenly the room's perfumed with lust
the sheet's a slick and dangerous road
where coupes of French hoods fishtail
like downed power lines and lurch and zoom
and billboards—Giant! White! Immaculate!—
are flying past and the boglands are in bloom.

And now your curiosity begins to travel
like a caravan, each pack animal loaded
with its weight of questions. Why has
the Gare de Lyon bulging at the horizon
huge, manly, tough, turned out to be
a grandpa in his waders among the sycamores?

There in the dark oblong of the windshield
a field of wheat comes swarming toward you
and hicks with open arms welcome you
to Ely, its parlors filled with the little iambs
of Granny's rocker, its sky damp and gray and chilly.

Lost in this wilderness, American and corny,
you stare at the trees and compose new
stanzas of such extravagant uncertainty that,
like "Uncle Raoul" whom you watched on
your knees through the keyhole, who lit up
your life with his burnished lassoes, they groan,
Jesus, Jesus, enough, enough.

ELINOR NAUEN

The Tucker Torpedo

Fierce as a bearcat I worry
You in the teeth of my love
Before I knew you I held out an arm
Saying dance little bearcat

Before you were born I loved you
In the back seat of an automobile
The party between my legs
I sat on your lap in a car named Blue

His forgotten face broods
In a swelter of promise
Unclaimed as prairie grass
Deep as last week

At times you can't help
But sentence 'em
Thoughts in the fire
Of the king of the road

My love cannot touch
Your lips titanic
Your concrete silence my love
Cannot touch love

If I were your teeth could I know
Your mouth better than my wild tongue
Before I knew you I held out an arm—
Say goodbye little bearcat

JEREDITH MERRIN

Autumn Drive

—FOR DIANE

Newly arrived in the Midwest
in mid-age, we drive under
pewter, lowering clouds
that presage an early
winter—past fields where dun
sparrows and occasional
rabbits glean; past wine trees,
copper, yellow, scarlet;
more walnuts, *Juglans,*
all in gold—exoticisms
almost shocking in the midst
of earnest houses, raked lawns,
pumpkins on the porch.

Different trees each season
move with their transformations
into the foreground, the way
members of each human
generation at different ages
come into relief. What was masked
by greenness now emerges:
following the first cold snap,
the delicate, sweet-butter-
colored ashes, the sudden
short-lived raging of
Euonymous, the burning bush.

But along the rain-pocked river,
the limbs of sycamores
are like mammoths' bones;
and there's a dead,
curled-up opossum
by the road. I'm tired
lately, so much of the time,
afraid I'll die without
having done what I intended —
just a body, just
one more unlucky beast.

Driving back to our still-strange
apartment, staring at red
tail-lights of cars,
dreamily in our own car
merging with that separately
yearning stream, passing
phone-booths (blue-lit,
almost elegant), it seems
we could go anywhere
or call up anyone:
a never-to-be-born
beloved child, dead parent,
or still unmet close friend.

Tomorrow, in early dark,
in this life-not-condoned
that the neighbors think exotic,
we'll write again at separate,
hopeful desks; below mine,
out the window, ornamental
crabapples line the street —
small, round green
trees turning ruddy slowly,
ripening like fruit.

ADRIENNE RICH

Song

You're wondering if I'm lonely:
OK then, yes, I'm lonely
as a plane rides lonely and level
on its radio beam, aiming
across the Rockies
for the blue-strung aisles
of an airfield on the ocean

You want to ask, am I lonely?
well, of course, lonely
as a woman driving across country
day after day, leaving behind
mile after mile
little towns she might have stopped
and lived and died in, lonely

If I'm lonely
it must be the loneliness
of waking first, of breathing
dawn's first cold breath on the city
of being the one awake
in a house wrapped in sleep

If I'm lonely
it's with the rowboat ice-fast on the shore
in the last red light of the year
that knows what it is, that knows it's neither
ice nor mud nor winter light
but wood, with a gift for burning

LOUISE MCNEILL

The Hard Road

When the roads first came,
When they looped and curled through the rocky cuts,
When the cars first whirled,
When the roads first came with their silvery gray,
When the houses far in the hills away
Came down to it in their huddled rows
Along the edge where the silver flows—

When the schoolhouse leaned and began to move,
When the church came in from its maple grove,
When the barns moved down with their lean-to sheds
And all stood close where the silver threads—

When the silver threads with its strands of gray
When the young folks smiled,
When they went away,
When the plow horse died in the tractor's row,
And the ballad changed to a radio—

When the roads first came,
When they looped and curled through the rocky cuts,
When they brought the world,
When they leaped the gorge,
When they lowered the hill,
When they brought the world with its good and ill—

FREYA MANFRED

American Roads

I

In spring
   snow geese going north
clatter on the slough.
   I'm off
along the road
again.

Lean back,
   let go.
Hwy 90 slithers west,
   snaps into 29.

      Two giants sit in two oceans
      and grin at each other
      across the USA.
      Knees up around their ears,
      toes in a New Jersey estuary,
      toes in San Francisco Bay,
      they lift a flap of Hwy
      in their fists
      and shake it up and down.
        ...
I race beneath white clouds
   crossing the Middle West:
black cow in square beige field,
A&W hamburg,
muddy Missouri,
sweet alfalfa,
   long green beachhead, fixed in time.

On my 25th crossing
   South Dakota becomes more
than the flat name of one state,
   tells itself
in the sound of two words:

"Sou . . . sou . . ."
   wind fallen into hollows
   for night rest
   after racing all day across corn.

"eth . . ."
   the long watery throat of the Missouri,
   fat with mud grains,
   seethes across fallen cottonwood.

"Da—kota"
stea—dy
   crack hand on the bow,
   pheasant in the corn row.

"Da—kota"
   comes smooth and even
   as you drive—
   the way breath comes
   when you lie on your back.
      . . .
White clouds over Dakota
   shift,
   quicken within
   my brain.
The car
   booms
   into hot summer wind.

Between my eyes
a soft explosion:

Those clouds
are painted on!

You could chip them off
with your fingernails.

I ask my hitchhiker,
"What's behind flat clouds?"
    Nodding his lion's mane,
    he rubs his young pug
    and begins to discuss
existentialism:
    leaving me
    with the mutter of clouds . . .

As a child
I fancied I created sky
by breathing out as I was born.
At twelve
earth continued, circles that opened,
spirals that pivoted, sky that breathed
with its own blood-throb.

        And once before the neo-cortex
        wrapped itself around, I
        roamed ocean gardens as a fish—
        spawned, sucked and bit—
        till death swallowed me whole.
        I had no intellect, with
        which to swallow death.

Now traveling
with death
too fast,
    my mind is strict
    with clouds:
I fear and need the wholeness
of living sky.
        . . .
I ignore my friend
    discussing despair
at the wheel.

    I tell myself a story:

        Once a woman moved to Heron Lake, Minnesota,
        with her twin lilies
        and a golden retriever.
        Heron Lake lipped along all summer,
        syrupy, with many eyes floating in it,
        including the woman's eyes.
        But one day Heron Lake iced over,
        glass of winter, coat of wind;
        the woman saw a single frozen face,
            wearing thin:
        so she and her jeep headed for I-45
        to chase the road's end.
        . . .
Highway
tentacles:
    along them cities,
    towers, walls of schools,
    plastic palm trees,
    wastebaskets that shine in the dark.

No wonder I see
   the backdrop sky
as man-made.

Some people
   who claim
everything is "like"
   something,
say even the sky
   can be jailed in a word;
they resent Ocean.

   What does it think it's doing,
      Ocean,
   being like nothing else
      before or since?
   Incomparable, unregistered,
      won't speak when spoken to.

On a high bridge over Chicago
   my car's small shadow
obliterates the metal scratches
   on the rind of earth.
500 thousand people tried
   to put Illinois in order
but lost to the rivers and the swamp.

II

On the road, I keep rocks:
   The *Love Poems* of Pablo Neruda,
   The Dying Self by Charles Fair,
   and *The Poetics of Space* by Gastón Bachelard.

I keep
>a blood-red rock from the Midwest,
>a flat grey rock from Plum Island, Massachusetts,
>and a milk-white Pacific rock with a thumb-sized hole.

I arrange these
in an order that suits my mood
at each stop.
>I pause over the milk-white rock:
>>It wants to be near the others
>>but far enough
>>for its own dense thoughts.

>At sunset
>a tall dark ranger
>on a California beach
>stopped to admire
>my bronze belly, apricot ears,
>the way I recited "yes."
>He asked me to dinner.

>He turned out to be interested in
>throwing girls into swimming pools
>while other girls watched.
>So I walked home alone
>through an orange orchard
>reciting "yes,"
>>and found the milk-white rock.
>It is a horse's skull, rising through fog;
>it is the fish head
>I was, before
>I was born,
>the face with one eye
>who stared at me
>from my womb
>when I traveled inside, by dream.

Out of flailing gravel roads,
    flower rivers,
officials of gate and street and pulpit
    gesturing:
out of roads cut for the first time
    through alfalfa fields,
out of the freakish luster of freeway slabs,
    when I don't see anyone I know all day,
or any place I've slept before,
    comes the ordering
    of rocks.
            . . .
In this world
    which has been all day
    scattering and gathering,
my car
    is my cave,
the engine my fire.
    The rear exhaust
gives the world the finger.

My car smiles at me
    through chrome braces
when I emerge from an unfriendly restaurant.
    It's an adolescent,
half girl, half boy, shiny red,
    bugging everybody.

When I shift, I make letters,
L   H   U   and   O.
Devious Boston streets register
polysyllabic words, complex sentences.
New York City elicits
an abrupt, thrusting language.
Country roads in Dakota
transcribe long and clean.

I ride, an eye, staring
    from the bone socket of my car.
The land flies by in slivers
    under heavy rain.
Hail pounds the skull,
    but I curl
on red seats
    and spin my wheels.

III

Every morning
    I sever the umbilical cord
grown during the night
    between myself and the moon.
I learn to trust the moon
    more than any human face.
Its eye returns each midnight
    to follow my story,
folds inward once a month
    upon its own saga.

I identify
    with things going long distances
alone:
    the ant on the silo
    the eagle on the wind.

But I can't stop eavesdropping:

"Nice day!" "let 'er rip!" "hi ya!"
    "right on" "Amen" "holy haystacks"
        "faster'n shit through a goose."

I'm caught by features:
    vanilla dairy-queen hair-do,
        blue thread of seaweed throbbing
            at a baby's throat.

Overtaken by voices:
    ice-creaking-on-the-lake voice,
        steak-beaten-until-tender voice,
            oily black-olive voice.

Forced to remember
    the Texas country woman
    who mauls and heals
    her innocent soft-nosed son
    with her gutteral voice and her downy voice,
    pinching his arms, spooning gravy into his mouth.

In Boston a woman with one leg shorter than the other
    talks to a posh green lamp post.

In Las Vegas a man with vodka veins
    screeches for his panting husky to FETCH.

A Navaho boy lopes across the desert near The Big Rock
    Candy Mountain, stretching to catch a frisbee.

In Carmel, California, two men try to drown a duck
    with their kayaks. One has a seaweed toupee on
    his bald head.

Every Sunday in Ames, Iowa, an old lady with two
    invisible Indians flanking her, marches to church.

I try to be metal,
    a man-made node,
but the retarded child in Howard Johnson's

eats cheesecake,
gesturing to herself
   in cream language
and I must
do as I please to her
with my eyes
   while she does
   what she can
   with her inherited self.

IV

During an afternoon rainstorm in spring,
   I stood musing with ghosts
at a stranger's attic window.
   Now on the road, I remember
I left the window open.

Which thoughts left behind
   have escaped?
How long will they ghost from mind to mind
   looking for their source?

      Once I lived on Heron Lake, Minnesota.
      I sang like a cricket
      about an acre of earth
      that made its home in my body—
      through the food I grew,
      through the same dirt day after day
      under bare feet.
      At four in the afternoon
      every 10th of October,
      a certain slant of sun
      radiated gloom and cheer
      from the hearts of past Octobers.

On the road
    I am a hunter.
I salt the game I catch
    and carry it
over many rivers.
    I weave my song
with the skeins
    of many soils.

I lick time.
    The car licks up
white dashes.
    I unravel
but cradle some core
    of myself,
as each new place
    jogs my wheel.

When I need to cry out,
    I call on
something hungry
    that endures:
it roars like an ocean
    packed into a point of space,
a vacuum
    filling with all life.

Hawks circle
    in blue gaps between the Black Hills;
the flatlands of Iowa
    roll out of the Mississippi roll.
People shout and march
    along the super-freeways.
I speed away from them.

Slow times
when I choose no one
     are vital
to the stone I smooth inside.

V

I stop longest
in the flattest, most solitary space:
out in the middle
of the Middle West.

Let the clouds move, let them run.
I hold out both arms,
laughing my basic
prairie laugh,
my friendly
cornstalk-rustling laugh
(the laugh I hide in cities)
which invites every black and white rapist
to come across the Rockies and Alleghenies
and up from the Delta
and eat my corn.

   How far do you think they'd get?
   eating their way,
   burrowing black and white tunnels
   into the wide yellow fields,
   the big golden tummy of my Ma,
        mama USA.
   "Stop that tickling," I'd say,
   "I got plenty."
         . . .

The power in the stone
I smooth within me
grows.
　　In Oregon
my forehead broadens,
new wrinkles flowing with rivers of sweat.
　　In Kansas
I stroke row on row
of gold wheat sprouted on my thighs.
　　In Wyoming
my heart leaps: the Tetons!
those tall ones who will stand up
next to me.

　　　　From the 6th tier
　　　　of a Boston Celtics basketball game
　　　　one night
　　　　I look down,
　　　　and the thousands let go,
　　　　recoil
　　　　into my eyes,
　　　　like the geography map the 4th grade teacher
　　　　used to snap up
　　　　over the blackboard.
　　　　　　I am a map
　　　　snapped back into myself,
　　　　filling with stadiums of people,
　　　　lines, teams,
　　　　choruses of people.

I feel so big,
a road hog
　　spinning my wheel,
writing
　　to empty my pocket gopher cheeks,

writing
    to restore my normal size,
writing
    till I drive to my own bones.

I'll stop
someday
    and leave my car, dead,
    in a graveyard of cars:
American in America
    traveling
the road.

And I'll leave my skeleton
to protect these pages,
this black on white map,
    this heart given voice to,
    this hunger fed.

Part Two

When I drive anything can happen.
KATHERINE HARDING

ELISAVIETTA RITCHIE

Why Some Nights I Go to Bed Without Undressing

(For poets Josephine Jacobsen, Rod Jellema, Irene Rouse, Roland Flint, and David and Judy Ray, who lost sons and a grandson in automobile accidents.)

Even as my children climb
jungle-gym and pine,
they too are swinging toward silence.

In desperate dreams I try to save
my daughter from the flood of night.
Still she drowns and drowns

while both my sons
spin nightmare wheels
against a thundering sky.

This wet midnight terribly awake
I pace the living room. My youngest son
is driving his broken Toyota home

from The Grateful Dead Live In Concert.
The storm keeps pouring over icing streets.
Finally I go to bed

but toss, alert for doors, or else
strange strained voices on the phone,
and I do not undress.

JOSEPHINE JACOBSEN

Country Drive-in

Sudden around the curve a high-up and huge
face luminous as a clock blocks out a quarter-sky.
Small I move small in my small car below
the head of a giantess, unbodied as John's
on the screen's charger.
Blue as seas, its eyes release bright pools,
kidney-shaped tears slide down the vasty cheeks.
The lips' cavern parts on teeth
whiter and bigger than any bedded wolf's.
How can I fit her mammoth grief
into the dark below my matchstick ribs?

LYNN EMANUEL

Big Black Car

. . . anything with wheels
is a hearse in the making.
RICHARD MILLER

I thought, You'll never get me
anywhere near that motor's flattened
skull, the hoses' damp guts, the oil
pan with its tubes and fluids; I thought,
I'll never ride the black bargello
of the treads or be locked up
behind its locks and keys,
or stare at the empty sockets
of those headlights, the chrome
grill so glazed with light it blurs—
oily, edible, about to melt.
You'll never get me into that back seat,
the ruptured upholstery hemorrhaging
batting is not for me, nor the spooky
odometer, nor the gas-gauge letters
spilled behind the cracked,
milky glass. The horn, like Saturn,
is suspended in its ring of steering wheel;
and below it the black tongue of the gas pedal,
the bulge of the brake, the stalk
of the stick shift, and I thought, You'll never . . .
But here I am, and there in the window
the tight black street comes unzipped

and opens to the snowy underthings,
the little white stitches and thorns
of a starry sky, and there, beyond
the world's open gate, eternity
hits me like a heart attack.

PAULA SHARP

A Meeting on the Highway

Arthurine rarely spoke of Grandpa Bubba except in reference to the salmon pink Cadillac he had left her at his death. For a long time, her grandson, Stanley, knew little about him except that he was dead, and that he had not prospered in life. The son of North Texas Methodist farmers who never finished fifth grade, Bubba attended medical school. He witnessed with horror and fascination the brutality and chicanery of the medical profession and, after one year of practice, longed for the powdery pink clay that nestled in the Dust Bowl like rouge in a compact.

Arthurine threatened to leave Bubba if he let her become a farmer's wife. She convinced him that the Veterans Administration, unlike the AMA, had always worked in the service of mankind, and he enlisted. For eight years the family lived on squalid military hospital grounds all over the South, rarely staying longer than nine months in one place. When they moved to New Orleans, a soldier who had returned insane from the South Pacific wrapped his arms in a wrestler's embrace around Bubba's neck. Within a month Bubba died of a rare tropical ailment. He left Arthurine only a veteran's pension, which barely maintained his family above the poverty line, and a salmon pink Cadillac, fully paid for.

After Stanley failed fifth grade, his mother sent him to spend the summer with his grandmother. His cousin Netta's father, a university professor in New Orleans, had promised to help Stanley with his schoolwork. The day Stanley arrived at Arthurine's house, she showed him a picture of Bubba at medical school. He was a young man in a T-shirt and panama hat. He held a toothpick in his mouth, and the way the light cast shadows between his teeth caused them to look rotten. When Netta came to Arthurine's to greet Stanley, she told him that Arthurine hated the picture because it made Bubba look like a farmer. Arthurine had no second photograph to prove she had once been married to a doctor.

Grandpa Bubba was the only person Stanley had an affiliation with who was dead. In Stanley's mind, death and his grandfather were hence one and the same. He pictured death as a thin man wearing a short-brimmed straw hat who drove a pink car and smiled, friendly-like, exposing his bad, bluish teeth. Stanley distrusted him as he would a man who pulled up behind him on the road and offered him candy.

It was in Bubba's salmon pink Cadillac that Arthurine gave Stanley his first introduction to death, although Arthurine never acknowledged this service. On Stanley's eleventh birthday, Arthurine put on a billowing white dress and matching sandals, and decided to take Stanley and Netta out to dinner at the Palace Cafeteria. Arthurine curled her hair and rubbed circles of lipstick into her cheeks to bring out their color.

Netta rode next to her great-aunt in the Cadillac's front seat, but Stanley sat in the back, perched on the removable seat arm, with both side windows rolled down so that he would not have to smell the upholstery. Stanley had never smelled a car like it. The Cadillac's odor reminded him of Arthurine's house, where menthol cigarettes, perfume, coffee and whiskey, rose water and hair spray had tucked away their smells year after year. If you entered one of her closets and opened a shoe box as narrow as a coffin, moments before you saw the sandals inside an odor would burst out and fill the room, a smell which may have hidden there for two decades waiting to be released. The car had powerful smells. Each ashtray had its own odor, the plastic seat cover stank vaguely of spoiled crab, the removable seat arm lowered with it a bad tar odor—not the rich scent of tar on a highway in the middle of summer, but the choking petroleum smell of newly poured asphalt.

The smells in the car cautioned any intruder that the Cadillac was Arthurine's inalienable property. She took the car with her even if she went only a block; she sat in it sometimes when she wanted a cigarette; and she kept handkerchiefs and magazines in the glove compartment. In the summer, she took naps in the front seat with the windows rolled down, her head wedged in a triangle of sunlight until her face turned the color of mustard, so that

Stanley had to wonder how she kept from suffocating in the heat. Never, however, in all the years Arthurine had given to making the car a second home, did it occur to her to learn how to drive.

This was precisely the concern of her grandson as Arthurine, heading for the Palace Cafeteria, eased her Cadillac past the divider onto the left side of a six-lane highway. She pressed her foot on the accelerator until the speedometer's fluorescent needle paused at forty. A car approaching in the same lane from three blocks away veered swiftly into the neighboring lane and whipped past the Cadillac.

Stanley looked at Netta, trying to summon the meaning of his eleven years into his mouth, trying to taste who he was before he died.

"Arthurine," Netta said, "you're going the wrong way down a six-lane divided highway."

"Don't tell me how to drive," Arthurine answered. She slowed her car to a steady twenty miles per hour, and glanced at the other cars whizzing away from her in the side mirror. Her own yellowish face smiled at her from the window glass.

As Stanley watched his grandmother's hands on the wheel, a bitter taste rose in his throat. He thought to himself that he had no more control over Arthurine than over the car, which he also did not know how to operate. The car, like the memory of Stanley's grandfather, belonged to Arthurine, and she could twist its purpose however she wanted.

Netta was watching the road. About forty yards up, an opening appeared in the divider. "Arthurine," Netta advised with the insolence of someone who expected to be ignored, "turn here, there's a divider break."

Arthurine paid her no mind. Cars buzzed past them without honking. Honking was for vehicles that ran red lights or loitered at green ones, for lazy pedestrians or stray dogs or wild bicycles, and not the approaching mirage of a salmon pink Cadillac plunging through waves of Louisiana heat.

Netta grabbed the steering wheel and turned it to the right.

The car cut through the opening in the divider as miraculous as new life, and continued down the road on the other side.

Arthurine continued as if nothing had happened. Netta looked at Stanley with relief. But Stanley stared at Netta with awe. It would never have occurred to him to turn Arthurine's steering wheel. He felt dizzy and liberated, as if he suddenly had been freed from a burdensome superstition.

"I hate this ugly old car," he said almost audibly.

"What?" Arthurine's face appeared in the rearview mirror.

"I said this ugly old car belongs in a junkyard."

Arthurine pulled into the Palace Cafeteria without answering her grandson. Except for acknowledging her relationship by paying for the children's meals, Arthurine made no gesture which indicated she was aware of Stanley and Netta's presence. She focused on a far point of horizon, just beyond the third row of tables in the cafeteria. When Stanley's lemon pie arrived with a horsefly embedded in the buckskin-colored meringue, she did not call over the waitress and order him a fresh piece.

On the trip home, Arthurine drove down the same side of the highway on which she and the children had come most of the way. When they reached the first bend in the road, the Cadillac snagged its fin on the chrome siding of a blue car traveling next to them, and bent the metal stripping from the hindmost to the front edge of the vehicle. The man behind the wheel was so close Stanley could see the individual hairs of his mustache arching over his mouth. The man's mouth was open in an O-shape, like a ghost in a picture book.

"You just scratched that man's car," Netta said. "From one end to the other."

"I did not," Arthurine answered. She drove off the highway onto the road home and continued for almost ten blocks. The blue car shadowed them the whole way. When they came to a stoplight, Arthurine leaned her head out the window. The man may have thought she was going to call something out to him, but her eyes were directed toward a house across the street.

Stanley and Netta saw a girl of around seventeen in an island-green dress, sitting on her front steps and eating a honeydew melon, her legs spread to catch the pulp and rinds. She did not have on any underwear.

Arthurine looked at Netta and muttered in a tone indicating this piece of wisdom would serve as a lifeline in the hard years ahead: "That girl should have more sense than to let herself be fucked by the eyes of every piece of trash passing down her street." Arthurine returned to diving.

Stanley and Netta both stared at Arthurine thunderstruck. They had never heard an adult utter the word that longed to slip through their mouths as easily as the word *no*. If Arthurine had talked in her coffin in the middle of her own funeral, the children would not have been half as impressed. For a moment, Netta and Stanley forgot about the blue car trailing them like a bloodhound. When they turned around to get another glimpse of the woman in the green dress, Stanley and Netta saw Arthurine had picked up speed, leaving the man's car fifty yards behind her.

Stanley found himself hoping that Arthurine would go on racing down the highway, police sirens lighting up behind her. Years later, when Stanley borrowed Arthurine's Cadillac for a three-day joyride—an event which ended with her sending him to stay with Netta's grandmother—this moment on the highway would return to him. He would recall Arthurine smiling at the black road ahead of her, the wind in her hair, and ask himself not what drove people to break the law, but how it was possible that some human beings could pass an entire lifetime without ever committing a crime.

When the woman in the green dress disappeared from view, Netta regained her composure and told Arthurine, "You have to stop." Netta added, with clear interest in the possibility, "You'll be put in jail for a hit and run."

Arthurine pulled the Cadillac into a vacant lot. Stanley watched the blue car follow them, sniffing their taillights. A young man stepped out of it onto the sidewalk to talk as Arthurine and the children emerged from the Cadillac. The man wore a straw hat and had crooked teeth. His cheeks were gaunt and pale. His face was so filled with expectancy that he reminded Arthurine of an insurance man or debt collector, come to demand his due.

She smiled at the man with a look which startled Stanley, and which would haunt Netta throughout her womanhood, a look at once helpless and coy that revealed Arthurine to be the very opposite of what she was. "*I* won't make you pay for my car if you've hurt it," she told the man.

"Arthurine," Netta intervened. "How can you tell him he hurt our car?"

Arthurine turned toward Stanley and the Cadillac, her face resettling into its accustomed expression of a tough old bird, her back to the man as she said, "Let's take a peek at my car." The man walked behind her with difficulty, because his hands were buried in his pockets. He opened his mouth as if about to say something, then closed it.

The man peered at the side of the Cadillac where Arthurine pointed to a three-year-old scratch bordered with rust. When he saw that the man was not going to say anything, Stanley wanted to shout, "But Arthurine, you ran into him!"

Stanley barely hid his jubilance as he traced a scratch on the blue car with a detective's accuracy. "There's no way he could have done that," Stanley said to himself. "Unless he backed up in the middle of doing forty on the highway."

Arthurine pinched him midway down his ribs, and Netta told her, loud enough for the man to hear, "Don't pinch Stanley."

The man walked behind the Cadillac to write down the license number on a ragged square of paper, but saw the plates were ten years old. He tugged at his hat so that it slid forward, hiding his face. He stared past the Cadillac for a minute, and then stuck the paper back in his pocket, climbed into his own car, turned on the ignition, and drove away. Not once in the exchange had he uttered a word.

Arthurine smiled victoriously as the blue car followed a pickup onto the highway. She and Stanley and Netta climbed back into the safety of the Cadillac and drove home without further incident. When they arrived, Arthurine shooed the children out of her car and locked herself in. She lay down, resting her head on her purse, and spreading her white dress around her so that she looked like a fried egg simmering on a skillet. She kicked off her sandals. She fell asleep thinking of that time long before Stanley was a baby when Bubba had shimmied along the street to her door, the new car leaping beneath him like a salmon escaping downstream from heaven.

EILEEN MYLES

Looking Out, a Sailor

The clouds looked made, & perhaps
they were. An angry little shelf
for the moon to have
some influence
on. I'm dying tomorrow

my car died tonight
a glorious explosion
then clunk.

Turning pages, turning pages
coming up on midnight
when the poet died.

It was his heart
not his
head.

The girl, she was say 27
covered in tattoo
a sauce her
boyfriend
made to cover
her sins

let's say she is glad tonight
to be dead. Her name?
Lorri Jackson.

So I push on & my
dog needs
a bath—don't sell Rosie
short says the
trainer & flattered
I won't.

I remember the last
night with my
car. Came home
& called the night
watery grave. Didn't
know why. Everyone
dying around
me now. But
not yet,
not me yet.

The lights all smeared &
gooey in an incredible
downpour like Lorri's
body I could see shadows
that I think were
persons, they were
the dead &
we were
alive, yes I think
it was that
way that
last night. So lucky
I didn't hit
one.

My pooch
by my side. This
is my life
when I grow
up I thought
as a child.
In my boat with
my dog, named
what, Rosie,
she barks
driving into
the night
god, we couldn't
see a thing
but we weren't
scared. Besides
we'd had
plenty of
life.

Prayed for a
parking space.
Funny turning
in the dark
those lights
back there
are cars I think.
Don't ask me
said Rosie.

But I wanted to sail
the rest of my
life. It was dumb.
I'd arrived
there was
my space.

Perfect & I pulled in
& this is the
saddest poem
I ever wrote.
What can I tell you about
sadness, the shapes
you find beneath it,
how you run from
it in your sleep,
bolting awake

early in my labors I
worked with
children, I was one
then but so
what the story goes.
Autistic kids, a
boy named
Bobby
who so loved
porcelain he leaned
his cheek on
it, a little
animal & his
cool white
mama

the things I warm my
hands by are not
true, someone
who holds her
head like
that forbidding
I think
is warm

I would lay my paw
on her icy bottle,
her icy dead
cheek, her red
legs

the red light rippled
in my watery grave
if I could paint
tonight I would
be the word
that fills the silence
after modern
following something
slow, red
changing lanes
it was utterly
silent my
painting, the
dog breathing
well, relentlessly
& they had
pulled my antennae
off long ago so
deep down

there was
some music
classical,
how to say
I was having
the pivotal
moment of
my life
with a
dog, all
the silence
had led up to
here & streamers
could be
followed to
the moment
of my
death,

what kind
could I be
some kind of
poet who
followed it
along, say it's
distant &
far off, or
right next
to me
now, I
do not know
or choose
to. I saw
the world
melt all
at once

I want to
go with
everyone
waiting for
everything
to shift back
to real &
it's stranger
& stranger
now—all
of my lies don't
lie anymore.
The car dies
& I drive
on. The rain
stops. He said
I would
surely outlive
my dog &
I know
that & I
took her
home. But
everyone. No I
didn't know
that. When
everyone
goes I
go. I'm
following
now, &
our truth
is dark

GAIL MAZUR

Poem Ending with Three Lines of Wordsworth's

The organ donor who smiles
in the leathery dark of my wallet
from a driver's license

has already struck one woman—
elderly, confused—
who stumbled off a Somerville curb

one January dusk
and became a sickening thump,
then a bleeding body

cradled in the driver's arms
until police and ambulance came.
That old woman lived

to sue the driver who now
takes a different route each week
to the supermarket,

and on her birthday,
in line at the Registry, decides
she's old enough, if not

for a Living Will, then to leave
her kidneys or heart or liver;
the little silver label below her

Polaroid portrait is the Registry's
donor code. She envisions herself
extricated one night

from crushed burning metal
by the jaws of life,
less lucky, finally, than her victim

whose two pocketbooks (maybe
she was a pursesnatcher?) flew
in opposite directions

and landed awfully far
from the eyeglasses and left shoe.
All the eyewitnesses

exonerated the driver.
They swore to what she won't remember:
the old woman fell,

or fainted to the fender;
the car was going five miles an hour.
Still, that impact was what she'd dreaded

all her tremulous years at the wheel
which she grips for dear guilty life,
concocting terms of a bargain—

she'll bequeath what she's got in her body
so whatever virtues she lacks,
she won't just be someone dead

unprofitably travelling toward the grave
like a false steward who has much received
and renders nothing back.

JOSEPHINE REDLIN

All the Carefully Measured Seconds

Back then I still believed it was possible
to prevent certain things, until that hot afternoon.
It was the middle of grain harvest, August of '54,
when Fred climbed down from his stalled combine
and took off for Montrose to buy a part.
Later I realized the part was a ruse of fate, like
something made up to get someone to a surprise party.
So many times I reran those last hours,
adding or subtracting a few seconds here or there.
Lingering a moment in the field, he could have
noticed the grain shiver as a cloud passed by,
he could have paused by the barn to admire the blue
and lavender flecks adorning the pigeons' throats,
he could have stopped by the house to finger
the soft leaves of the African violets
on the sill, he could have slipped his arm
around Ella's waist as she stood at the sink,
her hands in the dishwater.
But, he swatted the grain dust from his overalls
and climbed into his green Buick to keep
his appointment on Highway 38. Even then,
it was not too late. He could have floored
the car just this once, he could have let
the wind rush in, raising his sparse strands
of matted hair to dance in the breeze.

When I saw Fred's car again, it looked as if
it had been punched by the fist of some god
though surely not the same one who keeps

the earth spinning, the sun and moon rising,
passion ascending to fuse new life,
the rose unfolding with tenderness,
the worm tilling the orchard floor,
all the carefully measured seconds
adding up exactly to us.

In the Driver's Seat

It was the first funeral in ten years that Emma had been to without Fran. But in a way Fran was there, even if she was laid out in the other room with rosy cheeks like one of those alabaster Virgin Marys sold in religious shops. How they'd done it was a mystery because in real life Fran had skin more like wax paper that had been done to a turn in the oven.

All you heard were people sayin', "Now isn't she a picture?" or "Doesn't she look fine in death?" Jesus sake! Dead was dead. You weren't supposed to look like you was goin' to open your eyes an' go "Boo!"

If Emma hadn't been feeling so mad about it all, she would surely have fallen apart. For it was Fran lying there. Beloved Fran. Since their husbands had died some twenty years before, both men taken within a month of each other, there had been no sitting around for Emma or Fran. There had been bus tours of Europe and the British Isles, and right until Fran had her heart attack, neither of them had missed a single funeral, christening or tea in the Carlisle district and that was through wind, sleet or snow.

Emma did the driving and Fran sat back and enjoyed the scenery. The nice thing about Fran was that she never bitched or whined about a damned thing. In and out of ditches they'd been together, and once Fran had even been pinned when the car did a turn in Simmond's field, but Fran hadn't even complained then, just brushed herself off and laughed about the bruises.

"*I see us goin' real quick!*" she'd said once to Emma. "*Sort of flying, like on one of our trips, and we won't know what hit us.*"

"*Reckless!*" Emma's Bob had always called her driving. But she didn't care. She'd gotten them places for years and they'd survived. Only Fran had been wrong about them goin' together. She'd opted out early. She'd have been glad of that. They'd often talked about death and they'd made each other a solemn promise, no tubes and bottles an' things. *"Pull the plug real quick!"* Well someone had sure pulled Fran's quick enough, but who was going to pull hers now that Fran was gone?

She looked across the room at her daughter-in-law, Sharon. She'd be the last person. Sharon, strictly because of her principles of course, would keep her hooked up for an eternity like a spent battery waiting for a charge that wouldn't take.

Sharon in that same damned green pant suit, stuffing a piece of carrot cake into her mouth, licking off her fingers the way she always did: a fat rock lizard, the little red tongue flicking out greedily, making sure not to miss a crumb.

Sharon had started off pretty enough, but time hadn't been good to her. She'd been one of those soft-lookin' blondes with five-year-old voices, but the face was big and round now an' the voice had hardened in pitch so that it grated on the ears.

It was no use pretending about Sharon, they'd never liked each other from the word go. Sharon had thought by marrying Will she was entering some kind of competition, only there was none. Will, unlike Donald, her oldest, had always been a slow youngster: slow at everything, a week late bringing in the crops and then it would rain and they would lie soggy in the fields. Like all slow people the harder you push them the slower they go. Sharon had been too dumb to know that. Later, when she'd realized she was wasting her time nagging, her frustration had turned into bitterness.

Sharon came across the room to her. "Well, Mother-in-law, you'll have to put the car on blocks now." Her little eyes glittered with enjoyment.

"Not a darned thing wrong with the car that I know of," Emma smiled.

"Won't be the same on your own, will it?"

Marge Jedzinsky joined them and put a hand under Emma's elbow. "You'll miss her?" Marge said with sympathy.

"I was just sayin' that," Sharon said, pushing more cake into her mouth. "I sometimes think Mother-in-law shouldn't be on the roads. Some people just don't know when to quit."

"Oh, I don't know," Marge said with a grin. "She couldn't drive worth a darn forty years ago, nuthin' much has changed."

"It wouldn't do her no harm to stay home for a while." Sharon wiped a wrist across her mouth. What she'd wanted to say was, *"Stay home and clean up,"* Emma guessed, but she didn't have the nerve to say it. You couldn't set a foot in Sharon and Will's house without having to take off your shoes. The whole house was covered in plastic from top to bottom. What in God's name she was saving it all for was a mystery to Emma.

Sharon exchanged a look with Marge, but Emma didn't give a hoot. She'd never been one for housekeeping, but it hadn't bothered Bob, her husband, one bit. What she had done was cook good meals and raise the boys as best she could.

Donald was a professor in the city now an' she was proud of that. There was no denying that she had a lot more in common with Donald. They could talk about anything together, but there was also a special feeling there for Will because he'd been so helpless in so many ways. Donald, she knew, would always manage by himself; it would be Will who would have the struggle, and God help him, with Sharon he wouldn't get much comfort.

Will came over to her house a lot these days and lay around the living room with his legs stretched out, leafing morosely through old magazines. Emma reckoned he came for peace and quiet because the T.V. was on over at his place from morning to night. He probably came too to put his bum down on some honest-to-God fabric for a change. Lord knows it must be horrible to have to sit on plastic all the time.

Emma closed out the buzz of voices in the other room. *"Hey! Remember the time we went to New York?"* She heard the familiar voice distinctly, but she didn't open her eyes, she just smiled.

"Them cab drivers drove just like you, Emma. I felt right at home. Remember you could see them eyeballin' us in the mirror to see if we was gonna pass out from fright and there we was sittin' up tall and havin' a good smile?"

"What you doin' in here talkin' to yourself?" a green shadow by Emma's elbow asked.

"I wasn't talkin' to myself. I was having a talk with Fran," Emma said defiantly.

"It isn't healthy talkin' to the dead."

"Who said I was talkin' to the dead?"

Gone off her rocker! Definitely gone off her rocker! There'd be the voices whisperin'.

Will jogged her elbow. "You'd better come in the other room, Mother. Have some more tea," he said.

"I've had all the tea I'm gonna have. An' I'd appreciate it if you'd leave me to pay my last respects."

"It's no use being morbid, Mother."

"Who's bein' morbid?"

"Sharon says you've been talkin' away to yourself."

"I wasn't talkin' to myself, Son, I was talkin' to Fran."

"That's even worse," Will said. Sharon nodded in agreement.

Emma sighed. "I've been talkin' to Fran for forty-five years, Son, old habits die hard. Now if you don't mind I'd like to be alone."

The next couple of weeks were horrible. Emma got some kind of chest infection and had to stay in bed. The worst thing of all was having to be beholden to Sharon who came and went with trays of food: steak turned into shoe leather, swimming around in a morass of red-clay gravy; or meat loaf that turned to sawdust in the mouth.

The only good thing was that Fran kept coming and they went over all the good times they'd had together. She tried to keep Fran away when Sharon was there, but sometimes Sharon came sneaking in on them. She came in on them when she an' Fran were having a good gas about the Picasso exhibit they'd seen in Montreal.

"At it again, Mother-in-law?"

Sharon shoved the tray down on the side table, knocking a book onto the floor. Yanking out a tea towel she'd brought with her, she tied it like a bib around Emma's neck.

"I don't need this thing." Emma tried to take off the bib.

"Yes, you do, you'll drop all over yourself."

"I wish you'd stop treatin' me as if I'm demented."

"Maybe when you stop talkin' to yourself."

"Just because you can't see no one doesn't mean no one's there," Emma said.

"You think there's someone there?"

"Not someone! Fran."

Sharon sat back with a piece of chicken impaled on a fork and stared at her mother-in-law. Emma could see she'd gone too far. It was shortly after that they brought in the nurse, a female with a breath worse than Reggie, the farm dog's.

Emma's cough wouldn't go away, it wore her out when she got into one of the spasms. She knew she was a lot worse when Will came and sat with her for about an hour every day. She wasn't sure why he sat because they didn't have much to say to each other, but she liked him there and he did hold her hand.

Days had a way of folding into one another, dawn rolling into dusk, lights on and lights off, voices coming and going. Vaguely she heard, "Mother, there's going to be a storm an' we're scared we'll get locked in down here an' you not gettin' any better. Dr. Bell thinks we should take you into the hospital."

"I'm not goin' anywhere!"

"Donald's on his way."

"That's nice, but he's wasting his time. I'm not going to no hospital."

"Mother we can't look after you here if you get any worse." An' she knew he wasn't talking about her cough, she knew he was goin' on about her conversations with Fran, although God knows why he should have been worried about those. They didn't harm anyone and they kept her from being lonely.

Donald came finally, trying his best to hide his worry, but that would be because of Sharon's lies. He gave her a hug and sat down beside her.

"Hello, Mother!"

"Hello, Donald!"

"Will says you're being difficult."

"He's the one being difficult."

"We're all worried about you."

"About what?"

"Your cough."

"An'?"

"And nothing . . . your cough."

She knew it was no use to argue. They would use any trick to get her out, and she didn't feel she had enough energy for the battle. The nurse helped her dress, breathing her awful dog breath in Emma's face. At least they would have young ones in the hospital with fresh breath.

The awful thing was that as they left the farm she had a sudden, terrible feeling she was leaving Fran behind. When Donald had settled her into the car and gone to say his good-byes to Will and Sharon, Emma asked,

"Are you still there, Fran?"

"Darned tootin' I am. You don't think I'd leave you now?"

"I wasn't so sure."

"You're makin' a mistake, you know."

Emma frowned, *"You don't have to tell me, but I couldn't fight 'em all."*

"Don't see why not. This way it's the last time you'll see the place. They turf you out and then Sharon will come in with a scrubbing brush."

At that point Donald climbed into the car beside her and patted her blanket-covered knee. "Are you OK, Mother?"

Emma nodded, she was feeling anything but all right. It had already begun to snow outside, those big heavy cotton balls of snow that promise snowdrifts. Donald drove cautiously out of the driveway. It was already getting greasy the way it always did with the first layer.

"Looks like we just started in time."

"In time for what?"

"Before the storm comes in full force."

Donald drove just the way his father had, ten miles an hour, as if he expected to meet the worst around every corner. They were silent. She could see Donald needed his concentration, but there were things on her mind.

"I don't want them to put no paint on my face," she said finally.

"Paint on your face? What do you mean?" Donald didn't take his eyes off the road and had his "humor her" voice in place, although it wasn't as casual as usual.

"When I go, I don't want them makin' me up like I was some sort of china doll."

"Mother, you're not going anywhere but to hospital."

"No paint, mind!"

She was content she'd said what she had to, and she knew he'd paid attention even if he'd pretended it wasn't worth thinking about.

Sometime later, they turned into a service station for some gas. The attendant came out and he and Donald commiserated about the weather. She heard them only vaguely, because she wasn't feeling too good, like there was a big band tightening around her chest. Donald mumbled something about new wiper blades for the windshield and was gone somewhere. Suddenly she heard Fran's voice clear as a bell.

"So you're just gonna sit there an' let him take you to hospital? Just like that?"

Thank God it was Fran. Emma smiled, she knew that Fran would never abandon her.

"What else can I do?"

"You've got a car, get goin', hightail it back before the witch gets her shovel in to clear out your place."

"It don't seem right."

"It's not, but what they're doing isn't either. Come on, girl! Get a move on!"

Then she was in the driver's seat without even knowing where she'd found the energy to move and somehow the car was going.

"Way to go, girl!"

"You know I reckon all those years you've been eggin' me on, Fran?"

"Never needed too much urgin', that's for sure."

There was a lot of buzzing going on in her head.

"You're sure gettin' cautious in your old age. Remember how we talked

about flyin'? You still have a chance, you know. Perfect time to do it, nothing but soft landings."

"Fran, you old rascal."

But she was right about soft landings. Even now she felt as if she were inside a vast ball of wool, cushioned from any kind of hurt or danger. Where she was didn't really matter. She was conscious of the windshield wiper moving uselessly back and forth. Donald had been right, it was no earthly good, it cleared things for only a second, long enough for her to see someone's face peering at her, maybe Donald's, maybe not. Not, it couldn't be Donald, she was on the highway, she could feel the car moving beneath her.

"Atta girl! I knew you could do it!" Fran's voice said.

She could see big white tracks in front of her just like the snow plow made when it came in up the lane to the farm, and what sounded like Reggie's barking when he always ran out to greet her when she got back from one of her trips. Then it was like she was on a runway and everything around her was flying past and she was soaring, soaring and in the background Fran was laughing and urging her on ... An' the weirdest thing, somehow Reggie was hangin' over her an' she was trying to avoid his breath.

"Atta girl! Atta girl!"

KAREN LATUCHIE

from Counting Backward

I slept in my car last night. There had been a noise in the kitchen again. An explosive noise that grabbed me out of sleep. Sitting up in bed, my heart pounding, I listened to some new creature—it *had* to be larger than a mouse—rummaging across a kitchen shelf, making its way in my general direction. I'd been paralyzed, unable to think of what to do. If I got up to close the door I might meet it halfway. If I got the door closed, how would I know when it was safe to come out? I was trapped in the house, in my head. I pulled on my bathrobe, grabbed the flashlight I keep by the bed, and ran outside, pulling the bedspread around me. I was barefoot, there were stones, the flashlight cut a narrow path to the car.

I've spent a little time sitting on the patio now, still holding the bedspread and flashlight, seeing myself huddled inside the car a few hours ago. I'd quickly forgotten the noise and moved on to demons: imagining them jigging around the car, trying to breach its metal circumference. I couldn't see them but I knew that if I could catch a glimpse of them, any one of them, I would see Anne. That's what I imagined, sitting in the car, steadying my breath, trying to feel the safety of the enclosure and knowing that if one of those demons could have stopped its whirl for long enough, it could have looked in the window and seen me sitting quietly, clutching a bedspread like a security blanket.

But then Anne did come to me, in a dream. She sat with me in the car, in the front seat while I spread out in the back. We were catching up with each other. I was laughing, happy. I knew she understood why we were in the car instead of the house. When we were finished talking, she got out of my car and drove away in her own.

Her car. It was like something *she* would have dreamed, as if she'd come into my dream early, before I had it, and designed the car for herself. It was huge and ungainly, bigger and more power-

KAREN LATUCHIE ◆ 127

ful than anything she could actually buy. As if she'd planted the image in my dream to transport me away from this moment, back to a simpler one, twenty years ago when she told me the Lincoln story, made me laugh with it. How, newly arrived from Afghanistan in 1959, where her father had been stationed and she'd been born, she'd taken notice of her first American car: her father's new Lincoln Continental parked in their driveway. How she'd walked slowly around it while her parents stood off to one side, and then, pointing at it, asked her father: "Anybody home?"

"I was ripe for the revelation of American automotive prowess," she'd said to me, and she had remained a sucker for it. Once she was out of college she kept herself in used cars that approximated the size and power of the Continentals of her youth. She called them pigmobiles, and that was how she'd shown up in the dream: driving the greatest of all pigmobiles—

But that's a mistake. She didn't show up in the dream. I put her there. I invented that car for her to drive in and out, all shine and bloat, something imagined and changeable, to divert me from the real scene which I can only imagine in one way and can't help imagining now, again and again.

I imagine Anne driving the Oldsmobile Fire Chief: 1972, cream puff, mint condition, all that chrome against unblemished white, a hint of fins, red interior. She had driven up the Taconic Parkway, swaying the wheel through the curves, and then Route 22 north, past the spot where almost twenty years earlier we'd been stopped by the cop wondering if we were runaways. Did Anne remember it when she drove by? Remember how hard I laughed as we pulled away, thinking of the dime bag of grass in my backpack, and how long it had taken me to realize that she wasn't laughing at all? Or had she forgotten the spot, the incident, everything about the beginning of our friendship? Or if she hadn't forgotten, would she have pretended she had? I imagine that's what she would have done. I imagine that she saw no latent detail in the expanse of the Little Hoosic River valley as she drove up Route 22, until she sighted the Petersburg traffic light in the distance. The only light between New Lebanon and Hoosick Falls, the only place she would have had to slow down much at all and she would have known how to time it so that she'd make the green light. She would have reached for her cigarettes as she eased up on the accelerator, leaned over, searched the dash for matches since the lighter was so slow to heat, the one part of the car that showed its age. There would have been no matches (there never were) and she would have searched her bag next to her on the seat, relegating caution to instinct.

I was told that the car that hit her "came from nowhere," that her death was instantaneous. I find both things impossible to imagine no matter how often I try since the intersection is wide open and nothing is hidden on any of the approaches. Instead, I imagine that Anne would have looked up from her bag in time to see that even if she swerved it would do no good. She would have known that she had miscalculated, that the light was still seconds away from turning green and that the other car was racing to beat a yellow signal. She would have known that she was about to have a collision and, in that instant, her death would have begun. Which is not, I think, what they meant by instantaneous.

LINDA KITTELL

michael

It is Vermont mud that covers my boots. I pull out the day's mail, rip into the envelope with a Montana postmark. Inside there are xeroxed copies of Michael Cantrell's obituary, the death notice and accident reports:

. . . a computer technician for Glasgow Office Supply . . .

Carrump. The clean hit of cue against solid. Cowboy hats, elbows at right angles—all tables away. Michael steadily chinks balls into pockets, the quiet stalk of man around green felt. His fingers move constantly around the stick as if it were the size of a cigarette. "C'mon," he tells me. "Try this one here. Touch it right above center. It'll follow. C'mon, c'mon, a little higher and kinda loose. That's it."

The Cantrell car, a 1976 Chevrolet, driven by Michael Paul Cantrell, 33, of Wolf Point . . . was westbound and crossed the center line striking . . .

"Shit." He jumps out and kicks the car, the tire. We three others climb out in slow motion. Karen and I, laughing, walk out into the field.

"I gotta. Pee."

All our eyes must be puffed red and shining as if covered with bubbles.

"Geez. Us. Lookit the stars." We pull up our jeans and zip, a perfect unison. At the car, Michael is rummaging through bottles and clothes.

"God, Mike." His girlfriend snaps her gum and grabs the leather satchel she calls purse, searches through it and pulls out two different brands of cigarette.

. . . died Thursday in Billings' St. Vincent Hospital of injuries he sustained in a car-semitruck accident near Wolf Point Jan. 10.

The vacuum is mostly in pieces on his workbench. But Michael finds more pieces, cleaning each one as he digs further into the machine towards the motor.

"With Kirbys it's always the armature, if it's anything. But I know enough to get into the guts of these things. Even if some of these ladies are sure it ate their kids' Legos."

He works quickly, sometimes talking, sometimes picking up the melody of the song coming out of a small plastic radio that sits on the window sill. There are parts everywhere, screws that roll around the table ready to fall to the floor. Michael unwinds a long string of dental floss that's wrapped its way around a one by two inch rod.

"Jesus, her kid must have had a blast."

He holds up the part to show how the rod spins easily. Then as quickly as the machine has come apart, it comes back together, a kind of magic. In moments, the vacuum is whole again. He clicks it on to demonstrate. "It's always the armature."

The semi, loaded with several thousand gallons of sulphuric acid, was forced off the road into a field.

"Get it away. Bad medicine." A small snake makes him jump away from the potato patch. Michael does a comic dance, but he is really afraid. He must be remembering his boyhood in Oklahoma, a small boy from the reservation gone wrong. His memory is a circle around his mother's house in a big, blue Ford, Oklahoma dirt blown up around the house, to try to bury the family's bad medicine.

"It's just a garden snake, Chief," Ron tells him.

His white friend calling him "Chief" makes Michael smile. "They give me a choice. Nam or jail. So I pick Nam, where I can be free. They called me Chief there. And I was the radio man. See, I thought they were supposed to cover me. I remember running up hill and dropping behind that fucker. Heavy bastard, but big enough to hide behind."

Mr. Cantrell was a Vietnam Veteran.

"So one of the guys calls the old Chief out. And I'm in the jungle, vines hanging around thick." His thick arm cuts the air and reaches across the kitchen table after Tabasco sauce. "And then," he points the bottle toward his son, Merle, a miniature Michael whose chin touches the table top. "And then," Michael jumps up from the table, "I see this huge baboon. Bright. Orange. Sonovabitch. Those big baboon eyes staring me right in the face. All the guys laughing." And Merle laughs, banging his empty soda can against the table. Michael goes into a gorilla routine and his boy yells "Geegee. Geegee," his father's word for ghost, for boogey man.

In 1975 he married Karen McChesnie in Roundup.

"Hop in, Babycakes. They already down in Billings. I'm Edna. Have a cigarette. They been expecting you guys all day. The wedding, eh? Chri. Rusty you ole peckerhead, pull in here an' get us some brandy. Come on, Babycakes, have a cigarette. You gotta nice smile. Like me, we both got big teeth. Back there's Malcom and Leona, their kid Marla Rae. The fat one's Maggie. Chri, shut that kid up with one of them cokes and hand us two of them paper cups and some brandy."

The Cantrell car spun sideways and remained on the highway.

"Karen, get that doobie outta your purse there. This is some really good stuff. Hold on! I gotta get something outta the car." Michael paces the linoleum, fiddling with a glass, an empty can, a bottle top. "Merle, why dontcha go get Daddy's book."

"I can't believe you spent that much, Mike. Fifteen dollars." Karen passes him the joint.

"Didn't I tell you it was good?" Michael says, inhaling. Merle runs in with the book. Michael roughs up Merle's hair—"I am the Greatest. Ali. My man—" then gives the boy a high five.

. . . if the tank holding the sulphuric acid had burst, an evacuation would have been necessary for a several mile radius.

"Can me and Otto sleep here? It's late. You know what I tole you about the ole Chief and firewater." They climb in next to Ron, but do not bother to take off even their boots before crawling down under the covers and falling into a loud sleep.

Highway Patrolman Mike Frellick said there were actually two accidents which occurred. The first involved . . . Michael and Ron out fishing, walking along the river until the trees open up and row after row of herons rise up, great blue-grey birds whose rookery they've come upon and take as a sign of magic. Neither of them speak until later they can joke with their girlfriends over a beer in a run-down bar in Milltown.

Survivors include his wife:

"'I'm not going to sit around listening to some goddamn dumb Indian whine about his gut', that's what his doctor told me. And two days later they found gangrene. Geezus, all over his insides. I'm in Kalispell now, with the kids."

two sons, Michael III and Merle and a daughter Nicole;

"I had to make the decision. Now the whole family's not talking to me."

his father of Wolf Point; seven brothers, Michael Joseph, Courtney Jr., and Rubin, all of Wolf Point; Verle in Kentucky, Christopher, Tony and John all of Los Angeles, Calif.; nine sisters . . .

"I thought it was right. I thought it's what Mike would want."

The second accident involved . . . the two friends going too far back into the country by the river, not stopping to think about how soon dark comes in winter. They both misjudge the firmness of the ice, but only the white man winds up wading part way across the slim stretch of river. Michael somehow flies to the other side.

There he lays down the combined paper in both their wallets: a bank statement, some baseball cards, a picture of an old girl-friend, a Kirby business card, then builds a fire on top of a door pulled off a shanty. And when the fire has risen knee high and cracking, the white man strips naked and lays his clothes and boots to hiss dry. Together they drink, with the steam of stale coffee, the last of the brandy.

DENISE McCLUGGAGE

Ruth Levy, Me, Nassau

from AutoWeek *March, 1988*

It was memorable to those who saw it. Even after some thirty years
people tell me it was the most exciting race they ever did see. Most
recently, Walter Cronkite told me that. I had run into him at Skitch
Henderson's surprise 70th birthday party in New York. (Now
there's an opening for you: Two heavy names, both sports car buffs
of yore, and one heavy location.) But enough of this, let's cut to
the race. I wish I could have seen it, but I was in it. It was at Nassau
Speed Weeks and it was primarily between Ruth Levy and me. In
two heats.

This needs some scene setting.

Among the few women driving race cars in those days, I was
considered superior on the East Coast and on the West Coast it
was Ruth Levy. I kept hearing her name, she kept hearing mine. I
was curious. Was I faster than Ruth Levy? Could I beat her?

When it came to competition I have a strange advantage. I had
a dual childhood. I played dress-up and poured sugary tea for as-
sorted dolls and teddy bears. I went to birthday parties in puffed-
sleeved dresses with a big bow smack in the middle of my head.
But I also raised hell with cap guns, jumped off the garage roof
with an umbrella and played tackle football with the boys. I had to
"rassel" a few of them who moved into the neighborhood bearing
a notion that girls shouldn't be allowed to play real football, but
once the point was made we were all friends in the huddle. What
I'm saying is, I was used to being best friends with my best competitors. Something, I keep reading, that is still lacking in today's
corporate woman. Well, there are benefits to having a *boyhood*
whether you're male or female.

Friendship in competition was strange to Ruth. She told me
that the "ladies" races in California were near "hair pulls." And the

guys stirred the competitive pot, rather as if we women drivers were pet pit bulls. *Mine* can beat *Yours*, that sort of thing. And that's the vein in which a meeting between the two of us was being pushed. Ruth of the West Coast and me of the East Coast.

But I wasn't having any of this hissing-cat on the back fence routine. I had never met Ruth, but I phoned her with an invitation to co-drive with me at the Grand Prix of Venezuela in a Porsche RS. And after that event, I was privately satisfied that I was faster (I didn't ask how she felt), but I knew that it probably had to come to *mano-a-mano* some place to settle the matter.

That place was Nassau. At Speed Weeks I had the right to a guest and again I invited Ruth. As it turned out we would both have a Porsche RS for the "Ladies Race." I was never fond of "Ladies Races," but I drove them because they gave me yet one more chance at any given meeting to *race*. And that's what I liked most in the world to do—*race*. But the pressure was uncomfortable because in the "ladies races" I was *supposed* to win and I didn't like *supposed* to's.

Ruth was not only my chief adversary at Nassau, she was my roommate, a situation I handled better than she did. I suspect she needed to work up a hate for her opponent, and how could she hate me when I was so damned *nice* to her? (Hey, there's more than one way to psych out a rival. Right? Though I can't claim to being that clever.) Then Ruth came back to the room one night after she had been out with Stirling Moss, who had taken quite a shine to her. How was she going to tell me this? Instead of the 1500cc Porsche she was scheduled to drive, she was now going to drive the three-liter factory Aston Martin that was Stirling's ride in the big race. Did I mind too much? How could I forgive her? Etc.

Forgive her? Actually, I discovered I was rather pleased. Now that we were in unequal cars I had my preferred underdog role back. I would be up against a car twice the size of mine. Great!

The race course was partly old airport, wide open in some turns, and marked off with oil barrels. I don't recall who else was in the race—four or five others—but it was essentially a match between Ruth and me.

I know that Ruth blasted away first at the start. And I know that I went too wide in the first swooping turn and found myself skittering along in marbles—small stones and tiny chunks of asphalt. And I spun. But I think I'm the only one who knows that. I completed a fast, lucky, 360 and resumed the chase. Before the first lap was done I was back in the midst of it. I knew then I could win; it was just a matter of picking the right place to pass so Ruth couldn't get me back with the Aston's superior acceleration and out-drag me to the finish line.

And, too, it was a matter of staying out of Ruth's way. Her West Coast reputation had a streak of wildness and here she was, sending oil barrels flying. (John Wyer of Aston Martin was to wonder between heats where the dents came from. Ruth told him some tale with little resemblance to what I had seen, but she believed it.)

Anyway, I tested my passing scheme to be sure it would work. It would. So I bided my time, picked my spot and zipped past for the last time just where I had planned—three turns before the finish. We crossed under the checkered flag with the Porsche's nose no more than two feet ahead of the Aston's. Great cheers all around.

Then we had to do it again. Heat Two was coming up and Stirling was giving Ruth pointers. Well, I'd stay out of the marbles this time.

I can't remember how much passing and repassing we did in the second heat, but etched in my mind is the last turn of the last lap. It was two turns, really, a two-part hairpin taken as one that opened up rapidly to the finish line 100 yards along. I had to be neat and fast through this turn or Ruth could simply follow me around, tromp on the Aston and out-gun me to the line. And the first heat had given me only an eye-blink cushion.

Going into that turn I led Ruth by several car lengths, but she just kept coming, getting larger in my mirror as I was setting up for the turn. There in the mirror the green Aston growing bigger and greener. Already I was beyond my cut-off point and she kept coming on the inside—*accelerating*, not braking. I wasn't about to turn in front of her, she'd collect me as a hood ornament.

So I held my straight line deep into the turn, braking to a near stop. And *whoosh!* Ruth whipped by me, straight off the end of the pavement, and disappeared into the brush. I scrambled around the turn, took the checker and then dashed back to the place where Ruth had put a large dark hole into the underbrush. She wasn't seriously hurt, but Stirling's Aston was totaled. (He had to borrow a Ferrari for the race, and he won in it.)

In the hospital someone asked Ruth if she'd run out of brakes. "No," she said. "Brains."

World of Heroes

I try not to look at the stars. I can't bear to see them. They make me remember the time when I used to look at them and think, I'm alive, I'm in love and I'm loved. I only really lived that part of my life. I don't feel alive now. I don't love the stars. They never loved me. I wish they wouldn't remind me of being loved.

I was slow in starting to live at all. It wasn't my fault. If there had ever been any kindness I would not have suffered from a delayed maturity. If so much apprehension had not been instilled into me, I wouldn't have been terrified to leave my solitary unwanted childhood in case something still worse was waiting ahead. However, there was no kindness. The nearest approach to it was being allowed to sit on the back seats of the big cars my mother drove about in with her different admirers. This was in fact no kindness at all. I was taken along to lend an air of respectability. The two in front never looked around or paid the slightest attention to me, and I took no notice of them. I sat for hours and hours and for hundreds of miles inventing endless fantasies at the back of large and expensive cars.

The frightful slowness of a child's time. The interminable years of inferiority and struggling to win a kind word that is never spoken. The torment of self-accusation, thinking one must be to blame. The bitterness of longed-for affection bestowed on indifferent strangers. What future could have been worse? What could have been done to me to make me afraid to grow up out of such a childhood?

Later on, when I saw things more in proportion, I was always afraid of falling back into that ghastly black isolation of uncomprehending, solitary, oversensitive child, the worst fate I could imagine.

My mother disliked and despised me for being a girl. From her I got the idea that men were a superior breed, the free, the fortunate, the splendid, the strong. My small adolescent adventures and timid experiments with boys who occasionally gave me rides on the backs of their motorbikes confirmed this. All heroes were automatically masculine. Men were kinder than women; they could afford to be. They were also fierce, unpredictable, dangerous animals: One had to be constantly on guard against them.

My feeling for high-powered cars presumably came from my mother too. Periodically, ever since I can remember, the craving has come over me to drive and drive, from one country to another, in a fast car. Hearing people talk about danger and death on the roads seems ludicrous, laughable. To me, a big car is a very safe refuge, and the only means of escape from all the ferocious cruel forces lurking in life and in human beings. Its metal body surrounds me like magic armor, inside which I'm invulnerable. Everybody I meet in the outside world treats me in the same contemptuous, heartless way, discrediting what I do, refusing to admit my existence. Only the man in the car is different. Even the first time I drive with him, I feel that he appreciates, understands me; I know I can make him love me. The car is a small speeding substitute world, just big enough for us both. A sense of intimacy is generated, a bond created between us. At once I start to love him a little. Occasionally it's the car I love first. The car can attract me to the man. When we are driving together, the three of us form one unit. We grow into each other. I forget about loneliness and inferiority, I feel fine.

In the outside world catastrophe always threatens. The news is always bad. Life tears into one like a mad rocket off course. The only hope of escaping is in a racing car.

At last I reached the age of freedom and was considered adult; but still my overprolonged adolescence made me look less than my age. X, a young American with a 2.6 liter Alfa Romeo and lots of money, took me for fifteen or sixteen. When I told him I was twenty-one, he burst out laughing, called me a case of retarded development, seemed to be making fun of me in a cruel way. I was frightened, ran away from him, traveled around with some so-called friends with whom I was hopelessly bored. After knowing X, they seemed insufferably dull, mediocre, conventional. Obsessed by longing for him and his car, I sent a telegram asking him to meet us. As soon as I'd done it, I grew feverish with excitement and dread, finally felt convinced the message would be ignored. How idiotic to invite such a crushing rejection. I should never survive the disappointment and shame.

I was shaking all over when we got to the place. It was evening. I hid in the shadows, kept my eyes down so as not to see him—not to see that he wasn't there. Then he was coming toward us. He shook hands with the others one by one, leaving me to the last. I thought, he wants to humiliate me. He's no more interested in me than he is in them. Utterly miserable, I wanted to rush off and lose myself in the dark. Suddenly he said my name, said he was driving me to another town, said good-bye to the rest so abruptly that they seemed to stand there, suspended, amazed, for the instant before I forgot their existence. He had taken hold of my arm, and was walking me rapidly to his car. He installed me in the huge, docile, captivating machine, and we shot away, the stars spinning loops of white fire all over the sky as we raced along the deserted roads.

That was how it began. I always think gratefully of X, who introduced me to the world of heroes.

The racetrack justifies tendencies and behavior which would be condemned as antisocial in other circumstances. Risks encountered nowhere else but in war are a commonplace of the racing drivers' existence. Knowing they may be killed any day, they live in a wartime atmosphere of recklessness, camaraderie and heightened perception. The contrast of their lighthearted audacity and their somber, sinister, menacing background gave them a personal glamour I found irresistible. They were all attractive to me, heroes, the bravest men in the world. Vaguely, I realized that they were also psychopaths, misfits, who played with death because they'd been unable to come to terms with life in the world. Their games could only end badly: Few of them survived more than a few years. They were finished, anyhow, at thirty-five, when their reactions began to slow down, disqualifying them for the one thing they did so outstandingly well. They preferred to die before this happened.

Whether they lived or died, tragedy was waiting for them, only just around the corner, and the fact that they had so little time added to their attraction. It also united them in a peculiar, almost metaphysical way, as though something of all of them was in each individual. I thought of them as a sort of brotherhood, dedicated to their fatal profession of speed.

They all knew one another, met frequently, often lived in the same hotels. Their life was strictly nomadic. None of them had, or wanted to have, a place of his own to live in, even temporarily, far less a permanent home. The demands of their work made any kind of settled existence impossible. Only a few got married, and these marriages always came unstuck very quickly. The wives were jealous of the group feeling, they could not stand the strain, the eternal separation, the homelessness.

I had never had a home, and, like the drivers, never wanted one. But wherever I stayed with them was my proper place, and I felt at home there. All my complicated emotions were shut inside hotel rooms, like boxes inside larger ones. A door, a window, a looking glass, impersonal walls. The door and the window opened only on things that had become unreal, the mirror only revealed myself. I felt protected, shut away from the world as I was in a car, safe in my retreat.

Although, after winning a race, they became for a short time objects of adulation and public acclaim, these men were not popular; the rest of humanity did not understand them. Their clannishness, their flippant remarks and casual manners were considered insulting; their unconventional conduct judged as immoral. The world seemed not to see either the careless elegance that appealed to me, or their strict aristocratic code, based on absolute loyalty to each other, absolute professional integrity, absolute fearlessness.

I loved them for being somehow above and apart from the general gregarious mass of mankind, born adventurers, with a breezy disrespect for authority. Perhaps they felt I was another misfit, a rebel too. Or perhaps they were intrigued or amused by the odd combination of my excessively youthful appearance and wholly pessimistic intelligence. At all events, they received me as no other social group could ever have done—conventions, families, finances would have prevented it. Straightaway, they accepted my presence among them as perfectly natural, adopted me as a sort of mascot. They were regarded as wild, irresponsible daredevils; but they were the only people I'd ever trusted. I was sure that, unlike all the others I'd know, they would not let me down.

Their code prohibited jealousy or any bad feeling. Unpleasant emotional situations did not arise. Finding that I was safe among them, I perceived that it was unnecessary to be on my guard any longer. Their attitude was at the same time flattering and matter-of-fact. They were considerate without any elaborate chivalry, which would have embarrassed me, and they displayed a frank, if restrained, physical interest, quite willing, apparently, to love me for as long or short a time as I liked. When my affair with A was finally over, I simply got into B's car, and that was that. It all seemed exceedingly simple and civilized.

The situation was perfect for me. They gave me what I had always wanted but never had: a background, true friends. They were kind in their unsentimental racetrack way, treated me as one of themselves, shared with me their life histories and their cynical jokes, listened to me with attention, but did not press me to talk. I sewed on buttons for them, checked hotel and garage accounts, acted as unskilled mechanic, looked after them if they were injured in crashes or caught influenza.

At last I felt wanted, valued, as I'd longed to be all my life. At last I belonged somewhere, had a place, was some use in the world. For the very first time I understood the meaning of happiness, and it was easy for me to be truly in love with each of them. I could hardly believe I wasn't dreaming. It was incredible; but it was true, it was really happening. I never had time now to think or to get depressed, I was always in a car with one of them. I went on all the long rallies, won Grand Prix races, acted as co-driver or passenger as the occasion required. I loved it all, the speed, the exhaustion, the danger. I loved rushing down icy roads at ninety miles an hour, spinning around three times, and continuing nonstop without even touching the banked-up snow.

This was the one beautiful period of my life, when I drove all over the world, saw all its countries. The affection of these men, who risked their lives so casually, made me feel gay and wonderfully alive, and I adored them for it. By liking me, they had made the impossible happen. I was living a real fairy tale.

This miraculous state of affairs lasted for several years, and might have gone on some time longer. But, beyond my euphoria, beyond the warm lighthearted atmosphere they generated between them, the sinister threat in the background was always waiting. Disaster loomed over them like a circle of icy mountains, implacably drawing nearer: They'd developed a special attitude in self-defense. Because crashes and constant danger made each man die many times, they spoke of death as an ordinary event, for which the carelessness or recklessness of the individual was wholly responsible. Nobody ever said, "Poor old Z's had it," but, "Z asked for it, the crazy bastard, never more than one jump ahead of the mortuary." Their jargon had a brutal sound to outsiders. But, by speaking derisively of the victim, they deprived death of the terror, made it seem something he could easily have avoided.

Without conscious reflection, I took it for granted that, when the time came, I would die on the track, like my friends: And this very nearly happened. The car crashed and turned four somersaults before it burst into flames, and the driver and other passengers were killed instantly. I had the extreme bad luck to be dragged out of the blazing wreckage only three-quarters dead. Apparently my case was a challenge to the doctors of several hospitals, who, for the next two years, worked with obstinate persistence to save my life, while I persistently tried to discard it. I used to look in their cold, clinical eyes with loathing and helpless rage. They got their way in the end, and discharged me. I was pushed out again into the hateful world, alone, hardly able to walk, and disfigured by burns.

The drivers loyally kept in touch, wrote and sent presents to the hospitals, came to see me whenever they could. It was entirely my own fault that, as the months dragged on, the letters became fewer, the visits less and less frequent, until they finally ceased. I didn't want them to be sorry for me or feel any obligation. I was sure my scarred face must repel them, so I deliberately drove them away.

I couldn't possibly go back to them: I had no heart, no vitality, for the life I'd so much enjoyed. I was no longer the gay, adventurous girl they had liked. All the same, if one of them had really exerted himself to persuade me, I might . . . That nobody made this special effort, or showed a desire for further intimacy, confirmed my conviction that I had become repulsive. Although there was a possible alternative explanation. At the time of the crash, I had been in love with the man who was driving, and hadn't yet reached the stage of singling out his successor. So, as I was the one who always took the initiative, none of them had any cause to feel closer to me than the rest. Perhaps if I had indicated a preference . . . But I was paralyzed by the guilt of my survival, as certain they all resented my being alive as if I'd caused their comrade's death.

What can I do now? What am I to become? How can I live in this world I'm condemned to but can't endure? They couldn't stand it either, so they made a world of their own. Well, they have each other's company, and they are heroes, whereas I'm quite alone, and have none of the qualities essential to heroism—the spirit, the toughness, the dedication. I'm back where I was as a child, solitary, helpless, unwanted, frightened.

It's so lonely, so terribly lonely. I hate being always alone. I so badly need someone to talk to, someone to love. Nobody looks at me now, and I don't want them to; I don't want to be seen. I can't bear to look at myself in the mirror. I keep away from people as much as I can. I know everyone is repelled and embarrassed by all these scars.

There is no kindness left. The world is a cruel place full of men I shall never know, whose indifference terrifies me. If once in a while I catch someone's eye, his glance is as cold as ice, eyes look past eyes like searchlights crossing, with no more humanity or communication. In freezing despair, I walk down the street, trying to attract to myself a suggestion of warmth by showing in my expression ... something ... or something. ... And everybody walks past me, refusing to see or to lift a finger. No one cares, no one will help me. An abstract impenetrable indifference in a stranger's eye is all I ever see.

The world belongs to heartless people and to machines which can't give. Only the others, the heroes, know how to give. Out of their great generosity they gave me the truth, paid me the compliment of not lying to me. Not one of them ever told me life was worth living. They are the only people I've ever loved. I think only of them, and of how they are lost to me. How never again shall I sit beside someone who loves me while the world races past. Never again cross the tropic of Capricorn, or, under the arctic stars, in the blackness of firs and spruce, see the black glitter of ice in starlight, in the cold snow countries.

The world in which I was really alive consisted of hotel bedrooms and one man in a car. But that world was enormous and splendid, containing cities and continents, forests and seas and mountains, plants and animals, the North Star and the Southern Cross. The heroes who showed me how to live also showed me everything, everywhere in the world.

My present world is reduced to their remembered faces, which have gone forever, which get further and further away. I don't feel alive any more. I see nothing at all of the outside world. There are no more oceans or mountains for me.

I don't look up now. I always try not to look at the stars. I can't bear to see them, because the stars remind me of loving and of being loved.

LESLEY HAZLETON

Berlin, a Fast Car, Nightmares

This summer, I flew to Berlin to test-drive a new BMW. I justified
this act of jet-set bravado as part of my new persona of automotive columnist, a role I first discovered some five years ago and
have since grown into with an alacrity that has alarmed and dis-
mayed friends who knew me as a socially and politically concerned
reporter.

Flying to Berlin to drive a fast car seemed wholly in keeping
with the new spirit of the place. I thought of the city as most people seemed to: an exciting, sophisticated center of the arts and an
intellectual beehive — one of the places to be, all the more so since
the wall had come down. With neo-Nazi violence still in its early
stages, it was quite easy to push aside questions that my earlier
self would have placed uppermost.

Besides, Berlin had always attracted me. I had lived for 13 years
in another divided city, Jerusalem. Division was both familiar and
interesting. And then, if you had pressed me very hard, I might
even have acknowledged that the place gained extra allure from
the fact that I am Jewish, giving it an element of the risqué, something of enemy country, even after close on half a century.

But nobody was pressing me hard, and the thought of a dashing BMW sports convertible not on the market in the United
States overrode everything else. At least, in my consciousness.

My unconscious was something else.

I arrived in the morning and picked up the car. The day was
clear and sunny, perfect for a fast drive out to the country. But
suddenly, to my own surprise, there was something I had to do
first. I found myself headed right into the center of the city, where
I parked the car in a dusty unpaved alley, nose up against the eastern side of a short section of the wall left standing as a memorial.

I skirted the wall and headed for a large abandoned lot on
the other side, off Wilhelmstrasse. A rather crudely designed sign-

board read "Topographie des Terrors." A dirt track led across the lot and up a mound of rubble, grown over with weeds and a few forlorn saplings rooted in unlikely soil.

This mound consists of the stones of the neo-classical buildings, including the grandiose Prince Albert Palace, which were once Gestapo headquarters. They were bulldozed into a huge heap some time after World War II and then simply left there, as though nobody dared touch them any further.

Here and there, around the vast empty lot, cellars have been excavated: torture cellars. The excavators were students who began this project in the early '80s and found a sympathetic archeologist to declare the lot an archeological site and therefore protected from development. They set up a small prefab hut on the far side as a museum. Nearly everything in the museum, which houses a documentary collection of photographs of the site and what went on there in World War II, is labeled in German only. This is not a tourist attraction and, on a weekday afternoon, there are only a couple of other visitors. Somehow, this makes it all the more haunting.

It is haunting in the same way as Claude Lanzmann's film *Shoah*, less because of what it shows than because of what it does not.

There is no way to describe how it feels for anyone, let alone a Jew, to stand on top of the rubble of the Gestapo. There is a small sense of victory, perhaps, but a bitter one. A sense of completion, maybe, but incomplete. A feeling, somehow, that a small right has been applied to a great wrong. And an unpleasant frisson that comes from standing on a place where you know what happened but see little sign of it left. You sense that the stones of this rubble somehow hold the moans and screams of decades ago.

What you do hear are the sounds of modern Berlin: the bustle from the west, the relative silence from the east. Though the wall has come down in all except this and one other place, when you walk from one side of the city to the other, you are still walking through an invisible wall, from a lively, colorful, hyper, thriving city into a drab world of fortresslike apartment blocks.

If the mound were a little higher, you might even be able to see a couple of miles to the east, where the huge concrete block of the Stasi headquarters still stands, part of it now a museum, with swastikas daubed around the base making the obvious, if misleading, comparison between Nazi rule and Communist rule. That is why this section of the wall has been left standing, of course: the remnants of two kinds of dictatorship, side by side, the one full of brightly colored graffiti, blaring its messages of resistance and opposition, the other just weeds and stunted trees growing out of the rubble, whispering to you, in the voice of the breeze.

I walked away from there, got back into the car, and allowed myself to become caught up in the business of being a regular visitor to Berlin. I drove out to Potsdam and strolled the palaces and fig gardens of Frederick the Great, dined under the trees in a lakeside beer garden, ate white asparagus at the opera house.

But there was nothing regular about my dreams: one a night, three nights in a row. In the first, someone had booby-trapped the driver's seat of the car with a crossbow. In the second, a New York City policeman attacked me and Mayor David Dinkins with a knife. In the third, a disgruntled former student whom I didn't recognize came at me with a hatchet.

I'd never had such dreams before. "I don't know where they're coming from," I protested to myself. But after the third one, I finally had no choice but to make the obvious connection. And once I had made it, the dreams stopped.

I told a friend about these dreams—an Israeli intellectual and cosmopolite par excellence. "You should know better," he said. I knew what he meant: it is sobering to go somewhere in the spirit of chic cosmopolitanism only to find that your unconscious focuses on something else. That it insists, in fact, on being most unchic—almost, in today's world, downright provincial.

I had come to Berlin to do such a simple thing: to drive a car. To kick up my heels and have fun and get speeding tickets I'd never have to pay. But my unconscious had rigged up that crossbow in the driver's seat. Accustomed to being the fast-moving traveler, I found that I was still, above all, a Jew in Berlin.

JILL AMADIO

Run, Rabbit, Run

"... The last shall be first. And the first, last ..."

I never really wanted to be a racecar driver, although most journalists who cover auto racing itch to get behind the wheel at a racetrack, even if it's only while the car is in the pits. As a novice reporter, the closest I ever came was the time I was on a plane to the West Coast and we flew over Indianapolis just four days before the running of the 1975 Indy 500.

All that changed three months later when, during a steamy October weekend at Watkins Glen, New York, on the same internationally famous Grand Prix racetrack that Niki Lauda steered his Ferrari to victory, I completed two and a half laps in the most sensational car race of my rather short racing career. Very short. I never took to the track again.

Volkswagen Worldwide Corporation was staging its Stingy Driving Race, whereby each participating member of the press was provided with a 1975 Rabbit, a precisely measured thirty-two ounces of gas, and let loose on the track. The winner would be the driver who squeezed the most mileage from this meager ration of liquid gold. With my dainty little foot pressing softly on the accelerator I figured I was a cinch to tiptoe my Rabbit to a first-place win.

Assigned identically set up cars, twenty-two journalists stood dutifully at the starting line. Taped to the passenger side window of each Rabbit was the glass vial containing the precious gas. A narrow plastic tube ran from the vial, across the hood and into the engine like an I.V. line dripping life-saving fluids into a heart patient. Such drama. I was tingling with excitement.

Jim McGlone, of Jim McGlone Motors in Croton-on-Hudson, was brave enough to sponsor me and supply my sparkling white VW Rabbit sedan. He advised me to attack the race barefoot. That way, he said, you can better feel the accelerator and thus control your destiny. But this posed a problem.

Since the start was to be a LeMans-type start, where drivers line up about fifty yards away from their cars, dash across the gritty track at the signal, leap in and charge off, I couldn't make my mind up whether to loosen the laces of my sneakers and risk tripping, go nude-footed, or simply throw the sneakers out the window as I careened around the track.

Fortunately, the dilemma solved itself. The hour preceding the race was so fraught with amazing sights—semi-nude showgirls, three-tiered cakes shaped like Formula 1 race cars, behemoth-sized balloons that resembled bottles of beer—that I completely forgot Jim's advice and only remembered when I eventually took my muddy shoes off late that night.

Anyway, here we were, queued up very neatly like the British when they're waiting for a bus. There were supposed to be three of us females competing, along with twenty-one men. One lady was disqualified for reasons unknown to me. The second never showed up. Thus I found myself unwittingly representing the whole world of women drivers in the Bunny Hop VW Rabbit Race at Watkins Glen.

When I realized the honor that had been bestowed upon me, I decided I really wasn't worthy. I've never been much of a women's libber, and the feminist movement was still in its infancy in the 1970s. I dreaded the thought of what might happen if I let my side down. Would I be chased through the streets by angry women waving signs reading: "Jill's a Dumb Bunny?"

I offered to step down. I pleaded to step down. But by this time genial Chris Economaki, the gravelly-voiced ABC-TV race commentator, had already pushed a microphone under my nose.

"How will you handle the chicane?" he asked me.

I'd never, ever, heard of a chicane. What the heck was it? How did one spell it?

"Oh," I replied airily, "That's going to be a surprise. It's my secret weapon!"

Chris peered at me, a pitying look on his face, and moved on down the line, interviewing other journalists. Next to me was Ahmad Sadiq, art director for *Penthouse* magazine. He'd brought along a stable of voluptuous models who draped most of their bare flesh all over the hood of his fire-engine red Rabbit.

Nearby stood a carless driver, Junius Chambers, who wrote for the New York *Amsterdam News*. He was unable to participate because the Rabbit he'd been given to race was stolen from in front of his apartment in Manhattan the night before. Was he going to sprint toward my entry and try to beat me to the door? Or was he here simply to drool at the models?

Time for the race to start.

The popgun popped and we all ran madly toward our cars. We jumped in (no one got in the wrong car; I knew mine was white) and fastened our belts. Or at least, I tried to. I got my elbow caught in the shoulder strap and ended up starting the car with the seat belt harness doing a great job of hanging my left arm uselessly in the air as I clumsily changed gears and steered with one hand.

No matter. I was on my way around the track for the first lap. The only problem was, we were supposed to drive as slowly as possible to preserve the gas and achieve high mileage. Here we were on one of America's most famous racetracks and to win we were to dawdle all the way. Well, women never like to follow the crowd, just ask any husband, so I must admit I gave in to temptation and led the rest of the field at first, all twenty-one of the men behind me.

The circuit is 3.377 miles and goes up hill and down dale in a zig-zaggy fashion, twisting and looping most of the time.

Thousands of spectators — most of them still bleary-eyed from a night spent out in the open in the infamous Snake Pit swamp — were camped on the hillsides, a veritable tent city spread out behind them.

These fans were obviously not too keen on watching twenty-two silly Rabbits hopping along at a snail's pace. They'd traveled here from far and wide to watch Grand Prix champions tear up the track at better than 180. But they were good sports.

Halfway around, my car coughed, choked, bucked a couple of times, then sputtered to an ignominious stop. Nonplussed, I wondered if the Rabbit was going to roll over on its back and expire. What's happening? Was I a victim of the dreaded chicane?

"Hey, lady," shouted one of the rather rude spectators, "step on the gas!"

The gas! I looked at the transparent hose. Aha! An air bubble was blocking the flow from the bottle to the engine. What to do? My Rabbit needed an emergency transfusion.

I was soon surrounded by a gaggle of hung-over hippies who'd jumped over the guard rails and were offering to push the car home. Alas, the damage was done. My poor little Rabbit was gasping for gas.

Dodging my competitors who drove past sedately, shaking their heads, a track mechanic ran over. "Get a move on, lady! You can't stop there!" he yelled. Did he think I'd stopped to do some sightseeing?

"Oh," he said brightly. "You've got an air bubble. Here, I'll try to blow it out."

This brilliant man put the plastic tube between his lips and took an almighty breath. Instantly, the air bubble disappeared. It had been sucked into his mouth along with half my bottle of gas.

"Hey! You've swallowed my ration!" I shrieked.

His face turned green as he spat out some of the gas he'd stolen from me. "I knew it was a mistake to let women on this track . . ." he muttered, stalking away.

With what was left of my thirty-two ounces I restarted the Rabbit and continued around the track, accompanied by hoots of derision from the fans. I decided to enjoy the scenery, waving to my fellow drivers and trying to eke out as many miles as possible from my seriously denuded gas supply.

The Watkins Glen circuit is a sweet grid and if you're not in a hurry, as I certainly wasn't, there's a lot to see. The first curve is a ninety-degree turn which gets you all psyched up for that infamous chicane, and after all my fears it turned out to be merely a banked segment to slow the field down and ideally allow only one car at a time to pass through it. So what was the big deal? The chicane is followed by a very nice straightaway from which one may observe the lovely fall foliage on the surrounding hillsides. Then the track sends you along a tortuously twisting loop that can be hazardous if you're not paying attention, to set you up for the wiggling corners that wind up to the finish. It was a pleasant way to spend a Saturday afternoon in the fall, upstate New York, I must say.

So I ambled along, all pressure off, watching the bottle of gas finally gurgle out its last few drops. Halfway back to the finish line, my Rabbit slowed to crawl and, with a lurch, stopped dead in its track. I had to be towed back to the start/finish line.

After the officials tallied up our scores, they discovered I had managed to go around the track two and a half times, averaging thirty-six miles to the gallon.

Boy, I thought, was Volkswagen ever going to be surprised! So was the Environmental Protection Agency, both of which had boasted these cars had an official rating of thirty-nine miles to the gallon. Took a woman to show them the error of their ways.

The winner of our Bunny Hop was Bill Turney of the *Hartford Courant* who feather-footed his Rabbit gently enough to get 72.8 miles per gallon. Second was Jim Patterson of the *Long Island Press*, at sixty-four miles per gallon. They won all-expense-paid trips to the Bahamas. Neither invited me along.

After I gave my Rabbit back to my sponsor, Jim McGlone, I never heard from him again. I don't know if the guy who selfishly swallowed my gas perished or (sorry, God) merely suffered several extremely painful spasms. Curiously, I was not invited to race again. I never wanted to be a race driver anyway. So there.

MAGGIE DUBRIS

You Can't Spell Mess Without E-M-S

I stood in a line of men out front of the EMS building in Queens. We had just finished our orientation, which consisted of being handed a list of what did and did not constitute a uniform, watching a movie where an EMT in Kansas drove a glass of water around without spilling it, and receiving a tour of the 911 dispatch center where a bunch of fat ladies in green dresses ate caramels and plucked index cards with calls scrawled on them from an endlessly revolving conveyor belt.

"Gibbs, Sanchez, Taylor." Three men stepped forward. "Kings County." The men walked off.

"LaBella, MacAllen, Ortiz. Queens General."

"Brown, Delaney, Frank. Bellevue."

One by one the men around me vanished, until I was the only one left. The fat man looked me up and down.

"DeLaCroix, get a haircut. No hair below the collar."

"But I'm a girl, sir."

"Not anymore. You'll be working at Metropolitan. Take the elevator down to the morgue there, find a man named Rodale. He'll be the only one lying on a metal table that's still alive."

"But what does he look like?"

"Just keep shaking the bodies till one of them moves. That'll be your new partner."

I found him stretched out on an autopsy table, snoring like an airplane about to take off.

"Excuse me," I said. He didn't move. He looked like a pleasant old fellow; maybe fifty or so, with cottony hair.

"Excuse me! Excuse me!!"

Nothing. I shook his skinny arm, shouted in his ear, pinched his nose shut. He slumbered on. Finally I rolled him off the bench. He hit the floor with a loud thump, screamed, and leapt to his feet.

He didn't look quite so pleasant when he was awake. I stuck out my hand.

"Pleased to meet you," I said. "I'm your new partner."

He pulled a pack of Luckies from his back pocket, stuck one in his mouth and tried to light it. His hands shook so violently the match kept blowing out.

"My name is Mister Rodale," he barked, "you call me Rodie, I don't tolerate anyone calling me Mister Rodale."

"Sure. I'm—"

"I'll call you partner. I can't be learning all these new names at my age. If you last more than a week, then I'll learn your name."

"I'm an MVO," Rodie said as he got behind the wheel. "The Fat Man tell you about me?"

"Sure."

"What'd he say?"

"Nothing."

"Good. I drive. That's what MVO stands for. Motor Vehicle Operator. See this?" He held up a walkie-talkie. "This is our radio. But it isn't ours. It's mine. If you hear them calling us, and I don't appear to answer, notify me. Don't touch the radio. I ever see you touch it, I'll report you to my union, which is not the same as your union, and you'll be fired. I, and only I, answer the radio. Got it?"

"Sure."

"I have good luck with radios," he muttered. "I don't need anyone jinxing me."

He drove to the smoke shop, a bakery, some bashed-up metal door where he vanished for half an hour, then parked in front of a smoky-looking tenement where he had to visit one of his lady friends. The radio was glued to his hip. I sat in the front of the ambulance, trying to look important, wishing I had brought something to read.

When he came out of the tenement he was in a much better mood. He had one cigarette hanging from his lip and another between his fingers, and his white hair stood out like a dandelion.

"How you doing, partner?" he slapped my thigh gaily.

"What's wrong with you?"

"Can't a man be happy? Where does a sad sack like you live, anyway?"

"Downtown."

"In the Village?"

"Kind of."

"Hmm. You one of those pot-smoking types?"

I shook my head. He looked disappointed.

"It doesn't matter. You know, I love working with women," he said. "Did I ever tell you about Miss Montalvo? I treated her so good, she used to say 'Rodie, you are the only man I will ever work with.' Cause some of the other men, they can be a little, I don't know what you'd call it, backwards I guess. Like, they won't let a woman carry nothing. But I had a woman explain to me once that that's actually insulting. You see, I'm a man who understands what a woman wants. A woman just wants to do her share, isn't that right, partner. I wish they had more women here at EMS, I tell you I cried for a week when Miss Montalvo left me, but she had bigger fish to fry. You know what she did? She saved up her money and opened up a numbers parlor for elderly people right there on 124th Street. Isn't that nice? She was a beautiful person. A beautiful, beautiful person. In fact, I'm going to take you up to 124th Street right now. You're awfully sour-pussed for a young Village girl. You meet Miss Montalvo, then you can see how a woman's supposed to be."

He pulled in front of a shuttered storefront and banged on the rippled door. A slot opened at eye level, then winked shut. From behind came the sound of metal on metal, then a space appeared, just wide enough for us to turn sideways and squeeze through. The air was dark, thick with meat frying, sweat and beer soaked into pine flooring, we followed our guide down a narrow hallway that opened into a long saggy room where thirty or so old people sat at folding tables.

"Miss Montalvo," Rodie called. A woman rushed toward him

arms outstretched. She was about five feet tall, six inches of which consisted of pitch black hair whipped into stiff peaks. Her nails were long and blood-red, her lips an alarming shade of pink, and she had the thickest false eyelashes I had ever seen, teetering on her lids like two enormous caterpillars. He lifted her in his arms and swung her around. She had to be at least seventy years old.

"Rodie Rodie Rodie." She pinched his leathery cheek. "You're looking good, your face so big and round and shiny. You—"

She caught sight of me. The caterpillars undulated, creeping upward to reveal two rheumy brown eyes.

"That's my new partner," Rodie said. "Doesn't have much of a personality. This is her first day."

Miss Montalvo tottered toward me and grasped one of my hands in both of hers. "My my my, that calls for a drink. What department were you thrown out of, dear?"

"I wasn't thrown out of anywhere." She seemed to think I was a cane or something. I couldn't seem to extricate myself from her grip as she clumped me over to a cabinet in the corner.

"Now don't be ashamed, just hold your head up, the ambulance is a fine place to be and don't let anyone tell you any different," she chattered. "I was working in hospitals since before you were born, there's not a thing that surprises me. You see, I started in housekeeping, now I won't lie to you, housekeeping was never one of my strong points, they transferred me to clerical but for some reason that didn't last so they made me an orderly, imagine that, whoosh in no time I was off to credit and collections, then central supply, then I think it was laundry, then dietary where I got to know Rodie, and there was no place left to send me so out I went to ride the ambulance. Oh I liked that pretty well, and then we had the accident and my lawsuit came through and here I am!" She beamed and held out a shot glass of something green.

"No thanks."

She tapped her foot and narrowed her overburdened eyes. "Are you still on probation?"

"Yeah I think so."

She handed the shot glass to Rodie, who downed it in one gulp.

Two hours later Rodie had switched to vodka. The old people around us didn't even talk. All they did was play poker and stare at the racing sheets. After a few rounds Rodie and Miss Montalvo had pronounced me a good egg, but they passed that stage rather quickly and went on to reliving moments that consisted of Miss Montalvo raising her head from the table and intoning, "Remember when Moosh and Mishter Robinshon tried to rob, tried to rob—" as Rodie draped one rubbery arm around her shoulder and slurred, "I thought that ol' Carusho washh going to fire ush all, the lasht shtraw haw haw haw haw . . ."

I fiddled with the radio, which I had plucked from Rodie's belt after the first hour. A steady rain of calls fell in the areas around us but we remained untouched, as if someone had popped open an invisible umbrella, shielding us from the mayhem that filled the summer city night. I closed my eyes and thought about how impressed my ex-boyfriend would be if he could see me. Sitting in a real numbers parlor in my uniform, waiting for danger to strike. Of course, I wouldn't want him to be able to hear Rodie or anything, just catch a quick glimpse, like a movie seen briefly from a car window, of my glamorous new life that he could never be a part of.

Suddenly the radio vibrated in my hand. Cow-like tones emanated from the speaker. I shook it. Rodie smiled blearily and sucked down another slug of vodka.

"Moonk moonk moonk. All units be advised we have a report of a ten-thirteen involving an EMS vehicle at 126th Street and Lenox, units to respond? All units, moonk moonk moonk."

I leapt up. Rodie remained stationary.

"Come on," I said, "isn't that right near here?"

He stared happily at his hands.

"Rodie, get up. Rodie. Rodie! Rodie!!"

He blinked. "Huh?"

I wrestled him to his feet, Miss Montalvo cheering me on. "You show him whoshe bosh, girl, thas right, Rodie don' give that poor girl shuch a hard time."

I tried to think of him as a soccer ball. I just had to keep him in motion and everything would be all right. We crashed through the sleepy herd of old people, rolled down the hallway and out the door to the street where I shoveled him into the passenger seat. He promptly fell asleep.

I got behind the wheel. Nothing looked very familiar. I hadn't driven since I was sixteen and got my license. But from what I remembered, there wasn't much to it. Rodie had left the ambulance running, so all I really had to do was hit the gas pedal. I floored it. The engine sounded like it was about to blow up, but we didn't move. I took my foot off the gas and studied the dashboard. It was just a bunch of dials and mysterious lights. Finally I found the shift. Some genius engineer had stuck it behind the steering wheel. R was for reverse, P for park, I couldn't remember what D stood for so I threw it into 1 and hit the gas. We took off with a tremendous roar.

The bus slowed momentarily, I heard the sound of splintering wood, and we picked up speed again. Rodie had aroused from his stupor. He was looking at me and his mouth was moving, but no words came out. I wondered what I had hit. I felt great. I was driving an ambulance, it didn't matter what I had hit. Whatever it was, it was supposed to get out of my way. I sped past the projects. The ambulance was a little wider than it looked from my seat, I kept banging Rodie's door into things. I fiddled with the siren until it came on and followed a cop car up a wide avenue, figuring they must be going to the ten-thirteen.

The engine was making a loud noise as if we were drag racing, a summer night coming down in all its splendor as I chased the red eyes of the cop car along Lenox Avenue, past the corner boys turning in admiration and terror, my siren rattling from the walls of the tenements, cars splitting before me as pedestrians leaped to flatten themselves along against grated storefront windows just like the old Dick Tracy cartoons, and I controlled it all.

I leaned back in my seat and took one hand from the wheel, pushing back my hair. The wind flew in my window smelling of barbecues from the park, the cop car grew smaller and I pressed my foot into the accelerator, willing us to go faster faster into the hot Harlem night. A constellation of red brightened before me, I leaned forward.

"Oh shit," I screamed.

It was a mess of cop cars, ambulances, fire trucks, and people. And it was coming at me awfully fast.

"Rodie, how do I stop?"

He didn't answer. He was curled into a ball on the floor in front of his seat, his hands covering his eyes.

I knew there was a brake somewhere, but what was the brake and what was the clutch? Or maybe this kind didn't have a clutch. I wished I had paid more attention at my driving test. I took my foot off the accelerator and cut around a fire truck, up on two wheels, landing with a hard thud, took the bumper off a cop car and kept going, up the median and back down, sparks flying from beneath the hood, into a crowd that scattered like pool balls and onward to the center where an EMS ambulance was flipped on its side being beaten by a gang of men in Halloween masks. They turned screaming as I hurled toward them, ran past the boundaries of my windshield. Only the naked ambulance stood in my path.

I turned off the engine and bounced from the steering wheel as the front end exploded, blue flame shooting across the hood vanishing into a snarl of black smoke as we jerked to a stop and I rubbed my chest and blinked and wondered why it was so quiet all of a sudden. Rodie trembled on the floor beside me, still curled up.

"Hey Rodie," I said.

He curled tighter.

"Hey Rodie. I'm okay. Are you okay? Is there anything we're supposed to do now?"

My door opened. A green-hatted head peered in.

"That was something, Rodie, I can't believe the balls—Rodie? You're not Rodie. Where's Rodie?"

I pointed to the floor.

"Rodie, get up, there's some crazy girl driving your ambulance!"

"I'm not a girl, I'm an EMT," I said.

He leaned across me and poked at Rodie. "Rodie, this girl put you to shame!"

I sighed. Rodie began to uncurl. The man threw his arm around my neck. "Baby, you are some driver. I never seen an ambulance go like that!"

"Oh. Thanks," I said. "I'm just getting used to it, you know, this is only my first day. If it was tomorrow, I would have got here even faster."

He helped me out the door. I seemed to be all in one piece. My bumper had stopped inches from the roof of the tipped ambulance. Men gazed at me, awestruck, as I dusted myself off. Cops, firemen, other EMS workers. I smiled graciously.

"Well," I said, "do I have to fill anything out or can we go back on patrol?" Rodie staggered from around the hood and leaned against me. The ride seemed to have sobered him up a little.

"Get in the ambulance," he said. "We got to get out of here before the captain gets here."

One of the EMS men tossed him a bottle of White Out. "Rodie where'd you get that Evel Knievel girl?"

Rodie flipped him the bird. "You know, I love working with women. You don't have the faintest idea how good life can be, this girl is a beautiful person. A beautiful, beautiful person."

I stuffed the radio into my belt, basked in the glory for a few seconds and swaggered toward the driver's side. Rodie had somehow gotten there before me. He tipped his head toward the passenger seat and revved the engine.

"We ain't got all day, girl. I trained that captain that's after you. You better step lively."

He drove to the top of Mount Morris Park. I held the flashlight as he carefully painted over every scrape with White Out.

"This'll hold till the rain comes. Then they won't know who to pin it on," he said as we inspected his handiwork. "Give me the radio."

"I'm a good driver, aren't I," I said.

"Give me the radio, we get off in ten minutes." I threw it to him, hard. He caught it in one hand and swung it by the antennae, smashing out a particularly obvious dent.

Then he got back into the bus and shoved the radio between his legs. When we got to the hospital he cut the engine and exhaled dramatically.

"You coming back?" he said.

"Yeah."

"I got seniority, I can call in sick anytime I want."

He slammed the door. I trailed after him.

"Don't call in sick," I said.

"Maybe I will, maybe I won't. But you better not. You're still on probation. You know how long probation lasts?"

I shook my head.

When he got to the locker room door he turned and raised one hand. "Nobody does. One day they just staple a note to your paycheck and you're off it."

HETTIE JONES

Paleface

I am driving down the Connecticut Turnpike in a thirteen-year-old
    car whose name is Geronimo
An Apache chieftain born 1829 died 1909, forty-four years
    before the start of the car which goes
 Valiantly down the Connecticut Turnpike, land of the Pequod
    not the Apache, but
Stalwart and brave, as the children in the back seat are
    stalwart and brave
And young. Their eyes are black. Their eyes are beautiful.
    Their eyes
Are glittering with the anger of at least four traceable
    generations
And they will not allow it to happen to anybody else. Oh, my,
    children
Are so beautiful and stern on the Connecticut Turnpike, they
    have caught my heart
In a net of silk strings that sways in the center of my body
    even as they did once,
And the heat of it, my heart swinging at sixty miles an hour,
    Geronimo, Geronimo
Take me home and contain me or let me flourish in the eyes of
    my children,
Let this speed go out of me into their soft arms,
Let me rest, I am tired of the Connecticut Turnpike, of
    Indians who fought so valiantly
But did not win, let it be quiet, it's too hard to get
    anything done with all this swinging
And banging, Geronimo, the Apache, the eyes of my children,

There's no end but surrender and I cannot surrender
It's not right to die on any man's reservation, oh
Chief of the Chiricahua, terror of Arizona, 1882,
On the Connecticut Turnpike in the land of the Pequod,
    1966.

HETTIE JONES

Ode to My Car

It's not as if you were the first.
Before you I loved, one by one,
the fifty-three Plymouth in sixty-five,
the wagons, all three, the Ford and both
Ramblers, the Valiant, the fifty-six Chevy
stolen in Newark in sixty-nine, and lastly
the old green Maverick, which ran bravely
until it died and brought me to you,
my darling blue Honda, you of the brand
new look, the perfect, unmarred facade,
the powerful motor. And your secrets!—the
fifty-nine thousand miles you'd gone before
me. I drove you home as if enclosed in sapphire,
a piece of the sky, an ocean current, my hands
on your sturdy blue wheel, my feet at once
at home on your pedals, the highway a ribbon
laid out for our honeymoon. Since then
we've been in sun and rain, on ice, under
snow that threatened to bury us. We've lost
much—my teeth, your grill—pieces of us
flung into space, back to the earth
from which we both spring. Let me say
it's coming on winter now. We've traveled
sixty thousand more miles, our paint is peeling,
we have rusty corners, tears in our upholstery.
But still we ride, oh Crystal Blue Persuasion,
past daylight's haphazard fabrics into the
long snake of night, your throbbing voice
a lull of reassurance, your dented shell
my loved cocoon, my egg. Take me, friend,
onto life's inviting byways, fold me into

your small roomy body, bear my luggage,
my groceries, my precious children. Take me
surely to where I am now, in this perfectly
rounded silence, at this table of women
writing. Because of you we can, and we do.

ANNE WALDMAN

Jurassic

You think time had lost its way for you
You laughed before you thought this

Then the earth rolled under your wheels as
You drove across Route 80 blinded by sun

Putting on shades you startled Ute and Shoshone
(Jim Bridger settled later as the beaver trade dried up)

Muskets, bright feathers, phantom beadwork, bulldozers
Are all implements that turn the wheel

They spoke to you as no other history did
And you "cracked" the window to breathe fresh air

It adds up to a fraction of any life and yet
You are not the Dallas Cowboys, the Denver Broncos

You are not the Washington Redskins or New York Giants
(In the growing incredulity of these names)

You are She's-Driving-A-Car-On-A-Saturday
Observing a dirt-truck kick up a mirage

You are moving down the incline too
Curious and smaller than the rest of the dinosaurs

Perhaps this is the last light you will ever see
Lining the beautiful earth.

MARCIA LAWTHER

Driving the Central Valley

The road climbs out of Gilroy up Mount Madonna,
a single red-tailed hawk shadows the blond hill, the road
sidewinding into Watsonville, where the air
holds the sweet acid smell of canning tomatoes,
carries the high whine of the four o'clock whistle.
Cannery women, their hair still paled with netting,
men in tan Sears pants, open shirts stream
onto asphalt, pile into '67 Fords, '56 Chevy low-riders,
shag dice dangling from their rearview mirrors.

It is Friday and they will drive, maybe
to the San Luis Reservoir, park at the water,
low now it's August, watch speedboats pull
waterskiers. Or just drive, Los Banos, Chowchilla
to every bar that plays music, eat chili Colorado,
drive, drinking Budweiser into oncoming headlights
onto 99, through fields of peppers, alfalfa,
straight for the grid lights of Fresno to
Billy's pink blinking-neon date palm for tequila
loco phone calls to Dinuba, John's sister
Evangelina, living there in her yellow stucco
one bedroom, front yard filled with
glow in the dark datura, welter of
prickly pear cactus, junked cars,
dogs yapping, the phone ringing
left there ringing across
Tulare County, as they drive at 80, at 90
honking to the music, the Wolfman's rasp
out of L.A. They are
whooping to the stars, to the moon looming
into their windshield, as they swerve

tractor-trailers, as they luminate
the fields, spread out silver beside them.
They are sucked into engine
into burr of tires. They are
driving the line, the steady black
into solid air.

VIOLA WEINBERG

California Driving

Traffic. Cars. People. Fumes. Split rubber and bad mags. Animals loose on the road. Hitchhikers. Trucks and buses. Consenting adults. Dark death in the headlights. Rain and paint and chocolate syrup and blood on the pavement. You have seen it all.

It's California Driving, not California Dreaming, and it seems like the whole damn state is doing it. The media blames it on the economy, and there's something to that. California's boom went bust a while back, and now you take the work where you can get it and live where you can afford it. You drive hundreds of miles a day in a swollen stream with others of your ilk who live in idling cars and grind their teeth and wish to God the scenery was flying by. No matter how often you must crawl on the roadway during rush hour, you will drive on and on, for it's California and that's what we do here.

California—a jungle of vinelike blacktop—begins at the coast and seeps inland, capillarylike, to muddy rivers that trickle south and east into the desert. California has big mother earthquakes and colossal mudslides, and forest fires in the cities, and riots in the ghettos. Lots of things are wracked by disaster and can only hang in midair: bridges, twisted rail tracks, extra lanes, concrete dividers. You will survive and adapt, learn to navigate road craters and make alternative routes when freeways pancake and sinkholes swallow unlucky commuters, or a freeway sniper gets out a deer rifle.

It makes you wonder how anybody gets anywhere, a thought that occupies you as you passively meditate in the deathless lemming field called rush hour—slow moments when you notice your neighbors on the paralyzed roadway are doing things. They yak on car phones, balancing their checkbooks, curling their hair, learning Italian, shaving slack jaws, reading complete novels—like a trapped animal nervously washing the insides of its captivity with its nasty musk.

Rush hour is not forgiving, and soon cars will die of thirst and get pushed to the sides. Some simply fall in the middle of the road like the carcass of a dead heifer in the slow rolling tide of a cattle drive. Tempers will flare, middle fingers pop up. Sweat will form on the forearms of small, faded women in wagons. Small, rocket-powered sports cars will gnaw at the heels of mud-decked four wheelers.

Suddenly, and without warning, it's you that's breaking down, gut-shocked and frantic as your car craps out in the wild rapids of evening traffic that bilge out of urban arteries. Your gauges are tapping hot as you slither through the gateway to the valley below. Suddenly an emergency light flares on the dash like NORAD Control during an air attack. The car is moving but nothing is working, not the brakes, not the windows, not the radio, not the steering, and no one will let you over. You are caught in The Big Interchange where a sestina of Federal and State six-laners converge in a hivelike maze. One wrong move can send you north to Redding as metal salvage.

There are many, many lanes between you and the safe side of the road. It's so bad that you are forced to plow your car into the median, braking it by bouncing off the rubber cans that separate you from certain death, head-on. You crawl from the driver's seat to the passenger door and grab your purse on the way, wondering if it has any money in it.

As you work your way around the car, screaming tires and honking horns whiz by. From the divider, you compare one escape route to another. On the one side, nine lanes to cross, including two major freeways shooting in on cantilevers. Then, you will have to walk perhaps five miles via overpass that spans the streak of racing motorists to the truck stop on the other side of the highway.

Much more direct, but not for the weak of heart, lie the westbound lanes. You could spit and hit the truck stop across that little patch of highway, but first you have to outrun five lanes of cars throttling up the side of the hill. Beyond that, there's a deserted fruit orchard which trims frontage road like nappy rickrack that nothing can kill.

Without much thought, you jump the divider in your dress and heels, clutch your purse strings and run like hell for the Lazy J Truck Stop. You fly like you've never flown and you don't look back, because if you did, you would surely be road kill.

You open your eyes and let your breath go. You have arrived miraculously across the lanes to slug your way through four feet of Canadian mud lawn growing between the old pear trees. You spy the tipsy "J" from the Lazy J Truck Stop sign through the bare sticks in the heads of dead trees in your path.

In a few hundred yards, you can make out a phone booth with a dangling phone book, and you dash the last fifty feet. You have a broken heel and foxtails in your panty hose, and you have to dig deep to find a quarter for the tow truck. You call one, then another, and another, and another. They are all too busy to help because the traffic is furious.

You call a friend who can't help for three hours. You shake your head and hobble to the truck stop, fighting tumbleweeds as they fly across pits in the asphalt. All around you, semi-trucks are rolling ahead to the two-story diesel pumps. Their drivers are thick-necked men with tattoos and long greasy hair and shit on their boots. On the highly chromed bumpers of their rigs are bumper stickers that say things like "Kick their ass, Take their gas," or "I love spotted owl (scrambled and smothered)." Nobody looks up. They ain't got no time for a woman like you, and nobody stops to help.

Ahead, through plate-glass windows that jump with the rumble of trucks, you see her with her statuesque hair and her well-packed uniform. You can almost feel the violent snap of her gum against her tongue and teeth. She is poised with her ticket book folded out in a fan above the flat heads of the men she serves. Never taking her eyes off you, she jots down the order, absently sweeping the menus under her left arm as she strides toward the cash register where you have collapsed over the glass cabinet of Tums and floss and chewing gum.

Her name tag says "Dot." You take a breath and inhale the fumes of Tabu. You sense that this woman is poured into a girdle from Sears, that she pulls a double shift twice a week, that she dusts between the breasts with lilac talc, that her hairdo is wound in toilet paper at night and revarnished in the mornings. As she lowers her head to yours, she raises her eyebrows. You look into her face and see the dimple first.

As she looks at you, the corner of her mouth curls up like the trim on an old circus wagon. She keeps chewing her gum and asks "Road trouble?" in a voice made of loose gravel and cheap red wine and generic filter-tip cigarettes. Clenching a membership card, you nod desperately and point to the hulk of your car roof which gleams from the Interstate not so far away. Drawing yourself up to your full height, you tell her what happened, how you broke your heel, how no one would stop, and now, how no one will tow you away.

"No problem, kiddo," she chirps in a helpful way as she nods at the three other women working the counter and booths of the Lazy J. "Girl," she chuckles real low, "give me your Triple A card, and I'll call a guy who owes me." Three other waitresses at their stations wink and laugh. One taps the countertop with the eraser end of her pencil and wearily asks—"Good Lord, when will it all end?"

You get the feeling that this is the debt of a lifetime, bigger than you can imagine. Your desperation overwhelms the nagging question that begs at your wallet. You even say "please." With a triumphant snort, Dot wraps her phony red nails around a pencil until it looks like a barber pole and dials a number she knows by heart.

She speaks in monosyllabic sentences as she warms up for the pitch. "Hal. Dot. Yah, yah. Naw. C'mon. Really. Nice lady. Coil, maybe. Huh? Naw. Try fifteen." As she hangs up, she throws the receiver in the cradle and shrugs. "No problem."

You start to go outside to wait in the sweltering heat, but she halts you with a cool, plump hand and directs you to the counter where you can sit under the air conditioning and drink her fine coffee. At first sip you realize why she serves it all day. It's really durable.

As she pours, she leans over confidentially and her cleavage bubbles at eye level. "Just so you know, Hal is a dwarf. Japanese dwarf at that. Just so you aren't surprised." You wonder what would surprise you now.

In a few minutes, Hal tools in and escorts you to the big yellow truck that scoops up your abandoned car with a winch. Hal's good. He's really a dwarf and unmistakably Japanese. He runs the tow truck with panel levers rather than foot petals. He's up and down on the rig more times than you can count until the sling strap rests under the front axle and your dangling car points at the waning sun.

As Hal prepares to pull out across all those lanes of traffic he sizes you up, asking if you want to learn how to "shoot the hoop." He's already heard how you threw your big leg over the freeway divider and sprinted to the Lazy J. He laughs and tells you he knows you're game. He just does it, without telling you how he does it. He slips into traffic on a forty-five-degree angle that swings your car and makes it moan. In slow motion, he lets the stream of cars and trucks work around him. Steadily he gets toward the exit ramp and makes for a back road that leads to an industrial area of a city you have never visited.

As you enter the region, you can see that it was once a big meadow, although it's now covered with asphalt and warehouses that face each other in flimsy rows. "I got a friend," says Hal. "Two guys. Father and son. They're gonna stay open and get you rolling again." You marvel at the efficiency of your misfortune. You begin to thank him and suddenly see the small faded heart tattooed on his forearm, and the name under it, scratched out crudely with black ink. Dot. The sound of her voice comes back to you as if she were psychically telling you that everything is going to be all right. You certainly hope to God she's right.

As you approach the garage, Hal makes a call on the truck radio, and the steel and chain dock door reels up. Two large men step forward and shake your hand. They pull your dusty cruiser into the repair bay and promise to set a record. With their greasy caps on backward, they delve into the engine and remove the broken part with their bare hands. Hal pulls away to rejoin the rush-hour army of tow trucks on the freeway, and the guys go to it. In the back of the shop, a shadowy figure pushes a broom. As he approaches you shyly, you see he is a middle-aged mongoloid.

Suddenly, the repair is done, but you realize you are fifty dollars short and you don't have a single credit card with you. You suggest that a friend could drive some cash to you, but not until later. The men laugh and shake their heads no. You wonder what you will have to do. Your heart nearly stops when you suddenly think they might try something.

Bobbing their heads like dogs, they turn their caps around and say, "Just send us a check for the balance when you get home. Ain't never been took yet," they nod.

To clarify their gallantry, the men tell you they "have wives," as if this explains it. They laugh and claim they've never been sorry about someone they've rescued. They write out the invoice and you notice they haven't charged for labor even though they've kept their shop open for you. As you pull your car out into the parking lot and look for the way back to the freeway, they wave goodbye with their hats. It's dark now, but the car is fixed and you are invincible again. To celebrate, you pull on the running lights and slam the gas pedal.

You check your watch, and whistle. The whole thing has taken forty-five minutes and you're coming up fast on an empty rig clattering along in the passing lane. You blink your headlights and glide by at seventy-five, not once thinking about the speed limit, breathing deep and shaking out your hair. The truck pulls over and lets you by. You kick ass in passing gear. You know then it's not just a car you're driving; it's you and your restless spirit that loves the air, the space, and the insatiable mouth of the road that opens before you.

As you pull ahead, the trucker blinks his lights chivalrously as he bounces back into the fast lane. You surge away and cross into the next county as night casts a vague net of stars overhead. A honey-tongued breeze flows through the vents and you throw your head back, windows down, and yodel as loud as you can.

DEANNE STILLMAN

You Should Have Been
Here an Hour Ago

*We are at a scenic overlook somewhere in the Mojave Desert. A Ford Taurus
station wagon is parked there. We see three of its four inhabitants: Mom
(thirties); Janey (fourteen); and Joey (nine), three-fourths of a typical
family among the dozens of families currently finding themselves part of
the twenty-first century Hooverville along the highway.*

*As their old Ford Taurus station wagon is the worse for wear, so are the
family's clothes. Mom is in a tattered calico Ralph Lauren outfit; Joey in
a very dirty Hard Rock Cafe T-shirt, shredded jeans, and LA Gear high-
tops with flapping soles; Janey is in heavy-metal fan garb, which is perfect for the homeless life, although certainly her clothes, like everyone
else's, need to be Martinized. Dad, who appears later, wears what's left of
a Brooks Brothers suit. The fact is, if their teeth weren't so perfect, they
could easily be living over a heating grate in Manhattan.*

*A crude fire flickers; a bitter gust of wind sweeps through the camp. Janey
is on the phone under the car. Joey puts several slices of bread on a stick,
then moves closer to the fire to make toast. The family is relentlessly
happy and cheerful.*

JANEY (*under car*): . . . No, living here isn't so bad. I don't have to
make my bed because I don't have one, there's a cute, roving band
of inner-city youths that prey on everyone, and—

MOM (*checking her watch and looking under car*): Young lady, get off
that phone this instant—

JANEY: Call you later. Bye.

*Janey hangs up, crawls out from under the car, and hands Mom the
phone. Mom takes it as if it's the Hope diamond, examines it, gives it a
light dusting, then places it atop a pedestal—the hood of the car.*

MOM: I've told you time and time again to stay off the phone when we're expecting our call from the National Focus Group Survey. Do you have potatoes in your ears?

JANEY: Sorry, Mom.

MOM: Now go help your brother make toast. Your father's been away all night and I'm sure he'll be ready for a good, hot breakfast when he gets back.

JOEY: And appreciative of how thoughtful we are.

Janey moves to help Joey.

JANEY: It's not like I was being negative, or anything.

MOM: I know you weren't, Janey. You're a perfect daughter and Joey's a perfect son . . .

She moves to inspect the toast.

MOM (*cont.*): And this toast looks almost . . . perfect.

She becomes even more cheerful at the thought of her own little word jokes.

JOEY: Medium-brown, just like Dad likes it.

JANEY (*nostalgically*): Number four on the toaster.

The three of them ponder this for a moment.

MOM: Now that's enough wallowing in the past! Let's count our blessings . . .

Mom looks around, sees no blessings, looks again—this time at the desert, and immediately re-perks.

MOM (*cont.*): We live in . . .

JANEY/JOEY (*a routine chant*): . . . a scenic overlook.

MOM (*cheerfully continuing the chant*): Our lives are . . .

JANEY/JOEY: . . . suitable for framing . . .

ALL: And we've never gone a day without toast.

JOEY: That's because you're the best mom in the world, Mom.

MOM (*looking at ground and shuffling*): Aw, thanks, sweetie, but let's be fair. I owe it all to those calls from the National Focus Group Survey. (*as an afterthought*) And your father, of course.

JANEY (*concerned*): I wonder where he is. It's not like him to be late for an appointment with a pollster.

MOM: Young lady, turn that frown upside down. I'm sure your father's fine. Although you're right. It's not like him to be late for an appointment with a pollster.

JOEY: I'm sure he's fine. (*trying to be encouraging*) Maybe he stopped off to sell some blood, like last time!

They are buoyed by this thought. The phone rings. Joey leaps to answer it.

JOEY: Hello? . . . (*annoyed*) Bobby, I told you, I can't talk on Wednesday morning.

As she listens, Mom droops.

JOEY (*cont.*): That's when the Survey Group calls and asks for our opinion!

At the mention of "Survey Group," Mom recovers, pretending that she is a puppet and pulling herself up with an invisible string.

JOEY (*cont.*): Bye!

He hangs up the phone and Mom inspects it to make sure it's working properly, then puts it on top of the car.

JOEY (*cont.*): Sorry, Mom. Some people just don't understand the importance of being polled.

MOM: That's right. Polls are important. Polls are used to determine important decisions. Polls tells us that . . . (*now, a total change of character, as Jesse Jackson*) . . . We are somebody!

Janey and Joey exchange a look and Mom realizes that she just cracked, then quickly regains her composure and moves to the fire to check the toast.

MOM (*cont.*): Not a moment too soon!

She starts to wrap the toast in a towel. But the phone rings and Mom leaps to grab it. The toast goes flying.

MOM (*midair*): Children, make more toast. (*into phone*) Hello? . . . (*excitedly*) Yes, this is the Doakes family . . . the National Focus Group Survey? . . . Well, hello! May I tell you how synchronistic this is? I was just willing you to phone us . . . Of course, I believe in synchronicity. Is that what you're asking in today's poll? . . . You can't tell me because you need to talk to the head of the household? . . . (*stalling and scanning horizon*) Well, three out of four Doakeses are ready to be asked for our opinions, children, line up for the Survey people . . .

Janey and Joey line up.

MOM (*cont.*): . . . and say hello . . .

Janey and Joey ad lib hellos into the phone. It doesn't help. Mom is almost completely unglued.

MOM (*cont.*): . . . You know, Mr. Doakes will be here any second, as you may recall, he's got an impeccable record when it comes to being polled, he's always on hand for your call, in fact, you could say, it's the reason he gets up in the morning, that goes double for all the members of our family . . .

Janey and Joey cheerfully nod in agreement.

MOM (*cont.*): . . . Well, couldn't you call back? Mr. Doakes has so many opinions, and we already know what they are, so of course he's anxious to share them with you, in fact, the last thing he said to me was, "Honey, you know what really rings my chimes? . . . (*reacting to the line going dead*) Hello? (*shaking phone*) Is anyone there?

Mom frantically takes the phone apart and quickly puts it together again to see if it's working.

MOM (*cont.*): Did you kids do something to this phone?

JANEY: Of course not, Mom.

JOEY: I'm sure they'll call back.

MOM (*attempting to re-perk*): Oh, I'm sure you're right. You're always right. Except of course when your father—

Dad now enters, shell-shocked. Mom rushes to him, grabbing the stick with toast and offering it.

MOM (*cont., totally re-perked*): Toast?

DAD (*waving it away*): Five-thousand men showed up to write one line of ad copy. It started raining. They wouldn't open up the gates. Fights broke out. They sent in the dogs. It got ugly. I left.

A beat as Mom, Janey, and Joey frown.

DAD (*not liking their frowns, attempting to re-perk*): But I didn't miss our phone call, did I?

Mom, Janey, and Joey now exchange angry, sullen looks.

DAD (*cont., now deflated again*): Don't tell me. Correctly assuming that I would return jobless, Mom did a hoochie-koochie dance for the highway patrol, Joey broke down and sold his Pete Rose rookie card, and Janey was tied up and tongue-kissed by that roving band of inner-city youths.

JOEY (*well-meaning*): We couldn't help it, Dad—

MOM (*quickly cutting Joey off*): —The point is, honey, I've got some good news . . .

Dad smiles.

MOM (*cont.*): . . . And some bad news.

Dad frowns.

MOM (*cont.*): The good news is . . .

Dad smiles.

MOM (*cont.*): . . . they did phone, so that means we still count . . .

Dad does a little end-zone victory dance.

DAD: Team Doakes!

MOM: And the bad news is . . .

Dad stops dancing, then frowns.

MOM (*cont.*): . . . they only wanted to talk to the head of the household and you weren't here . . .

DAD (*disbelieving*): Well, couldn't you get them to phone back? They've never asked specifically for me . . .

JANEY: Maybe that's because you always answer the phone.

MOM: Zip your lip, young lady. I won't have any of that smart talk in this house.

Janey "zips" her lip and exchanges a look with Joey.

Dad starts pacing around the camp. Mom plants the stick with the toast over the fire.

DAD: I suppose I didn't have to go off on another wild-goose chase job hunt . . .

MOM: Sure you did, honey, because that's the kind of guy you are.

Dad re-perks, as Mom begins to deflate.

MOM (*cont.*): . . . I suppose I could have disguised my voice and said I was the head of the household . . .

DAD: But, honey, that would have been dishonest, and that's not the kind of gal you are.

Mom re-perks, as Dad deflates again.

DAD (cont.): . . . Well, I suppose if I had a real head on my shoulders, I would have taken our family nest egg out of the bank, and put it in our king-size Serta sleeper and then removed it before the bank collapsed and the bed was repossessed. But thanks to my famous short-sightedness, I didn't do that.

MOM: Hey, hey, hey, honey, you're not Nostradamus!

Dad does not re-perk. Mom begins a cartwheel.

DAD: Well, I should have read Nostradamus. He predicted this whole shebang, didn't he?

MOM (*completing the cartwheel*): Maybe he did, maybe he didn't, but one thing's for sure. Back in his day, they didn't have toast!

Dad immediately re-perks, and the two of them move happily to the fire. The family huddles around.

DAD (*picking up the toast stick and examining the toast*): Mmmmm . . . medium brown . . . Number four on the toaster. If you want my opinion, I like it!

Everyone agrees, anxiously waiting for Dad to start eating so they can follow.

DAD (*cont., shouting into the void*): The Doakes family likes medium-brown toast! Did you hear that, National Focus Group Survey? (*now sheepishly, to family*) In case they're listening.

JANEY/JOEY: We're listening, Dad. We like to hear your opinions.

The phone rings.

MOM (*midair*): It's working!

They all lunge for it and pile up on top of the phone. Dad tries to keep the toast stick clear of the jumble. From under the pile we hear Dad.

DAD (*excitedly*): Head of the household. What can I do you for? . . . (*dejectedly*) Oh, yeah, sure, what the hey . . .

The group reassembles around the campfire.

MOM (*hopefully*): Well?

DAD: The Coopers in the blue Le Baron. They said they have some preserves so I invited them over.

MOM (*looking around*): Might as well start meeting our neighbors.

Dad finally begins to take a bite of what's left of the toast. But a gust of wind blows it from his hand and offstage. Dad deflates.

MOM: Children, make more toast.

The lights fade.

Part Three

No one with a good car needs to be justified.
FLANNERY O'CONNOR, *Wise Blood*

LINDA PASTAN

Jump Cabling

When our cars	touched,
When you lifted the hood	of mine
To see the intimate workings	underneath,
When we were bound	together
By a pulse of pure	energy,
When my car like the	princess
In the tale woke with a	start,

I thought why not ride the rest of the way together?

KATHARINE HARER

Midas Muffler

Standing under the underside
of my car with the Midas Muffler man
did you say kiss me he asked
no I said Merry Christmas oh
I thought you said kiss me
I didn't say kiss me standing under my
oil pan although it was sort of intimate
under there and personal the loose
pipes I didn't want him to think I neglected
my car but I didn't say kiss me
although I stood close to him as he
bounced my rusted muffler deftly his
hand under my car
I didn't say kiss me or even think it then
although I looked at his face and imagined what
it would be like to kiss him
I didn't say kiss me but I wanted to say
what if I had said kiss me what if I had
and it was almost as though I had said it
although it was him not me

I felt very pink in that place my sleeveless
arms and pink toes I felt very calm
waiting in a pool of sun on the oily floor
I felt the sounds of kiss me very pleasant
opening and closing
inside my lips

ELOISE KLEIN HEALY

Changing the Oil

I get her up on the curb, two wheels off the street
and dive under with my tools—my favorite blue-handled
wrench and a drop-forged hammer with a no-slip grip.

Her, her, her—always the female car. And now I'm under,
lying on the news of the day before yesterday, slowly turning
the warm nut. She's above me like a womb or heaven
about to rain. I'm slowly turning my way into her
black blood, slipping on the wet bolt, diving into
the underworld we women crawl into with our new pride
fresh from the parts store. Turning the beautiful
implements over in my hands, tenderly
the oil spurts free—and I have done it.

LESLEÁ NEWMAN

Have femme Will Travel

"Tell me I'm dreaming," Flash moans. "Tell me this is a nightmare."

"This is a nightmare," I tell Flash. "But you're not dreaming." I shake my head at the sorry sight before my eyes: my beloved Flash sitting in her beloved car, the back tires on solid ground, the front wheels up to their hubcaps in sand.

How did this happen? This was not part of our vacation plan. The plan was to enjoy two long, luxurious, stress-free weeks on Cape Cod. Tonight we were supposed to drive into Provincetown for a show featuring the world famous drag queen, Lotta Sequins. I'd gotten all dressed up (not to be outdone by the boys) in my shortest shirt, longest earrings, highest heels, and biggest hair. Flash, looking dapper in her black silk shirt and chinos, steered into the parking lot and started searching for a space. The place was jammed, so she headed for the back of the lot, never dreaming that trouble lurked just around the corner in the form of a sand trap disguised as the last available parking space on the planet. Who could imagine that the Goddess would be so cruel?

"Maybe you should get out of the car, Flash," I gently suggest. "We'll see the show and deal with this later."

"Are you crazy?" Flash remains behind the steering wheel, a true captain ready to go down with her ship. All of a sudden I realize who I am dealing with here: a butch. In other words, a woman who appreciates a good truck as much as a good fuck. A woman who won't pick up a dust rag inside the house, but spends hours every weekend washing, waxing, buffing, polishing, and vacuuming her car (not to mention cleaning out the stick shift grooves with a toothpick). Flash has actually said that if she was going to be marooned on a desert island and could only take one thing with her (besides me, of course), she would take her car. I, on the other hand, would take my pocketbook, which is big enough to hold Flash, Flash's car and anything else I might possibly need, but that's another story. To me, a car is a hunk of metal someone else drives me around in. To Flash, a car is a thing of beauty and a joy forever.

Maybe this is hard for me to understand because I grew up in Brooklyn where nobody owns a car. That's because there's nowhere to put it unless you have enough money to pay for a garage space, which costs more than your rent, and if you had that kind of money, why in the world would you live in Brooklyn? When my family moved to Long Island, I spent years looking for the subway stops. It finally dawned on me that there weren't any because everyone's house came with a two-car garage. Which meant they had cars and all knew how to drive. Which meant I had to learn how to drive, too.

I signed up for driver's ed the day I turned seventeen. My teacher, Miss Ford, spent the entire first lesson teaching me how to get in and out of the car like a lady. For those of you who missed this important lesson, pay attention: first you gently lower your derrière onto the seat, keeping your back straight and your head high. Then, with your knees pressed tightly together, your thighs parallel to the ground and your knees bent at a perfect ninety degree angle, you use your stomach muscles to slowly lift your legs and *swivel* your gams into the car. I had to practice this maneuver for weeks, both on the driver's side (swiveling left to right) and the passenger side (swiveling right to left) before Miss Ford would actually let me take the car out on the road.

Then came the big day: my driver's test. Actually, it was a series of big days, since I had to take my road test five times. It wasn't my fault, though. The officer, Mr. Steel (named for his nerves) truly had it in for me. He asked me to parallel park on a hill. He told me to change lanes right as we were approaching a traffic light (of course I didn't see it was red; I was too busy looking in my rear view mirror). Mr. Steel made me so nervous, my three-point turn turned into a twenty-three-point turn. "We've got to stop meeting like this," I said to him as I got into the car for my fourth try. He didn't crack a smile, but immediately flunked me for sticking the key into the ignition *before* I fastened my seat belt, even though I hadn't even turned the car on yet.

That did it. Clearly, drastic measures were needed. On the day of my fifth road test I wore the shortest mini-skirt my mother would let me out of the house in, and proceeded to get into the car exactly like a lady shouldn't. Needless to say, Mr. Steel passed me with flying colors. And I'm proud to say that I have never been in an accident or even had major car trouble since. Of course I only drive to the shoestore and back. Oh, except for that one time I drove from Lesbianville to Boston and, on the way home, my muffler fell off. I did what any quick-thinking femme would do: I wiggled out of my pantyhose, tied the muffler back on with them, and drove home without a hitch. "You did what?" Flash asked, aghast. "Do you know how dangerous that is?" The next day she came home loaded down with maps, matches, jumper cables, jacks, flares, flashlights, gas cans, blankets, freeze-dried dinner packets, and a huge banner that says H-E-L-P which is what I needed to fit it all into my car. "And I got you this, too," Flash said, handing me a small gift box, exquisitely wrapped.

"What's this?" I gasped, tearing at the ribbon. Inside was a plastic card. "A charge card!" I squealed.

"Not exactly. It's a Triple A card. Do not," Flash said sternly, "ever leave home without it."

"Where's yours?" I asked.

"I don't need one," Flash boasted. Sure she can change her oil, change a tire, jump-start the ignition and jimmy a lock, but clearly she cannot tow her car. Luckily she always has her femme in tow, and luckier still, her femme always follows her butch's advice. I dig my Triple A card out of my pocketbook and flash it at Flash. "I'll be right back. Don't go anywhere," I say, trying to make her laugh. Her face is as uncrackable as Mr. Steel's.

I make my way through the parking lot into the theater. Before I have a chance to look around the lobby for a pay phone, I am bombarded by a middle-aged couple. Both husband and wife are decked out in matching outfits: Hawaiian-print Bermuda shorts and *My Son Came Out And All I Got Was This Lousy T-Shirt* T-shirts.

"Ooh, look, George. He looks just like a woman."

"You're wrong, Ethel. See his feet? They're *huge*. They say you can always tell by the feet."

I look around, and then realize to my horror that George and Ethel are talking about *me*. "I'm a woman, NOT a drag queen," I bark at them.

"Oh, it's definitely a man," George decides. "The voice is a dead giveaway."

"I am NOT a man!" I stomp my gigantic foot on the ground.

"He really believes he's a woman," George marvels.

"*She*, George, you're supposed to call them *she*. Take a picture, take a picture." Ethel puts her arm around my waist and smiles as George snaps away. Someone else asks for my autograph. In a moment of divine inspiration, I come up with my drag name: Dusty Tchotchkes. A crowd gathers. "You'll all have to excuse me," I apologize. "It's almost show time." And with those words I make a dash backstage into Lotta Sequins's dressing room.

"Darling, you look *fabulous*." Lotta kisses me on the cheek. "Oh that skirt, those earrings. Those *shoes*. I've just got to try them on." I kick off my shoes and Lotta slides her size twenty-five feet into them. They fit perfectly.

"Listen, Lotta," I say. "I'll trade you those pumps for the use of your phone."

"Oh my God," Lotta shrieks, "you're a girl!" At least Lotta knows a real female voice when she hears one. She puts her hands on her hips and glares. "What the hell is this, *Victor/Victoria?*"

I explain the situation and Lotta could not have been more gracious. She shows me to the phone where I spend fifteen minutes listening to Muzak before I get someone on the wire. "They'll be there within the hour," the dispatcher tells me. I race outside to tell Flash. The girl is up and out of her car, directing traffic. "You, in the white Toyota, back that baby up. This aisle has to stay clear. A tow truck's coming through." I watch my butch with pride. All those years working traffic control in Michigan had definitely paid off.

"Hey, where are your shoes?" Flash looks at my bare feet.

"Don't ask." I shake my head. "Listen, I've got good news. Triple A will be here in an hour." Yeah, right. And I'm Barbra Streisand. After exactly fifty-nine minutes have passed, I go back into the theater to call again. "Oh, you're in Provincetown?" the dispatcher says. "I thought you said Providence."

"Providence? You mean Rhode Island?" I try to keep my voice down, as Lotta Sequins is on stage, doing a soft Bette Midler number. The dispatcher assures me she'll send someone right away and I hurry outside to inform Flash. Just as Lotta starts belting out "Enough is Enough," the tow truck arrives.

"Hi, I'm Diesel." A woman with short black hair climbs out of the truck and shakes Flash's hand. I don't know why I'm surprised to see a dyke. I mean this is Provincetown, after all. Diesel looks like she could lift Flash's car out of the sand with her bare hands. She gets out the chains, drags them over to our helpless vehicle, and disappears underneath the car to assess the situation. Without saying a word to us, she gets up, goes back into the tow truck, revs the engine, and roars away. "My car!" Flash screams, envisioning her pride and joy jolted out of the sand and flying through the air like a cartoon.

"Relax, Flash, she didn't hook them on yet." I try to soothe my beloved, whose nerves are clearly shot. Diesel comes back. "I needed more of a lead," she explains, squatting down again. This time she attaches the chains to the car and then walks back to the tow truck to turn on the juice. Flash kneels to the ground. "C'mon baby, c'mon baby, you can do it baby, that's it, that's it, do it for me baby, yes, yes, yes," she croons as if she's egging me on to orgasm rather than coaxing her car out of the sand. Finally the car begins to move. A minute later all four wheels are on solid ground. Two minutes later, Flash is back behind the wheel and we head out of the parking lot, with Lotta Sequins's encore, "Everything's Coming Up Roses," ringing in our ears.

"God, that was a drag," Flash says.

"You don't know the half of it." I tell Flash all about George, Ethel, and Dusty Tchotchkes. She smiles for the first time all night. "Thank God they didn't ask you to sing," she says.

"R-E-S-P-E-C-T," I remind Flash, in my best imitation of a young, gifted, and tone-deaf Aretha.

"Please," Flash begs. "Tell you what. If you stop singing, I'll buy you a new pair of shoes tomorrow."

That shuts me up fast. I zip my lips and remain silent all the way home, glad that the evening didn't turn out to be a total loss after all.

EDNA FERBER

Hey! Taxi!

Nervous old ladies from Dubuque, peering fearfully at the placard confronting them as they rode in Ernie's taxi, waxed more timorous still as they read it. It conveyed a grisly warning. Attached thereto was a full-face photograph of Ernie. Upon viewing this, their appraising glance invariably leaped, startled, to where Ernie himself loomed before them in the driver's seat on the other side of the glass partition. Immediately there swept over them an impulse to act upon the printed instructions.

POLICE DEPARTMENT
CITY OF NEW YORK

ERNEST STEWIG

This is a photograph of the authorized driver.
If another person is driving this cab notify a policeman.

Staring limpidly back at one from the official photograph was a sleek, personable, and bland young man. This Ernest Stewig who basked in police approval was modishly attired in a starched white collar, store clothes, and a not-too-rakish fedora. Trust me, he said.

From a survey of this alleged likeness the baffled eye swung, fascinated, to the corporeal and workaday Ernie seated just ahead, so clearly outlined against the intervening glass.

A pair of pugnacious red ears outstanding beneath a checked gray and black cap well pulled down over the head; a soft blue shirt, somewhat faded; or, in winter, a maroon sweater above whose roll rose a powerful and seemingly immovable neck. Somewhere between the defiant ears and the monolithic neck you sensed a jaw to which a photograph could have done justice only in profile. You further felt that situate between the cap's visor and the jaw was a pair of eyes before which the seraphic gaze of the pictured

Ernie would have quailed. The head never moved, never turned to right or left; yet its vision seemed to encompass everything. It was like a lighthouse tower, regnant, impregnable, raking the maelstrom below with a coldly luminous scrutiny.

About the whole figure there was something pantherlike—a quietly alert, formidable, and almost sinister quality—to convey which was in itself no mean achievement for a young man slouched at the wheel of a palpably repainted New York taxicab.

Stewig. Stewig! The name, too, held a degree of puzzlement. The passenger's brain, rejecting the eye's message, sent back a query: Stewig? Isn't there a consonant missing?

Just here the n.o.l. from Dubuque had been known to tap on the glass with an apprehensive but determined forefinger.

"Young man! Young man! Is this your taxicab you're driving?"

"What's that?"

"I said, are you driving this taxi?"

"Well, who'd you think was driving it, lady?"

"I mean are you the same young man as in the picture here?"

Then Ernie, to the horror of his fare, might thrust his head in at the half-open window, unmindful of the traffic that swirled and eddied all about him.

"Me? No. I'm a couple of other guys," he might say, and smile.

In spite of sweater, cap, jaw, ears, and general bearing, when Ernie smiled you recognized in him the engaging and highly sartorial Ernest Stewig photographically approved by the local constabulary. Apologetic and reassured, the passenger would relax against the worn leather cushion.

About Ernie there was much that neither police nor passenger knew. About police and passenger there was little that Ernie did not know. And New York was the palm of his hand. Not only was Ernie the authorized driver of this car; he was its owner. He had bought it secondhand for four hundred dollars. Its four cylinders made rhythmic music in his ears. He fed it oil, gas, and water as a mother feeds her babe. He was a member in good standing of the United Taxi Men's Association. He belonged to Mickey Dolan's Democratic Club for reasons more politic than political.

In his left coat pocket he carried the gray-bound booklet which was his hack driver's license—a tiny telltale pamphlet of perhaps a dozen pages. At the top of each left-hand page was printed the word VIOLATION. At the top of each right-hand page was the word DISPOSITION. If, during the year, Ernie had been up for speeding, for parking where he shouldn't, for wearing his hackman's badge on his left lapel instead of his right, for any one of those myriad petty misdemeanors which swarm like insects above a hackman's head, that small crime now would appear inevitably on the left-hand page, as would his punishment therefor on the right-hand.

Here it was, November. The pages of Ernie's little gray book were virgin.

It must not be assumed that this was entirely due to the high moral plane on which Ernie and his four-cylinder, secondhand cab (repainted) moved. He was careful, wise, crafty, and almost diabolically gifted at the wheel. When you rode with Ernie you got there—two new gray hairs, perhaps, and the eye pupils slightly dilated—but you got there. His was a gorgeous and uncanny sense of timing. You turned the green-light corner just one second before the sanguine glare of the stop light got you. Men passengers of his own age, thirtyish, seemed to recognize a certain quality in his manipulation of the wheel. They said, "What outfit were you with?"

There were many like him penduluming up and down the narrow tongue of land between the Hudson and the East River. He was of his day: hard, tough, disillusioned, vital, and engaging. He and his kind had a pitying contempt for those grizzled, red-faced old fellows whose hands at the wheel were not those of the mechanic, quick, deft, flexible, but those of the horseman, bred to the reins instead of the steering gear. These drove cautiously, their high-colored faces set in anxiety, their arms stiffly held. Theirs were rattling old cars for which they had no affection and some distrust. They sat in the driver's seat as though an invisible rug were tucked about their inflexible knees. In their eyes was an expectant look—imploring, almost—as though they hoped the greasy engine would turn somehow, magically, into a quadruped. Past these, Ernie's car flashed derisively.

Up and down, up and down the little island he raced. New York swore at him, growled at him, confided in him, overtipped him, undertipped him, borrowed money from him, cheated him, rewarded him, bribed him, invited him to crime. His knowledge of New York was fearful. He forever was talking of leaving it. He complained of the dullness of business, of the dullness of life. He never talked to you unless you first talked to him, after which you had some difficulty in shutting him up. He had a sweet, true, slightly nasal tenor which he sometimes obligingly loaned to college boys with an urge to harmonize while on a New York week end. His vocabulary in daily use consisted of perhaps not more than two hundred words. He was married. He was fond of his wife, Josie. His ambition, confided under the slightest encouragement, was to open a little country hotel somewhere up the river, with a quiet but brisk bar and liquor business on the side. To this end he worked fifteen hours a day; toward it he and Josie saved his money. It was to be their idyl.

"Yeh, hackin', there's nothing in it. Too many cabs, see? And overhead! Sweet jeez, lookit. Insurance thirty bucks a month and you got to pay it. If you ain't got your sticker every month—yeah, that's it, that blue paper on the windshield, see?—you're drove off the street by the cops and you get a ticket. Sure. You gotta insure. Garage, twenty-five. Paint your car once a year anyway is fifty. Oil and gas, two-fifty a day. Five tires a year and a good shoe sets you back plenty. That says nothing about parts and repairs. Where are you, with anyway fifteen hunnerd a year and nearer two grand? No, I only got just this one hack. No, I wouldn't want no jockey. I drive it alone. They don't play square with you, see? It ain't worth the worry of an extra bus. Yeh, I see aplenty and hear aplenty. Keep your eyes and ears open in the hackin' game, and your mouth shut, and you won't never get into a jam is the way I figger."

Strange fragments of talk floated out to Ernie as he sat so stolidly there at the wheel, looking straight ahead:

"Don't! There! I've lost an earring."

"... five dollars a quart ..."

"... sick and tired of your damn nagging ..."

"... You do trust me, don't you, babe?"

Up and down, up and down, putting a feverish city to bed. Like a racked and restless patient who tosses and turns and moans and whimpers, the town made all sorts of notional demands before finally it composed its hot limbs to fitful sleep.

Light! cried the patient. Light!

All right, said Ernie. And made for Broadway at Times Square.

I want a drink! I want a drink!

Sure, said Ernie. And stopped at a basement door with a little slit in it and an eye on the other side of the slit.

I want something to eat!

Right, said Ernie. And drove to a place whose doors never close and whose windows are plethoric with roast turkeys, jumbo olives, cheeses, and sugared hams.

It's hot! It's hot! I want to cool off before I go to sleep!

Ernie trundled his patient through the dim aisles of Central Park and up past the midnight velvet of Riverside Drive.

One thing more. Under his seat, just behind his heels and covered by the innocent roll of his raincoat, Ernie carried a venomous fourteen-inch section of cold, black, solid iron pipe. Its thickness was such that the hand could grasp it comfortably and quickly. A jack handle, it was called affectionately.

Though he affected to be bored by his trade he deceived no one by his complaints; not even himself. Its infinite variety held him; its chanciness; the unlimited possibilities of his day's vagaries. Josie felt this. Josie said, "You'll be hackin' when you're sixty and so stiff-knuckled your fingers can't wrap around the wheel."

"Sixty, I'll be pushing you in a wheel chair if you don't take off some that suet."

They loved each other.

Saturday. Any day in Ernie's life as a hackman might bring forth almost anything, and frequently did. But Saturday was sure to. Saturday, in winter, was a long hard day and night, yet Ernie always awoke to it much as a schoolboy contemplates his Saturday, bright and new-minted. It held all sorts of delightful possibilities.

Saturday, in late November. Having got in at 4 A.M., he awoke at noon, refreshed.

Josie had been up since eight. She did not keep hackman's hours. Josie's was a rather lonely life. She complained sometimes, but not often; just enough to keep Ernie interested and a little anxious. A plump, neat woman with slim, quick ankles; deep-bosomed; a careful water wave; an excellent natural cook; she dressed well and quietly, eschewing beige with a wisdom that few plump women have. Ernie took pride in seeing her smartly turned out on their rare holidays together. A lonely and perforce an idle wife, she frequented the movies both afternoon and evening, finding in their shadowy love-making and lavishness a vicarious thrill and some solace during Ernie's absence.

His breakfast was always the same. Fruit, toast, coffee—the light breakfast of a man who has had his morning appetite ruined by a late lunch bolted before going to bed. Josie had eaten four hours earlier. She lunched companionably with him as he breakfasted. It was, usually, their only meal together. As she prepared it, moving deftly about the little kitchen in her print dress and wave pins, Ernie went up on the roof, as was his wont, to survey the world and to fool for five minutes with Big Bum, the family police dog, named after Ernie's pet aversion, the night traffic cop at the corner of Forty-fifth and Broadway. He it was who made life hard for hackmen between the hours of nine-thirty and eleven, when they were jockeying for the theater break.

The Stewigs' flat was one of the many brownstone walk-ups in West Sixty-fifth Street, a sordid and reasonably respectable row of five-story ugliness whose roofs bristled with a sapling forest of radio aerials. A little rickety flight of stairs and a tiny tar-papered shed led to an exhilarating and unexpected view of sky and other low-lying roofs, a glimpse of the pocket-edition Statue of Liberty on top of the Liberty Storage Warehouse, and even a bit of the Hudson if you leaned over the parapet and screwed your neck around.

Ernie liked it up there. It gave him a large sense of freedom, of dominance. He and Big Bum tussled and bounded and rolled about a bit within the narrow confines of their roof world. They surveyed the Western Hemisphere. Big Bum slavered and pawed and bowed and scraped his paws and wagged his tail and shimmied his flanks and went through all the flattering and sycophantic attitudes of the adoring canine who craves male company, being surfeited with female.

"Ernie!" a voice came up the airshaft. "Coffee's getting cold!"

Big Bum threw his whole heart into his effort to hold his master on the roof. He bared his fangs, growled, set his forefeet menacingly. Ernie slapped him on the rump, tousled his muzzle, tickled his stomach with a fond toe.

"Come on, Bum."

"Aw, no!" said Bum, with his eyes. "Let's not pay any attention to her. Couple of men like us."

"Ernie! Don't beef to me if your toast is leather."

"Come on, Bum." Down they went to domesticity.

"What time'll you be home, do you think?"

"How should I know?"

"You couldn't stop by for dinner, could you, late? Nice little steak for you, maybe, or a pork tenderloin and lemon pie?"

"On a Saturday? You're cuckoo!"

"Well, I just thought."

"Hey! Don't go bragging."

They had discussed a child in rare conjugal moments. "Wait," Ernie had said, "till we got the place up the river with a back yard for the kid like I had time I was little and lived in Jersey, and he can fool with Bum and like that. Here, where's he be but out on the street being run over?"

"Yes," said Josie, not too delicately. "Let's wait till I'm fifty."

She bade him good-bye now, somewhat listlessly. "Well, anyway, you're not working tomorrow, are you, Ernie? Sunday?"

"No. Give the other guy a chance tomorrow. We'll go somewheres."

They did not kiss one another good-bye. After seven years of marriage they would have considered such daytime demonstration queer, not to say offensive.

One o'clock. Over to the garage on Sixty-ninth for the hack. Gas, oil, and water. These services he himself performed, one of the few taxi men to whom the engine of a car was not as mysterious and unexplored as the heavenly constellations. It was a saying among hackmen that most of them did not know what to do when the engine was boiling over. Ernie's car had been cleaned during the morning. Still, he now extracted from beneath the seat cushion a flannel rag with which he briskly rubbed such metal parts as were, in his opinion, not sufficiently resplendent.

He had fitted the car with certain devices of his own of which he was extremely proud. Attached to the dashboard, at the right, was a little metal clip which held his pencil. Just below the meter box hung a change slot such as streetcar conductors wear. It held dimes, quarters, and nickels and saved Ernie much grubbing about in coat pockets while passengers waited, grumbling.

Out through the broad, open door of the garage and into the lemon-yellow sunshine of a sharp November Saturday. A vague nostalgia possessed him momentarily. Perhaps they were burning leaves on some cross street that still boasted an anemic tree or two. Saturday afternoons in Jersey—Jeez, it's a great day for football, he thought, idly, and swung into Sixty-eighth Street toward the Park.

Two elderly, gray-haired women twittered wrenlike at the curb in front of a mountainous apartment house near Central Park West. They looked this way and that. At sight of Ernie's cab they fluttered their wings. He swooped down on them. They retreated timidly, then gave him the address and were swallowed in the maw of his taxi.

Two o'clock. Ernie's Saturday had begun.

The number they had given was on Lexington Avenue in the Fifties. It turned out to be a small motion-picture theater.

"This where you meant, lady?"

They fumbled with the door. Ernie reached in, opened it. They stepped out, stiffly. The fare was fifty-five cents. One wren handed him a minutely folded green bill. He tapped the change slot three times and gave her two dimes and a quarter. The wren put the three coins into a small black purse. From the same purse she extracted a five-cent piece and offered it to him. He regarded it impersonally, took it.

A little superstitious shiver shook him. A swell start for a Saturday, all right. What those two old birds want to come 'way over here to a bum movie for, anyway! Curious, he glanced at the picture title. *Souls for Sale.* That didn't sound so hot. Oh, well, you couldn't never tell what people done things for. He tucked the folded bill into his upper left coat pocket. He always did that with his first fare, for luck.

Off down the street. Might pick up a matinee fare at the hotels on Madison. He came down to Forty-seventh, jockeyed along the Ritz. Little groups of two and three stood on the steps and came languidly down to the sidewalk at the Madison Avenue entrance. Orchids, fur, sheer silk stockings; British topcoats, yellow sticks: au 'voir, darling . . . awfly nice. . . . The doorman hailed him.

Two of the orchids skipped into his car. They waved good-bye to a coat. Whyn't the big stiff come along with'm, pay their fare and maybe a decent tip instead of the dime these kind of mice give a guy?

"Listen, driver, can't you go faster?"

"Doing the best I can. You can't go through the lights."

Turn around the middle of the street front of the theater if the cop wasn't looking. Yeh, he wasn't. "Forty-five cents."

"I've got it dear. Please let me. Don't fuss. We're so late."

Oh, my Gawd!

The winning orchid handed him a dollar. He flipped a nickel and two quarters into his palm, turned to look hard. "That's all right," said the orchid. They skipped into the theater. Well, that was more like it. Cute couple kids, at that.

He headed down Eighth Avenue toward the loft district in the Thirties between Eighth and Fifth. The fur and cloak-and-suit manufacturers were rushed with late Saturday orders to be delivered, to be shipped. Little dark men ran up and down with swatches, with bundles, with packages of fur and cloth and felt. Take me down to Tenth and Fifth. Take me up to Thirty-second and Third. I want to go to Eight-eight University Place.

It was tough driving through the packed, greasy streets. You couldn't make time, but they were generous with their tips. Ernie preferred to stay all afternoon in and out of the cloak-and-suit district. Being too far downtown, he headed uptown again toward the Thirties. In Thirteenth Street, going west, vacant, he had a call from a gimlet-eyed young man at the curb in front of an old brick building. The young man leaned very close to Ernie. He made no move to enter the taxi. He glanced quickly up and down the street. He said to Ernie, quietly:

"Take a sack of potatoes?"

"Sure," said Ernie. "Where to?"

"Broadway and Nine'y-foist."

"Sure," said Ernie.

The gimlet-eyed young man nodded ever so slightly toward an unseen figure behind him. There emerged quickly from the doorway a short, mild-looking blond man. He carried a suitcase and a brown-paper corded bundle. His strong short arms were tense-muscled under the weight of them. It was as though they held stone. He deposited these gently in the bottom of the cab. Glupglup, came a soft gurgle. The younger man vanished as the little fellow climbed ponderously into the taxi. He reappeared carrying still another brown bundle. He sagged under it.

"Fi' bucks for you," he said to Ernie. "Take Ninth Avenue."

"Sure," said Ernie.

The young man closed the taxi door and disappeared into the brick building. Ernie and the mild blond fellow and the suitcase and the two stout, brown-paper parcels sped up Ninth Avenue, keeping always on the far side of an occasional traffic cop and observing all road rules meticulously.

The uptown Broadway address reached, the man paid him his fare and the five dollars. Ernie sat stolidly in his seat while the little man wrestled with suitcase and bundles. Not him! They wouldn't catch Ernie carrying the stuff with his own hands. As the bundles touched the curb he stepped on the gas and was off, quickly. He headed down Broadway again.

A plump, agitated little woman in an expensive-looking black fur coat hailed him at Eighty-fifth. "Take me to Eight-fifty-five West End. And I'm late for a bridge game."

"That's terrible," said Ernie, grimly. She did not hear him. She perched on the edge of the seat, her stout silken legs crossed at the ankles, both feet beating a nervous tattoo.

Ernie whirled west on Eighty-fifth, then north up West End. The dressy woman climbed laboriously out. She handed Ernie his exact fare and scurried into the marble-and-plush foyer of Number Eight-fifty-five.

"And I hope you lose your shirt," Ernie remarked feelingly.

He took out the five-dollar bill that the man had given him for carrying the sack of potatoes, smoothed it, and placed it in his billfold. Then he remembered the bill in his upper left coat pocket—his first fare given him by the fluttery old ladies bent on seeing *Souls for Sale*. He fished down with two fingers, extracted the bill, smoothed it, and said piously, "For the jeez!"

It was a ten-dollar bill. His mind jolted back. He pieced the events of the past two hours into neat little blocks. Hm. Gosh! Fifteen bones clean, he could call it a day and knock off and go home and have dinner with Jo. There was no possibility of returning the ten-dollar bill to its owner, even if he had thought remotely of so doing—which he emphatically had not.

The blue-and-gold doorman, guardian of Number Eight-fifty-five, now approached Ernie. "What you sticking around here blocking up this entrance?"

Ernie looked up absently. He tucked his bills tidily into the folder, rammed the folder into his hip pocket. "Do you want me to move on?" he inquired humbly.

"You heard me." But the doorman was suspicious of such meekness.

Ernie shifted to first. He eyed the doorman tenderly. "And just when I was beginning to love you," he crooned.

Four-fifteen. He bumbled slowly around the corner on Eighty-sixth and across the Columbus. Might go home, at that. No, Jo wouldn't be there, anyway. A white-tiled coffeeshop. A great wire basket of golden-brown doughnuts in the window, flaky-looking and flecked with powdered sugar. Pretty cold by now. Ernie stamped his feet. Guess he'd go in; have a cup of hot coffee and a couple sinkers.

There were other hackmen in the steaming little shop with its fragrance of coffee and its smell of sizzling fat. They did not speak to Ernie, nor he to them. The beverage was hot and stimulating. He ate three crullers. Feeling warm and gay, he climbed into the driver's seat again. He'd stick around a couple hours more. Then he'd go home and give the other guy a chance.

Down to Columbus Circle, across Fifty-ninth, down Seventh, across Fifty-seventh to Madison. Down Madison slowly. Not a call. Nearly five o'clock.

A girl gave him a call. Tall, slim, pale. Not New York. She had been standing at the curb. Ernie had seen her let vacant cabs go by. As she gave him the number she smiled a little. She looked him in the eye. Her accent was not New Yorkese. She got in. The number she had given turned out to be an office building near Fortieth.

"Wait here," she said and smiled again and looked into Ernie's eyes.

"Long?"

"No, just a minute. Please."

It didn't look so good. Still, he'd wait a couple minutes, anyway. Wonder was there another exit to this building.

She came out almost immediately. "The office was closed," she explained.

Ernie nodded. "Yeh, five o'clock, and Saturday afternoon. Close one o'clock."

She got into the taxi, gave another number. Ernie recognized it as that of still another office building. That, too, probably would be closed, he told her. He turned his head a little to look at her through the window.

She smiled and put her head on one side.

"I want to try, anyway." Then, as Ernie turned to face forward again, his hand on the gear shift, "Could I trouble you for a match?"

Hm. Thought so. When they asked you for a match, anything might happen. He gave her a light. She took it, lingeringly, and kept the matches. You want me to take you to that number, girlie? Yes. She did not resent the girlie. He took her to the number. Wait, please. In a minute she was back. Her voice was plaintive, her brow puckered.

"Seems like everybody's away," she said. She got in. "I love riding in taxis. I'm crazy about it." Her *I* was *Ah*. Her *ou* was double *o*, or nearly.

"You from out of town?"

"I'm from Birmingham. I'm all alone in town. I guess you better take me to my hotel. The Magnolia Hotel, West Twenty-ninth."

He started for it, waiting for the next move from his fare. She pushed down the little seat that folded up, one of a neat pair, against the front of the taxi. She changed over to it and opened the sliding window, leaning out a little.

"My train doesn't go till ten o'clock tonight, and I haven't a thing to do till then."

"That's too bad," said Ernie.

"If I keep my room after six they charge for it. It's almost half-past five now. And my train doesn't go till ten and I haven't a thing to do."

"Yeh?"

"If I got my suitcase and checked out, would you be back down here at six?" They had reached the hotel entrance.

"Sure," said Ernie. She stepped out, her slim ankles teetering in high heels. She turned to go.

"Ninety cents, girlie," said Ernie. She gave him a dollar. Her hand touched his.

"Six o'clock," she repeated. "Right here."

"Sure," said Ernie.

He drove briskly over to the manufacturing section again. They were great taxi riders, those little paunchy men, and a fare there around six o'clock meant a good call up to the Bronx, or over to

Brooklyn. The manufacturers worked late now in the height of the season. Six o'clock and often seven. On the way he got a call to Twelfth Street, came back to the Thirties, and there picked up a Bronx call just as he had hoped. This was his lucky day, all right. Breaking good. Wonder was that Birmingham baby standing on the curb, waiting.

He drove briskly and expertly in and out of the welter of traffic. His fare wanted some newspapers, and Ernie obligingly stopped at a newsstand and got them for him—*Sun, Journal, Telegram*. The man read them under the dim light inside the cab, smoking fat black cigars the while. The rich scent of them floated out to Ernie through the tightly closed windows. A long cold ride, but Ernie didn't mind. He deposited his fare in front of a gaudy new apartment house far uptown.

"Cold night, my boy," said the man.

"I'll say!" A fifty-cent tip. The fare had left the newspapers in the taxi. Ernie selected the *Journal*. He drove to a near-by lunchroom whose sign said Jack's Coffee Pot. Another cup of coffee and a ham-on-rye. He read his paper and studied its pictures, believing little of what he read. Sometimes, though rarely, he discussed notorious tabloid topics with a fellow worker, or with a talkative fare, or a lunchroom attendant. His tone was one of sly but judicious wisdom. In a murder trial he was not deceived by the antics of principals, witnesses, lawyers, or judges. "Yeh, well, that baby better watch herself, because she can't get away with that with no jury. Blonde or no blonde, I bet she fries."

Seven-thirty. Guessed he'd start downtown and get around the Eighties by eight o'clock, pick up a nice theater fare. Wonder if that Birmingham baby was waiting yet. No. Too late. Looked as mild as skim-milk, too. Never can tell, and that's a fact. He'd have to tell Jo about that one. Uh—no, guess he wouldn't, at that. Mightn't believe him. Women.

Central Park West. He turned in at Sixty-seventh, picked up a theater fare for Forty-fifth Street. Hoped that big bum on the corner Forty-fifth would leave him turn right, off Broadway. From Fifty-first to Forty-fifth his progress became a crawl, and the crawl became a series of dead stops punctuated by feeble and abortive attempts to move. The streets were packed solid. The sidewalks were a moving mass. Thousands of motors, tens of thousands of lights, hundreds of thousands of people.

Ernie sat unruffled, serene, watchful at his wheel. He rarely lost his temper, never became nervous, almost never cursed. It was too wearing. Hacking was no job for a nervous man. It was eight-thirty when he deposited his fare in front of the theater. Sometimes, on a good night, you could cover two theater calls. But this was not one of those nights. He went west to Ninth Avenue on his way to dinner uptown. Ninth would be fairly clear going. But at Forty-seventh and Ninth he reluctantly picked up a call headed for a nine-o'clock picture show. Oh, well, all right.

By nine he was again on his way uptown. He liked to eat dinner at Charley's place, the Amsterdam Lunch, on Amsterdam near Seventy-seventh. He could have stopped very well for a late dinner at home. But you never could tell. Besides, Jo getting a hot meal at nine—for what! The truth was that his palate had become accustomed to the tang of the pungent stews, the sharp sauces, and the hearty roughage of the lunchroom and the sandwich wagons. When possible he liked to drive uptown to Charley's, out of the welter of traffic, where he could eat in nine-o'clock peace.

Charley was noted for his Blue Plate, 65¢. He gave you stew or roast and always two fresh vegetables. Spinach and asparagus; corn and string beans. His peas were fresh. No canned stuff at Charley's. His potatoes were light and floury. Josie was an excellent cook. Yet, on the rare occasions when he ate at home, he consumed the meal listlessly, though dutifully. She went to endless trouble. She prepared delicate pastry dishes decorated with snarls of meringue or whipped cream. She cut potatoes into tortured shapes. She beat up sauces, stuffed fowl. Yet Ernie perversely preferred Smitty McGlaughlin's lunch wagon at Seventh and Perry.

Charley's long, narrow slit of a shop was well filled. There were only two empty stools along the glass-topped counter. Ernie had parked his car, one of a line of ten taxis, outside the Amsterdam Lunch.

"What's good eating tonight, Charley?" Ernie swung a leg over the stool at the counter.

Charley wore an artless toupee, a clean white apron, a serious look. "Baked breast of lamb with peas and cauliflower and potatoes."

Ernie ordered it, and it was good. Rich brown gravy, and plenty of it. But even if, in Charley's momentary absence, you had made your own choice, you would not have gone wrong. Boiled ham knuckle, baked beans, Ger. fr., 50¢. Broiled lamb chops, sliced tomatoes, Fr. fr., 55¢. As you ate your Blue Plate there smirked up at you, through the transparent glass shelf below, sly dishes of apple pie, custards, puddings, cakes. Here you heard some of the gossip of the trade—tales of small adventure told in the patois of New York.

"I'm going east on Thirty-eighth, see, and the big harp standing there sees me, starts bawling me out, see? 'What the hell,' I says, 'what's eating into you?' Well, he comes up slow, see, stops traffic and walks over to me slow, looking at me, the big mick! 'Want a ticket, do you?' he says. 'Looking for it, are you?' he says. 'Asking for it? Well, take that,' he says, 'and like it.' Can you match that, the big . . ." There followed a stream of effortless obscenity almost beautiful in its quivering fluidity.

Usually, though, the teller emerged triumphant from these verbal or fistic encounters. "They give me a number up in Harlem. You ought to seen the pans on them. Scared you. When we get there it's in front of a light. So one of them pokes their head out of the window and says it ain't the place. It's in the next block, halfway. Well, then I know I'm right. I reach for the old jack handle under the seat and I climb down and open the door. 'Oh, yes it is,' I says. 'This is the right place, all right, and you're getting out.' At that the one guy starts to run. But the other swings back so I clip him one in the jaw. I bet he ain't come to yet—lookit the skin of my knuckles. . . ."

His fellow diners listened skeptically and said he was an artist, thus conveying that he was a romancer of high imagination but low credibility. "Come on!" they said. "I heard you was hackin' at Mott Street Ferry all evening."

Ernie paid for his meal, took a toothpick, and was on his way downtown for the theater break. Might as well make a day of it. Get a good rest tomorrow. It was a grim business, this getting in line for the eleven-o'clock show crowd. The cops wouldn't let you stand, they wouldn't let you move. You circled round and round and round, east on Thirty-eighth, back to Broadway, chased off Broadway by the cops, east again, back up Broadway, over to Eighth. "Come on! Come on! Come *on!*" bawled the cop, when you tried to get into Forty-fourth. "Come on! Come *on! Come on!*" chasing you up to Forty-sixth, on Eighth.

Ernie picked up a call in Forty-fourth. They wanted to go downtown to one of those Greenwich Village dumps. Pretty good call. Uptown again, and down again. He stopped at Smitty's and had a hamburger sandwich and a cup of coffee. Cold night, all right. How's hackin'? Good!

One o'clock. Might as well go over to the Sucker Clubs around the West Fifties. Saturday night you could pick up a 33⅓. One of the boys had cleaned up a hundred dollars one night last week. You picked up a call that wanted to go to a night club, a club where there was enough to drink. You took him in, if he looked all right to you, and you handed him over to the proprietor and you parked your hack outside and you came in, comfortably, and waited—you waited with one eye on him and the other on the cash register. And no matter what he spent, you got your 33⅓ per cent. One, two, three hundred.

Ernie cruised about a bit, but with no luck. Half-past one. Guessed he'd call it a day and go home to old Jo and the hay. Early, though, for a Saturday night. Pretty fair day.

He cruised across Fifty-first Street, slowly, looking carefully up at the grim old shuttered houses, so quiet, so quiet. A door opened. A bar of yellow light made a gash in the blackness. Ernie drew up at the curb. A man appeared at the top of the stairs. He was supporting a limp bundle that resembled another man. The bundle had legs that twisted like a scarecrow's.

"Hello, Al," said Ernie.

"Hey," called the man, softly, "give me a hand, will you?"

Ernie ran up the stairs, took the scarecrow under the left arm as the man had it under the right arm. The bundle said, with dignity, "Cut the rough stuff, will you, you big ape!"

Ernie, surprised, looked inquiringly at Al. "His head is all right," Al explained. "He ain't got no legs, that's all."

Together they deposited the bundle in Ernie's hack. Ernie looked at the face. It was scarred again and again. There were scars all over it. Old scars. It was Benny Opfer.

"There!" said Al, affably, arranging the legs and stepping back to survey his handiwork. "Now, then. The address . . ."

"I'll give my own address," interrupted Mr. Opfer, with great distinctness, "you great big so-and-so."

Al withdrew. The yellow gash of light showed again briefly; vanished. The house was dark, quiet.

Benny Opfer gave his address. It was in Brooklyn.

"Oh, say," Ernie protested, with excusable reluctance, "I can't take no call to Brooklyn this time of night."

"Do you know who I am?" Ernie was no weakling; but that voice was a chill and horrid thing, coming even as it did from the limp and helpless body.

"Yeh, but listen, Mr. Opfer—"

"Brooklyn." He leaned forward ever so little by an almost superhuman effort of will. "I'm a rich man. When I was fourteen I was earning a hundred dollars a week."

"That right!" Ernie responded wretchedly.

"Do you know how?"

"Can't say I do."

"Gunning," said Mr. Benny Opfer modestly. And sank back.

They went to Brooklyn.

Arrived at the far Brooklyn destination, "I ain't got any money," announced Mr. Benny Opfer with engaging candor, as Ernie lifted him out.

"Aw, say, listen," objected Ernie plaintively. He hoisted Mr. Benny Opfer up the steps and supported him as he fitted the key.

"Get you some," Opfer promised him. "She's always got fi' dollars stuck away someplace. You wait."

"I'll wait inside," Ernie declared stoutly.

Ernie stood outside in the cold November morning. He looked up at a lighted upper window of the Brooklyn house. Sounds floated down, high shrill sounds. He waited. He mounted the steps again and rang the bell, three long hard rings. He came down to the street again and looked up at the window. 'Way over to Brooklyn, and then gypped out of his fare! He rang the bell again and again.

The window sash was lifted. A woman's head appeared silhouetted against the light behind it. "Here!" she called softly. Something dropped at Ernie's feet. It was the exact fare. Benny Opfer, limp as to legs, had been levelheaded enough when it came to reading the meter.

Half-past three.

Ernie was on his way home, coming up Third Avenue at a brisk clip. A man and a girl hailed him. The girl was pretty and crying. The man gave an address that was Riverside at One Hundred and Eighteenth Street. The streets were quiet now. Quiet. Sometimes New York was like that for one hour, between three-thirty and four-thirty. The front window was open an inch or two.

"You don't need him," said the man. "He's all washed up. You stick to me and everything'll be all right. He never was on the level with you, anyway."

"I'm crazy for him," whimpered the girl.

"You'll be crazy about me in a week. I'm telling you."

An early morning el train roared down her reply.

Cold. Getting colder all the time. Sitting here since one o'clock today. Today! Yesterday. Ernie sank his neck into his sweater and settled down for the grind up to One Hundred and Eighteenth. Last fare he'd take, not if it was the governor of New York State, he wouldn't.

The man and the girl got out. The girl's head dropped on the man's shoulder. The man paid Ernie. She wouldn't sit so pretty with that bimbo if the size of his tip was any sign and, if it wasn't, what was?

No more hackin' this night. He turned swiftly into Broadway.

Tired. Dead-tired. Kind of dreamy, too. This hackin'. Enough to make you sick to your stomach. Taking everybody home and putting them to bed. Just a goddam wet nurse, that's what. One Hundred and Fifteenth, Tenth. His eye caught a little line of ice that formed a trail down the middle of Broadway. The milk wagons that came down from the station at One Hundred and Twenty-fifth Street. The melting ice inside these trickled through the pipe to the pavement, making a thin line of ice in the cold November morning. One Hundredth, Ninety-fifth.

Half-past four.

The sound of a tremendous explosion. The crash of broken glass. Ernie, relaxed at the wheel, stiffened into wakeful attention. It was still dark. He drove swiftly down to Ninetieth Street. The remains of a white-painted milk wagon lay scattered near the curb. Broken glass was everywhere. A horse lay tangled in the reins. The sound of groans, low and unceasing, came from within the shattered wagon. Fifty feet away was a powerful car standing upright and trim on the sidewalk.

Ernie drew up, got out. All about, in the towering apartment houses lining the street, windows were flung open. Heads stuck out. Police whistles sounded. No policeman appeared. Ernie went over to the cart; peered in. A man lay there, covered with milk and blood and glass. Chunks of glass stuck in his cheeks, in his legs. They were embedded in his arms. He was bleeding terribly and groaning faintly as he bled. More faintly. Men appeared—funny fat men and lean men in pajamas with overcoats thrown on.

"Here, give me a hand with this guy," commanded Ernie. "He's bleeding to death."

No one came forward. Blood. They did not want to touch it. Ernie looked up and around. He saw a figure emerge from the queerly parked automobile and walk away, weaving crazily.

"Hey, get that bird," Ernie cried, "before he gets away. He's the one hit the wagon. Must of been going eighty miles an hour, the way this outfit looks."

A slim, pale young fellow, fully dressed, detached himself from the crowd that had now gathered—still no police—walked quickly across the street—seemed almost to flow across it, like a lean cat. He came up behind the man who had emerged from the reckless automobile. Swiftly he reached into his back hip pocket, took from it a blackjack, raised his arm lightly, brought it down on the man's head. The man crumpled slowly to the pavement. The pale young fellow vanished.

The groans within the shattered wagon were much fainter. "Give me a hand here," Ernie commanded again. "One you guys. What's eating you! Scared you'll get your hands dirty! Must of all been in the war, you guys."

Someone helped him bundle the ludicrous yet terrible figure into the taxi. Ernie knew the nearest hospital, not five minutes away. He drove there, carefully yet swiftly. The groans had ceased. Men in white uniforms received the ghastly burden.

Ernie looked ruefully at the inside of his hack. Pools of red lay on the floor, on the cushions; ran, a viscid stream, down the steps.

At the garage, "I won't clean no car like that," declared the washer.

"All right, sweetness, all right," Ernie snarled. "I'll clean it to-morrow myself."

The washer peered in, his eyes wide. "Jeez, where'd you bury him!" he said.

Josie was asleep, but she awoke at his entrance, as she almost always did.

"How'd you make out, Ernie?"

"Pretty good," Ernie replied, yawning. "Made a lot of jack."

"You rest till late," Josie murmured drowsily. "Then in the after-noon we'll maybe go to a movie or somewhere. There's *Ride 'Em, Cowboy* at the Rivoli."

"The West," Ernie said, dreamily, as he took off his socks. "That's the place where I'd like to go. 'Ride 'em, cowboy!' That's the life. Nothing ever happens in this town."

DEBRA BRUCE

First Ticket

The cop's hips mean business
when they jut toward
my face before I can open
the door or say anything,
his whole body idling high
while I fumble for my license.
I already know his type—
22 or so, his fingers raw
since the winter he was 15
and hung out in back of school
and smoked. He'd drive breakneck
Saturday night with Linda Lyons or
some girl crumpled
against his chest. He'd pull off
the road, cut into her mouth
with his tongue, and later
marry her. Now he loves
law and order, loves to catch
a blonde going 5 miles an hour too fast
for her own good. He slaps me
with a mean fine and I'm stunned
and watch him walk off just
like that, with one hand
riding his hip, one hand
smoothing his hair.

SUSAN FIRER

Once I Threw Up Down My Blouse

In Sarah's red, black convertible topped VW bug.
1965, a cop had pulled us over on a pumpkin night,
on a River Hills road, under a Midnight In Paris
royal blue, star-peppered night sky. He was hunched
over, staring at us grinning fools. I knew
it was going to happen. (One can
only drink so much at 16 before it does.) I had
options: I could have leaned out the window,
done it on the black, rubber floor mat.
But, like always back then, I took a gamble:
the cop might be grossed out, sickened,
not want to get near me, or not want me to
get near him, or, even better, he might think
I was crazy that I'd stop at nothing, and he'd leave
us alone. I don't know which it was, but I put
my mouth down my blouse and let go, watching him
the whole time. He incredulously watched back,
sniffed, put his chin on his chest, raised it, made
his mouth a straight line, cocked his head,
lifted his eyebrows, turned around, walked
back to his car, got in, and drove off.
Sarah opened her car door, rolled out, lay
under the cut up stars, laughing until she peed
in her pants. We cleaned up in the servants'
quarters before we entered her French phoned house.
We slept with brush rollers the size of orange
juice cans in our hair; they were held in place
by pink plastic picks that stuck in our skulls,
leaving little indentations all over our heads.
We slept in bouffant capped hair dryers, their
electric lullabies our dreams' orchestration.

Our bodies were velour, our brains silly string.
We'd dress so boys could touch us. Every Sunday
the whole secular world shut completely down.
Everyone ate hot ham and hard rolls.
My sister punched my mother in the chest. Our
legs were vanilla phosphates and shaving scars.
At ballroom dancing lessons when we stretched
our legs, the instructor looked up our skirts.
Kitty K's father stuck his tongue down my
throat; my date laughed and said it was okay
because Doctor K. was a doctor. On Saturday
nights, my father high kicked to Lawrence Welk's
champagne music: bubble, bubble, bubble, bubble.
He always asked me why I couldn't be more
like Janet Lennon. (Where is Janet Lennon now?)
My oldest sister stole my mother's charge cards.
She charged a new bedroom set & 36 PAIRS of spike heels.
Mary Pat U. wore pastel striped candy colored sweaters.
After our Saturday morning swim & visit to her dad's
office, Candy H. & I overdosed
on Brandy Parfaits. Cookie H. was addicted
to tweezing her leg hair. But now, still,
25 years after I threw up down my blouse,
I love Sarah, the great girl love of my youth, who,
holding hands with me, jumped off buildings & play-
ground equipment just to hear our own sweet bones
break. Sarah who took too many drugs in Mexico
and killed herself after she shot her mother,
trying to get her son, Wind, back, all on a road
with a saint's name: Santa Monica. Sarah who arranged
an illegal, back alley, Boston abortion for me, trying
to save my fucked up adolescent life. (Maybe everyone
who dies should be stuffed where they fall, encased,
preserved in a glass box in their death moment, like bears
were on the Alaskan streets of my youth. A tape
recording could give all the pertinent information.

Possibly we'd all lead more thoughtful lives.) But
now, still, frequently, I think, Sarah, had you not
that one day done all that great awful mess,
we could have learned how to love the world together.
We could have figured out what made us so car-crashing crazy
while others were happy doing cartwheels, studying
geography, choosing nail colors. If you had stuck
around, I bet you'd be surprised by what we end up
loving that we never expected to: ghost sticks of yellow
warblers thin as dress patterns, window sills of lilacs,
Chinese red firecracker tree limbs, scallops,
children and solitude. It is spring again, and,
like always, the lilacs are corner-tavern crazy
with color and perfume, and I, like always, have filled
tea pots, vases, canning jars, and glasses with lilacs—
lilacs in every room. Still now, I save the very best
for the green, English candy jar Sarah gave me
for my birthday the year we both turned seventeen.
That summer we spent most of our time on Cedar Lake,
dreaming surfer girl dreams & guitar boys on a Wisconsin
kettle lake. Nights, after the adults were asleep,
we'd take the twin 75 Evinrude out on the lake
and crash it moon drenched & cloud crazy
into other sleeping families' night quiet piers,
trying to knock them lake-float off
their tightly secured family moorings.

CHERYL FISH

Freedom in Feet

Subtract the car from the woman
freedom in feet, no stick shift
I take trains, buses and bikes
the women in my family let the
husbands drive
dad gets his hands on the controls
mom and aunt are afraid to merge,
or pick up speed
but they direct traffic any way
it's a familial need

If you drive, I must follow your itinerary
feet want to feed on pavement
my license keeps on getting renewed
unticketed, unused
out of New York City, what kind of
adult might you be
never owned a car, got pulled over
or had a flat
what kind of grown up
won't pollute and make gridlock

Feet force you up and out
go get some grease and
push pedals
freedom in these crowded streets of
America
land of guns, roads and cars

Sometimes I want wheels to
break my dependency
but I'm still car free
take me with you
or walk along with me

OONA SHORT

One of Life's Passengers

September, 1994: We must be going ninety, maybe one-hundred miles an hour. If I loosen my grip on the steering wheel, the car will fly off the highway completely.

"I think you could go a little faster," says my boyfriend Imre. I take my eyes off the road long enough to glance at the speedometer. It's edging up toward forty-five.

A caravan of cars passes, their back seats crammed with children who point to me and laugh. "They're just playing," says Imre, massaging my hunched shoulders. "Don't take it personally." Imre went to divinity school, which was good preparation for teaching me how to drive: He knows how to counsel people in distress, and he believes in eternal life. "Did you happen to see that sign?" he asks.

I remember seeing something Jackson Pollack-like whizz by on the left. "Hidden driveway?" I suggest. "Traffic merging?"

Imre points up. "I meant the toll plaza," he says. He tears open a bag of Doritos and begins munching. "You have to put the clutch in now."

I draw a blank. "What does that mean, *clutch in?*" I ask. "Is the foot up or down?"

"Push the foot down—the *left* foot. Now go straight."

I head for the tollbooth like an arrow toward its bulls-eye. "Slow down, pull up, drop in the coin," I repeat to myself. "Slow down, pull up"—but wait, there's a hitch here: my window is closed. How do I open it if my left hand's on the wheel and my right hand's on the stick?

The tollbooth looms larger and larger as I search for the extra hand you need to pass a small, round coin through a large, sealed car. I hardly hear Imre's advice on shifting from fourth gear to third to second. I screech to a stop, but too late. The tollbooth is five feet behind me. I hang my head. There's no way I'm going to be able to back up. It's not in the stars.

"Honk the horn," says Imre.

"Where's the horn?" I ask. "Oh God, they heard me—"

Everyone with a horn is honking it.

"SHUT UP YOU ASSHOLES!" I scream above the din.

"Well, you've got the language down," says Imre.

I pull over to the side of the road. "I got closer to the booth that time," I declare with some bravado. Meanwhile, I'm thinking: Why am I going through this again? I don't need to drive. I live in New York, which has buses and cabs and subways. Someday there will be monorails. There will be little booster rockets we attach to our backpacks. I've made it through adolescence and well into adulthood without driving—I only have to hold out a little while longer before driving becomes obsolete.

Besides, not driving makes me so special! "I don't drive," I say, when pressed. Not, "I can't drive." I never say that. I say, "I don't drive." The implication is that I choose not to drive. I have to be taken. Like Cleopatra on a barge. *Moi, je ne drive pas.* I am transported. I am picked up and delivered. I am shipped. I settle into the car. I make no decisions. I assume no responsibility. It happens by magic. How can I give this up, become just like everyone else? If you want me to be somewhere, you'll have to do something about it. "Carry me," I say to the world. "I am one of life's passengers."

June, 1987: I'm sitting in a parked car waiting for my friend Dennis to pick up his date before dropping me off at home. I hear bells clanging. Dennis has left the car in front of a firehouse. A fire engine is pulling out, fire fighters swarming around it like bees. They motion me to move. "I don't drive," I tell them. One of the men jumps off the truck and into the car. The keys are still there. He speeds us around the corner to the fire.

Dennis comes out of the building, finds his car—and me—missing, and calls a cop. The cops find me at the scene of a suspicious fire, sitting in a car that's been reported stolen.

"No one had time to drive me back," I explain. "I don't drive," I add.

I am urged by uniformed representatives of the New York City Police and Fire Departments to learn how.

July, 1987: I get a driver's manual. I study it for three years. I believe everyone understands the rules except me. Everyone else remembers when to be fifteen feet from one thing or twenty feet from another. I study the road signs again and again. A straight black line means this. A squiggly black line means that. A straight line plus a squiggle—but my mind has already wandered to something I'm interested in, like how the Mets did last night.

I take driving lessons. I am launched onto the streets of Brooklyn. Pedestrians walk in front of me from between parked cars, against lights. Nothing looks the way it did in the little diagrams in the manual.

The thought occurs to me that if I'm behind the wheel of a car without having the slightest idea what I'm doing, others may be, too.

I take the required five-hour safety class in a basement room in Greenwich Village. The class is given in English, although not everyone in the room speaks it. Some talk among themselves in their native tongues or listen to rock music on their headsets, as slides of the bloodiest traffic accidents of the 1950s are projected on a streaky screen.

Erwin, our instructor, has had visions of the future that are almost too painful for him to share. "One day you'll take your eyes off the road," he intones, "and a child will jump into your path. You won't see her. She'll fall under your wheels, dead. Dead. And it will be because of you. You. Your fault. You'll have to live with it. You'll see her face for the rest of your life. A child dead. Your fault. Forever."

I let my permit expire.

October, 1991: I take a business trip to California. I look for round-the-clock buses and subways, and find none. "Can you give me a lift?" I ask near-total strangers day after day. "Can you drop me?" "Can I hitch a ride with you?" "Are you going my way?" "I'll wait outside . . . on the corner . . . wherever you want me . . . when are you leaving? . . . oh, so soon? . . . oh, not till then?"

"You seemed so independent!" says a colleague when I tell her I missed an important meeting because I couldn't find a way to get to it from my hotel. "Outside New York you're helpless!"

March, 1992: I'm introduced to Imre. Before long he's cheering for me at every softball game I play in. I find myself saying *"Eemreh"* over and over to myself—at first so I won't stumble over the name, and later to savor its sound. "Driving isn't any harder than playing softball," he says, over a game of catch. "I'll teach you how."

Soon after meeting him I dream I'm behind the wheel of a car moving rapidly along a winding road. To my surprise, I enjoy not knowing where the next turn will take me. I want the ride to go on and on. From outside the car, a voice screams, "Brake! Brake!" I awaken with my right heel kicking through the sheets.

Back at the toll plaza: Imre takes over at the wheel. He mentions that his oldest niece has just received her driver's license. "It's given her such a sense of accomplishment—" he says, popping open a soda.

I'm jealous. Imagine making such a fuss over someone just for driving! Anyone can drive. Practically anyone, anyway. Not me, of course, I don't need to.

"—and it'll do the same for you," Imre concludes. The man's confidence in me is unshakable. It's so *irritating.*

I stare idly out the window. Images form on passing trees and telephone poles. I see Dennis careening away from the fire, furious with me for causing so much trouble for him and his date. I see myself on a phone in L.A., offering feeble excuses to executives who never call me again. I see Imre—a week, a month, a year from now—keeling over at the wheel in exhaustion, as I say "I don't drive" and hand him bus fare to the nearest hospital.

Suddenly, I'm seized by an intense desire: I want to drive! I want to be alone in a moving car. I want to put the top down, even though I'm not in a convertible. I want to not be helpless. I want to show Imre he's right to believe in me.

Ten minutes pass. An arrangement of black-and-yellow shapes appears in front of me. I don't like its message. I fear it's a bad omen for us. "Imre," I say, pointing to it. "Our road will divide soon."

"Construction," says Imre. He bears left, then glances my way. "Oona," he says cautiously. "Did you just understand a highway sign?" For an instant, our eyes meet. We both grasp the significance of what's taken place. This is a breakthrough, a Helen-Keller-at-the-water-pump moment. "What else do you know?" Imre asks.

"Push the clutch in," I say, as I press my left foot against the floor mat. "Shift into third." My right hand curls around an imaginary knob. I talk him from third gear down through first, as we stop—"clutch out, parking brake on"—on the shoulder.

"Would you like to drive now?" asks Imre. He holds up the keys.

"Yes!" I shout. I hurry around to the driver's side as if a prize awaits me. As soon as I'm behind the wheel, though, my high spirits vanish. "I'm not going to be Cleopatra anymore," wails a voice in my head. "No more being carried on a barge."

I sit. Imre sits. Then I hear an even louder, more insistent voice from within. "Are you nuts?" it asks. "You're at the wheel of a brand new Toyota. Why do you want a *barge*?"

Imre coughs. "Are you going to take off the brake?" he hints.

"It's off," I say, as I yank back the lever. I feel its release with my whole body. "Where to?" I ask.

"You're the driver," says Imre, settling into his seat. He's still chuckling as I step on the gas.

LINDA MIZEJEWSKI

Stickshift

A thousand times I touched you the wrong way,
pressing too hard or not enough
into your clutch, my timing off,
knowing I'd failed when you wrenched and stopped.
We were supposed to fit together.
You were too heavy, all grill and frame.
I strapped myself in, did not feel safe.

No explanation could say enough—
not from books, nor from girls who knew,
nor from that first patient lover
who kissed me hard each time I stalled,
and who lifted the hood to let me see
that pumping center of coils, belts, oil—
the gaskets, the riggings, the secret
that the moving, shifting world was hooked
to the pedals under the large black shoes
of fathers, lovers, brothers with cars.

I learned you, slammed and locked myself in,
memorized your passages with one tight hand,
found by touch where your tensions bent and eased
under my feet. I learned what you like.
I pretended it was control, not need.
We bruised each other—breakdowns, scrapes.
There would be others, and I knew you knew.

It's taken me this long to love you,
suspecting sometimes you still feel nothing,
expecting you, still, to do me in.
We go too fast, break laws, run down,
while the accidents wheel around us,
and I'm belted to you—hip, shoulder, breast—
ready for our own.

LISA BERNSTEIN (LISA B)

Apricots

The valley was ripe with peaches, pink slurpees, apricot nectar poured from a can, its aluminum taste on the tongue. Exhaust diffused into the branches, the heart-shaped leaves. She and her girlfriends talked about love. The scent of fruit, carbon monoxide, the unmoving dusty ridges, everywhere lit freeways and stores. The intangible sweetness, as if a tongue put into the afternoon air would slice an apricot in half.

Her period was something no one wanted. She could taste it, the pulpy thin juice of it unmentioned, won from the month, the mouth of the culture. Ache in the lower back meant no one's baby, unadvertised, a ragged gesture. An unclenching resulting in liquid, but not wounded—renewed. To open inward and pulse down, unlike a gorge or freeway when it flooded. Soaked into, disappearing, the menses hers to speak of, the one measure.

Meanwhile the guys eased into the drivers' seats of their borrowed cars, revving the engine and fiddling with the radio dials. They sat inside a metal doll with no head or appendages, all viscera and compartments. She wanted to slide into it too, to play inside the chrome-covered, vinyl-sheathed body like the boys.

Why couldn't she have both, the body and the object. Trace the fine blond hairs on the haunch without surrendering the dashboard, the taste of rust, metal and wire cutting her gums. If she could disembowel the boy without pain, a sweetness so unreachable it had to be sliced from his gut, his concave belly tan and smooth like hers. To pare through the pulp into the pit. Like when she bled every month, an excavation, why couldn't she put her hand into his insides. And after, stroke his whole outward shape, lying in the car, the eucalyptus bent and rattling, one breast exposed, headlights passing, her skull pressed against the door.

MARY A. KONCEL

The Big Deep Voice of God

That morning Tommy Rodriguez heard a voice, so he piled his family into the car and headed down the interstate. "Take off your clothes," he ordered after a while. And because Tommy had heard the voice, maybe the big, deep voice of God, they all obeyed, watched shirts and underpants fly out the window, twisting and turning like strange desert birds.

Around noon, Tommy's wife began to wonder. She hadn't heard the voice but thought if she did it would call her "Sugar." "Sugar," it would say, "your thighs are hives of honey, and I am the Bumble Bee of Love." Quivering slightly, she pressed her left cheek against warm blue vinyl.

At home she often wondered too. There, on those late summer evenings, she leaned across the sink into still white clouds of steam and listened. Opening her mouth, she always took in more than air and water.

Tommy drove a little faster, beyond the vast and restless sand, a failing sunset, the tangled fists of tumbleweed. In the backseat, Grandpa whined, and Aunt Maria began to pee. Tommy closed his eyes. He was sure salvation was just one billboard or gas pump away, sure the voice was whispering now. "Drive like the wind," it was telling him, "like a wild saint in the Texan wind."

FLANNERY O'CONNOR

The Life You Save May Be Your Own

The old woman and her daughter were sitting on their porch when Mr. Shiftlet came up their road for the first time. The old woman slid to the edge of her chair and leaned forward, shading her eyes from the piercing sunset with her hand. The daughter could not see far in front of her and continued to play with her fingers. Although the old woman lived in this desolate spot with only her daughter and she had never seen Mr. Shiftlet before, she could tell, even from a distance, that he was a tramp and no one to be afraid of. His left coat sleeve was folded up to show there was only half an arm in it and his gaunt figure listed slightly to the side as if the breeze were pushing him. He had on a black town suit and a brown felt hat that was turned up in the front and down in the back and he carried a tin tool box by a handle. He came on, at an amble, up her road, his face turned toward the sun which appeared to be balancing itself on the peak of a small mountain.

The old woman didn't change her position until he was almost into her yard; then she rose with one hand fisted on her hip. The daughter, a large girl in a short blue organdy dress, saw him all at once and jumped up and began to stamp and point and make excited speechless sounds.

Mr. Shiftlet stopped just inside the yard and set his box on the ground and tipped his hat at her as if she were not in the least afflicted; then he turned toward the old woman and swung the hat all the way off. He had long black slick hair that hung flat from a part in the middle to beyond the tips of his ears on either side. His face descended in forehead for more than half its length and ended suddenly with his features just balanced over a jutting steeltrap jaw. He seemed to be a young man but he had a look of composed dissatisfaction as if he understood life thoroughly.

"Good evening," the old woman said. She was about the size of a cedar fence post and she had a man's gray hat pulled down low over her head.

The tramp stood looking at her and didn't answer. He turned his back and faced the sunset. He swung both his whole and his short arm up slowly so that they indicated an expanse of sky and his figure formed a crooked cross. The old woman watched him with her arms folded across her chest as if she were the owner of the sun, and the daughter watched, her head thrust forward and her fat helpless hands hanging at the wrists. She had long pink-gold hair and eyes as blue as a peacock's neck.

He held the pose for almost fifty seconds and then he picked up his box and came on to the porch and dropped down on the bottom step. "Lady," he said in a firm nasal voice, "I'd give a fortune to live where I could see me a sun do that every evening."

"Does it every evening," the old woman said and sat back down. The daughter sat down too and watched him with a cautious sly look as if he were a bird that had come up very close. He leaned to one side, rooting in his pants pocket, and in a second he brought out a package of chewing gum and offered her a piece. She took it and unpeeled it and began to chew without taking her eyes off him. He offered the old woman a piece but she only raised her upper lip to indicate she had no teeth.

Mr. Shiftlet's pale sharp glance had already passed over everything in the yard—the pump near the corner of the house and the big fig tree that three or four chickens were preparing to roost in—and had moved to a shed where he saw the square rusted back of an automobile. "You ladies drive?" he asked.

"That car ain't run in fifteen year," the old woman said. "The day my husband died, it quit running."

"Nothing is like it used to be, lady," he said. "The world is almost rotten."

"That's right," the old woman said. "You from around here?"

"Name Tom T. Shiftlet," he murmured, looking at the tires.

"I'm pleased to meet you," the old woman said. "Name Lucynell Crater and daughter Lucynell Crater. What you doing around here, Mr. Shiftlet?"

He judged the car to be about a 1928 or '29 Ford. "Lady," he said, and turned and gave her his full attention, "lemme tell you something. There's one of these doctors in Atlanta that's taken a knife and cut the human heart—the human heart," he repeated, leaning forward, "out of a man's chest and held it in his hand," and he held his hand out, palm up, as if it were slightly weighted with the human heart, "and studied it like it was a day-old chicken, and lady," he said, allowing a long significant pause in which his head slid forward and his clay-colored eyes brightened, "he don't know no more about it than you or me."

"That's right," the old woman said.

"Why, if he was to take that knife and cut into every corner of it, he still wouldn't know no more than you or me. What you want to bet?"

"Nothing," the old woman said wisely. "Where you come from, Mr. Shiftlet?"

He didn't answer. He reached into his pocket and brought out a sack of tobacco and a package of cigarette papers and rolled himself a cigarette, expertly with one hand, and attached it in a hanging position to his upper lip. Then he took a box of wooden matches from his pocket and struck one on his shoe. He held the burning match as if he were studying the mystery of flame while it traveled dangerously toward his skin. The daughter began to make loud noises and to point to his hand and shake her finger at him, but when the flame was just before touching him, he leaned down with his hand cupped over it as if he were going to set fire to his nose and lit the cigarette.

He flipped away the dead match and blew a stream of gray into the evening. A sly look came over his face. "Lady," he said, "nowadays, people'll do anything anyways. I can tell you my name is Tom T. Shiftlet and I come from Tarwater, Tennessee, but you never have seen me before: how you know I ain't lying? How you know my name ain't Aaron Sparks, lady, and I come from Singleberry, Georgia, or how you know it's not George Speeds and I come from Lucy, Alabama, or how you know I ain't Thompson Bright from Toolafalls, Mississippi?"

"I don't know nothing about you," the old woman muttered, irked.

"Lady," he said, "people don't care how they lie. Maybe the best I can tell you is, I'm a man; but listen lady," he said and paused and made his tone more ominous still, "what is a man?"

The old woman began to gum a seed. "What you carry in that tin box, Mr. Shiftlet?" she asked.

"Tools," he said, put back. "I'm a carpenter."

"Well, if you come out here to work, I'll be able to feed you and give you a place to sleep but I can't pay. I'll tell you that before you begin," she said.

There was no answer at once and no particular expression on his face. He leaned back against the two-by-four that helped support the porch roof. "Lady," he said slowly, "there's some men that some things mean more to them than money." The old woman rocked without comment and the daughter watched the trigger that moved up and down in his neck. He told the old woman then that all most people were interested in was money, but he asked what a man was made for. He asked her if a man was made for money, or what. He asked her what she thought she was made for but she didn't answer, she only sat rocking and wondered if a one-armed man could put a new roof on her garden house. He asked a lot of questions that she didn't answer. He told her that he was twenty-eight years old and had lived a varied life. He had been a gospel singer, a foreman on the railroad, an assistant in an undertaking parlor, and he come over the radio for three months with Uncle Roy and his Red Creek Wranglers. He said he had fought and bled in the Arm Service of his country and visited every foreign land and that everywhere he had seen people that didn't care if they did a thing one way or another. He said he hadn't been raised thataway.

A fat yellow moon appeared in the branches of the fig tree as if it were going to roost there with the chickens. He said that a man had to escape to the country to see the world whole and that he wished he lived in a desolate place like this where he could see the sun go down every evening like God made it to do.

"Are you married or are you single?" the old woman asked.

There was a long silence. "Lady," he asked finally, "where would you find you an innocent woman today? I wouldn't have any of this trash I could just pick up."

The daughter was leaning very far down, hanging her head almost between her knees watching him through a triangular door she had made in her overturned hair; and she suddenly fell in a heap on the floor and began to whimper. Mr. Shiftlet straightened her out and helped her get back in the chair.

"Is she your baby girl?" he asked.

"My only," the old woman said "and she's the sweetest girl in the world. I would give her up for nothing on earth. She's smart too. She can sweep the floor, cook, wash, feed the chickens, and hoe. I wouldn't give her up for a casket of jewels."

"No," he said kindly, "don't ever let any man take her away from you."

"Any man come after her," the old woman said, "'ll have to stay around the place."

Mr. Shiftlet's eye in the darkness was focused on a part of the automobile bumper that glittered in the distance. "Lady," he said, jerking his short arm up as if he could point with it to her house and yard and pump, "there ain't a broken thing on this plantation that I couldn't fix for you, one-arm jackleg or not. I'm a man," he said with a sullen dignity, "even if I ain't a whole one. I got," he said, tapping his knuckles on the floor to emphasize the immensity of what he was going to say, "a moral intelligence!" and his face pierced out of the darkness into a shaft of doorlight and he stared at her as if he were astonished himself at this impossible truth.

The old woman was not impressed with the phrase. "I told you you could hang around and work for food," she said, "if you don't mind sleeping in that car yonder."

"Why listen, lady," he said with a grin of delight, "the monks of old slept in their coffins!"

"They wasn't as advanced as we are," the old woman said.

The next morning he began on the roof of the garden house while Lucynell, the daughter, sat on a rock and watched him work. He had not been around a week before the change he had made in the place was apparent. He had patched the front and back steps, built a new hog pen, restored a fence, and taught Lucynell, who was completely deaf and had never said a word in her life, to say the word "bird." The big rosy-faced girl followed him everywhere, saying "Burrttddt ddbirrrttdt," and clapping her hands. The old woman watched from a distance, secretly pleased. She was ravenous for a son-in-law.

Mr. Shiftlet slept on the hard narrow back seat of the car with his feet out the side window. He had his razor and a can of water on a crate that served him as a bedside table and he put up a piece of mirror against the back glass and kept his coat neatly on a hanger that he hung over one of the windows.

In the evenings he sat on the steps and talked while the old woman and Lucynell rocked violently in their chairs on either side of him. The old woman's three mountains were black against the dark blue sky and were visited off and on by various planets and by the moon after it had left the chickens. Mr. Shiftlet pointed out that the reason he had improved this plantation was because he had taken a personal interest in it. He said he was even going to make the automobile run.

He had raised the hood and studied the mechanism and he said he could tell that the car had been built in the days when cars were really built. You take now, he said, one man puts in one bolt and another man puts in another bolt and another man puts in another bolt so that it's a man for a bolt. That's why you have to pay so much for a car: you're paying all those men. Now if you didn't have to pay but one man, you could get you a cheaper car and one that had had a personal interest taken in it, and it would be a better car. The old woman agreed with him that this was so.

Mr. Shiftlet said that the trouble with the world was that nobody cared, or stopped and took any trouble. He said he never would have been able to teach Lucynell to say a word if he hadn't cared and stopped long enough.

"Teach her to say something else," the old woman said.

"What you want her to say next?" Mr. Shiftlet asked.

The old woman's smile was broad and toothless and suggestive. "Teach her to say 'sugarpie,'" she said.

Mr. Shiftlet already knew what was on her mind.

The next day he began to tinker with the automobile and that evening he told her that if she would buy a fan belt, he would be able to make the car run.

The old woman said she would give him the money. "You see that girl yonder?" she asked, pointing to Lucynell who was sitting on the floor a foot away, watching him, her eyes blue even in the dark. "If it was ever a man wanted to take her away, I would say, 'No man on earth is going to take that sweet girl of mine away from me!' but if he was to say, 'Lady, I don't want to take her away, I want her right here,' I would say, 'Mister, I don't blame you none. I wouldn't pass up a chance to live in a permanent place and get the sweetest girl in the world myself. You ain't no fool,' I would say."

"How old is she?" Mr. Shiftlet asked casually.

"Fifteen, sixteen," the old woman said. The girl was nearly thirty but because of her innocence it was impossible to guess.

"It would be a good idea to paint it too," Mr. Shiftlet remarked. "You don't want it to rust out."

"We'll see about that later," the old woman said.

The next day he walked into town and returned with the parts he needed and a can of gasoline. Late in the afternoon, terrible noises issued from the shed and the old woman rushed out of the house, thinking Lucynell was somewhere having a fit. Lucynell was sitting on a chicken crate, stamping her feet and screaming, "Burrddttt! bddurrddtttt!" but her fuss was drowned out by the car. With a volley of blasts it emerged from the shed, moving in a fierce and stately way. Mr. Shiftlet was in the driver's seat, sitting very erect. He had an expression of serious modesty on his face as if he had just raised the dead.

That night, rocking on the porch, the old woman began her business, at once. "You want you an innocent woman, don't you?" she asked sympathetically. "You don't want none of this trash."

"No'm, I don't," Mr. Shiftlet said.

"One that can't talk," she continued, "can't sass you back or use foul language. That's the kind for you to have. Right there," and she pointed to Lucynell sitting cross-legged in her chair, holding both feet in her hands.

"That's right," he admitted. "She wouldn't give me any trouble."

"Saturday," the old woman said, "you and her and me can drive into town and get married."

Mr. Shiftlet eased his position on the steps.

"I can't get married right now," he said. "Everything you want to do takes money and I ain't got any."

"What you need with money?" she asked.

"It takes money," he said. "Some people'll do anything anyhow these days, but the way I think, I wouldn't marry no woman that I couldn't take on a trip like she was somebody. I mean take her to a hotel and treat her. I wouldn't marry the Duchesser Windsor," he said firmly, "unless I could take her to a hotel and giver something good to eat.

"I was raised thataway and there ain't a thing I can do about it. My old mother taught me how to do."

"Lucynell don't even know what a hotel is," the old woman muttered. "Listen here, Mr. Shiftlet," she said, sliding forward in her chair, "you'd be getting a permanent house and a deep well and the most innocent girl in the world. You don't need no money. Lemme tell you something: there ain't any place in the world for a poor disabled friendless drifting man."

The ugly words settled in Mr. Shiftlet's head like a group of buzzards in the top of a tree. He didn't answer at once. He rolled himself a cigarette and lit it and then he said in an even voice, "Lady, a man is divided into two parts, body and spirit."

The old woman clamped her gums together.

"A body and a spirit," he repeated. "The body, lady, is like a house: it don't go anywhere; but the spirit, lady, is like a automobile: always on the move, always . . ."

"Listen, Mr. Shiftlet," she said, "my well never goes dry and my house is always warm in the winter and there's no mortgage on a thing about this place. You can go to the courthouse and see for yourself. And yonder under that shed is a fine automobile." She laid the bait carefully. "You can have it painted by Saturday. I'll pay for the paint."

In the darkness, Mr. Shiftlet's smile stretched like a weary snake waking up by a fire. After a second he recalled himself and said, "I'm only saying a man's spirit means more to him than anything else. I would have to take my wife off for the weekend without no regards at all for cost. I got to follow where my spirit says to go."

"I'll give you fifteen dollars for a weekend trip," the old woman said in a crabbed voice. "That's the best I can do."

"That wouldn't hardly pay for more than the gas and the hotel," he said. "It wouldn't feed her."

"Seventeen-fifty," the old woman said. "That's all I got so it isn't any use you trying to milk me. You can take a lunch."

Mr. Shiftlet was deeply hurt by the word "milk." He didn't doubt that she had more money sewed up in her mattress but he had already told her he was not interested in her money. "I'll make that do," he said and rose and walked off without treating with her further.

On Saturday the three of them drove into town in the car that the paint had barely dried on and Mr. Shiftlet and Lucynell were married in the Ordinary's office while the old woman witnessed. As they came out of the courthouse, Mr. Shiftlet began twisting his neck in his collar. He looked morose and bitter as if he had been insulted while someone held him. "That didn't satisfy me none," he said. "That was just something a woman in an office did, nothing but paper work and blood tests. What do they know about my blood? If they was to take my heart and cut it out," he said, "they wouldn't know a thing about me. It didn't satisfy me at all."

"It satisfied the law," the old woman said sharply.

"The law," Mr. Shiftlet said and spit. "It's the law that don't satisfy me."

He had painted the car dark green with a yellow band around it just under the windows. The three of them climbed in the front seat and the old woman said, "Don't Lucynell look pretty? Looks like a baby doll." Lucynell was dressed up in a white dress that her mother had uprooted from a trunk and there was a Panama hat on her head with a bunch of red wooden cherries on the brim. Every now and then her placid expression was changed by a sly isolated little thought like a shoot of green in the desert. "You got a prize!" the old woman said.

Mr. Shiftlet didn't even look at her.

They drove back to the house to let the old woman off and pick up the lunch. When they were ready to leave, she stood staring in the window of the car, with her fingers clenched around the glass. Tears began to seep sideways out of her eyes and run along the dirty creases in her face. "I ain't ever been parted with her for two days before," she said.

Mr. Shiftlet started the motor.

"And I wouldn't let no man have her but you because I seen you would do right. Good-by, Sugarbaby," she said, clutching at the sleeve of the white dress. Lucynell looked straight at her and didn't seem to see her there at all. Mr. Shiftlet eased the car forward so that she had to move her hands.

The early afternoon was clear and open and surrounded by pale blue sky. Although the car would go only thirty miles an hour, Mr. Shiftlet imagined a terrific climb and dip and swerve that went entirely to his head so that he forgot his morning bitterness. He had always wanted an automobile but he had never been able to afford one before. He drove very fast because he wanted to make Mobile by nightfall.

Occasionally he stopped his thoughts long enough to look at Lucynell in the seat beside him. She had eaten the lunch as soon as they were out of the yard and now she was pulling the cherries off the hat one by one and throwing them out the window. He became depressed in spite of the car. He had driven about a hundred miles when he decided that she must be hungry again and at the next small town they came to, he stopped in front of an aluminum-painted eating place called The Hot Spot and took her in and ordered her a plate of ham and grits. The ride had made her sleepy and as soon as she got up on the stool, she rested her head on the counter and shut her eyes. There was no one in The Hot Spot but Mr. Shiftlet and the boy behind the counter, a pale youth with a greasy rag hung over his shoulder. Before he could dish up the food, she was snoring gently.

"Give it to her when she wakes up," Mr. Shiftlet said. "I'll pay for it now."

The boy bent over her and stared at the long pink-gold hair and the half-shut sleeping eyes. Then he looked up and stared at Mr. Shiftlet. "She looks like an angel of Gawd," he murmured.

"Hitchhiker," Mr. Shiftlet explained. "I can't wait. I got to make Tuscaloosa."

The boy bent over again and very carefully touched his finger to a strand of the golden hair and Mr. Shiftlet left.

He was more depressed than ever as he drove on by himself. The late afternoon had grown hot and sultry and the country had flattened out. Deep in the sky a storm was preparing very slowly and without thunder as if it meant to drain every drop of air from the earth before it broke. There were times when Mr. Shiftlet preferred not to be alone. He felt too that a man with a car had a responsibility to others and he kept his eye out for a hitchhiker. Occasionally he saw a sign that warned: "Drive carefully. The life you save may be your own."

The narrow road dropped off on either side into dry fields and here and there a shack or a filling station stood in a clearing. The sun began to set directly in front of the automobile. It was a reddening ball that through his windshield was slightly flat on the bottom and top. He saw a boy in overalls and a gray hat standing on the edge of the road and he slowed the car down and stopped in front of him. The boy didn't have his hand raised to thumb the ride, he was only standing there, but he had a small cardboard suitcase and his hat was set on his head in a way to indicate that he had left somewhere for good. "Son," Mr. Shiftlet said, "I see you want a ride."

The boy didn't say he did or he didn't but he opened the door of the car and got in, and Mr. Shiftlet started driving again. The child held the suitcase on his lap and folded his arms on top of it. He turned his head and looked out the window away from Mr. Shiftlet. Mr. Shiftlet felt oppressed. "Son," he said after a minute, "I got the best old mother in the world so I reckon you only got the second best."

The boy gave him a quick dark glance and then turned his face back out the window.

"It's nothing so sweet," Mr. Shiftlet continued, "as a boy's mother. She taught him his first prayers at her knee, she give him love when no other would, she told him what was right and what wasn't, and she seen that he done the right thing. Son," he said, "I never rued a day in my life like the one I rued when I left that old mother of mine."

The boy shifted in his seat but he didn't look at Mr. Shiftlet. He unfolded his arms and put one hand on the door handle.

"My mother was a angel of Gawd," Mr. Shiftlet said in a very strained voice. "He took her from heaven and giver to me and I left her." His eyes were instantly clouded over with a mist of tears. The car was barely moving.

The boy turned angrily in the seat. "You go to the devil!" he cried. "My old woman is a flea bag and yours is a stinking pole cat!" and with that he flung the door open and jumped out with his suitcase into the ditch.

Mr. Shiftlet was so shocked that for about a hundred feet he drove along slowly with the door still open. A cloud, the exact color of the boy's hat and shaped like a turnip, had descended over the sun, and another, worse looking, crouched behind the car. Mr. Shiftlet felt that the rottenness of the world was about to engulf him. He raised his arm and let it fall again to his breast. "Oh Lord!" he prayed. "Break forth and wash the slime from this earth!"

The turnip continued slowly to descend. After a few minutes there was a guffawing peal of thunder from behind and fantastic raindrops, like tin-can tops, crashed over the rear of Mr. Shiftlet's car. Very quickly he stepped on the gas and with his stump sticking out the window he raced the galloping shower into Mobile.

VIVETTE J. KADY

Lessons in Steering

Julia spoons ice cream into her mother's open mouth. Her mother blinks and smacks her lips together, frowns as her tongue pushes the ice cream around, closes her eyes as it slides down her throat. Vanilla drools down her chin. Julia dabs at it with a napkin.

"Lovely, isn't it?" Julia says, spooning in more whenever the mouth falls open. The eyes are dead, not bright impatient fledgling eyes.

"Maybe next visit we'll go for a drive," Julia says.

Her mother's hands lie stiff at her sides, wax paper skin and blue rope veins, motionless as stunned swallows bashed against a windowpane.

"We'll buy ice cream, and eat it by the lake."

Perhaps it's the smell of vanilla ice cream that prods Julia's memory. She'd forgotten those long-ago afternoon drives, cocooned in the old Ford wagon. Now a slow ribbon of images surfaces: the stickiness of ice cream dribbling down wrists; the Ford diffused with light; Aunt Mavis's hat bobbing as she chatters; the tilt of her mother's chin as she concentrates on negotiating the road while her beautiful hands stroke the steering wheel ("Don't wrestle the wheel," her father would have said when he taught her mother to drive, just as he taught Julia years later—"Handle it with style.")

Julia got carsick as a child—there were times when she leaned out the window to gulp fresh air, trying desperately not to throw up, but she can't remember any bouts of nausea spoiling those afternoons.

Julia must have been ten or eleven years old then. She was accompanying her mother on deliveries—her parents sold stationery, and while her father minded the store, her mother would deliver boxes of lined pads and carbon paper and typewriter ribbons to offices and factories—but her mother had the ability to transform what might have been a tiresome chore into an outing. They'd go after school, perhaps once a week or every fortnight, and they always took Aunt Mavis.

They'd pull into the parking lot of the Retirement Home and Julia would climb onto the back seat while her mother went in to get Aunt Mavis. Aunt Mavis was Julia's dead grandmother's sister, but Aunt Mavis was far from dead—she was alive and kicking, or so she regularly announced, "Probably because I was never quite foolish enough to marry." Julia couldn't imagine Aunt Mavis actually *kicking* anything—her thick calves were bound in elasticized stockings and her swollen ankles bulged from her sturdy shoes.

Julia's mother walked briskly to the front entrance, high heels tapping the tarmac, arms swinging alongside her skirt, and emerged a few minutes later steering Aunt Mavis by the elbow. Aunt Mavis's watery eyes shone with pleasure as she heaved herself onto the front passenger seat, and her false teeth shifted and clicked in her beaming mouth as she greeted Julia. She smiled and waved like a queen at any resident or staff member who happened to be nearby. She wore white gloves and a hat which was kept in place with a pearl-tipped hatpin. She carried a purse with a gold butterfly clasp, from which she regularly withdrew peppermints or Kleenex.

Aunt Mavis chattered away, interrupting her stories from time to time to yell at some driver, "You're a complete menace!" then she'd sweetly continue, "Now where was I? Oh yes . . ." as Julia's mother grinned into the rearview mirror.

Sometimes as they turned a corner the Ford shuddered and sputtered to a halt. "Oh darn, not again!" Julia's mother would say, rummaging through the glove compartment. "Now where'd that hairpin go?" and Aunt Mavis would sacrifice one of the pins that held her bun in place. Julia's mother would open the hood, fiddle around in the engine with the hairpin, slam the hood, get back in the car, wipe her hands on the Kleenex that Aunt Mavis offered, start the engine, and they'd be off again.

Their route depended on where orders had to be delivered. Julia's mother bit her lip and frowned as she slowed the Ford to look for landmarks or street names. If other cars sounded their horns, Aunt Mavis wound down her window and gave them a piece of her mind.

Unless her mother needed help carrying boxes, Julia stayed in the car with Aunt Mavis. She'd talk about her worst teachers and her best friends, or which books she'd read and which movies she'd seen, and Aunt Mavis would tell Julia about when she was young, or about Julia's mother when she was Julia's age. On warm days they'd wind down all the windows and Aunt Mavis would take off her gloves and fan herself with them. The backs of Julia's legs would stick to the seat and it hurt when she wriggled.

The last stop was the longest, and always at the same place: Benson's Manufacturing Co. always needed a stationery delivery, and Julia didn't have to help her mother with the boxes because Mr. Benson came out to help while her mother was still parking the car. Julia liked Mr. Benson. He had a nice smile and his forearms and face were tanned.

"What a beauty you're becoming, young lady. Just like your mother!" He put his hand lightly on the arch of her mother's back. "Here, Mrs. Shaw, let me get those boxes for you."

Her mother's eyes shone and her cheeks flushed. She fluffed her hair, which she'd already checked in the rearview mirror, as she followed Mr. Benson inside.

"Did you have lots of boyfriends when you were young?" Julia once asked Aunt Mavis while they waited.

Aunt Mavis twisted around in her seat to look at Julia. "I had my fair share," she said. "None I'd ever marry though. Peppermint?" Aunt Mavis had a habit of telling a story with a peppermint stored in her cheek, and the saliva would loosen her false teeth and make it difficult to hear her until she remembered to suck and swallow. "There was this one fellow, owned a music store downtown. A quiet fellow, nice enough I suppose. Funny-looking though; ugly as sin, actually—oh, I shouldn't say that, should I?"

Julia willed Aunt Mavis to swallow. She was getting good at mental telepathy—she'd been practicing on everyone. She willed her friends to phone her, strangers to cross the street, her piano teacher to have a headache and cancel her lesson. Aunt Mavis swallowed, and adjusted her teeth.

"Anyway, one night after a concert he took me for a drive in his new car. We drove up some remote hillside. He'd hardly said a word all evening. Drove slowly, too, and he looked so solemn you'd have thought we were in a hearse. Sure you won't have a peppermint?"

Julia shook her head and stared at Aunt Mavis. Aunt Mavis swallowed.

"Suddenly he stopped the car and got out. This was in the middle of nowhere, not a living soul for miles around, and pitch dark, so I began to get a little nervous. He took something out of the back of the car—I couldn't make out what on earth he was doing—then he came around to my side, opened my door, and opened this case he was carrying. I was ready to scream blue murder, to kick him where it hurts most and make a run for it, but then, as gently as if he were lifting a baby, he took a violin from the case and began to play." Aunt Mavis's eyes opened wide, then crinkled and moistened as she chuckled. "Fancy that—the poor shy man, serenading me on a hilltop. I had to bite my lip so hard to keep from laughing, I'm sure it must've bled. But my goodness, could he play! Beautifully, just beautifully. I never went out with him again, though."

Julia looked hard at the door of Benson's Manufacturing Co., promising herself that by the count of seventeen, her mother would come out.

Julia and Aunt Mavis didn't really mind the long wait at Benson's Manufacturing Co. because the best part of the afternoon lay ahead. After the deliveries they always stopped for ice cream at the Dairy Den Drive-Thru. In fine weather they took their ice creams down to the lake, and when the weather was bad they ate them in the car. They all chose vanilla—chocolate-dipped for Julia, a plain cone for her mother, and a paper cup with a wooden spatula for Aunt Mavis. They ate slowly, rolling the ice cream around in their mouths, nodding at one another, licking the spills.

"I hope this won't spoil your appetite for dinner, Aunt Mavis," Julia's mother would say.

"It's baked fish and tapioca pudding tonight—who gives a fig if it does!"

At the end of those afternoons, when Julia's mother took Aunt Mavis back to the Retirement Home, both women seemed suddenly weary. Aunt Mavis's hat had slipped to one side and the stray wisps of hair made her look uncertain, and much older. She leaned on Julia's mother and they walked slowly. The warmth of the car had gone, and Julia felt stifled and irritable. A strange sadness slipped over them and held them like a dark glove.

One day Aunt Mavis fell in a corridor of the Retirement Home and broke her pelvis. She died of pneumonia three weeks later, and the afternoon drives came to an end.

Julia turns the volume of the radio up high as she drives home from the nursing home. Pedestrians are walking as if their movements have been choreographed to the music, strangely synchronized to the rhythm.

One afternoon, after they had dropped Aunt Mavis back at the Retirement Home, Julia's mother suddenly said, "Let's drive to the sea. Wouldn't you love to go to the beach?"

The sun was low on the horizon, gilding panes of glass, flinging wisps of rose and orange over clouds.

"When? For our vacation?"

"Right now. If we kept on driving toward the sun, we'd get all the way to the ocean. In about five hours you'd be able to dip your toes into the waves."

Julia watched her mother's face for signs that she might be teasing. Her mother looked calmly ahead at the road.

"But what about Daddy?"

"Oh, we'll call to let him know where we are."

"But what about school?"

They stopped at an intersection. If they drove straight they'd get to the highway; if they turned left they'd reach home. Julia's mother looked at her for a moment, then smiled, "Don't worry, my love. We won't go if you don't want to," and turned left.

Julia floors the accelerator. She is driving on the highway with the car windows down. Her hair whips back, the white lines stream by. She pictures her mother, her beautiful hands caressing the wheel with exquisite style, riding the white lines like a tightrope walker, the engine roaring as she picks up speed.

A man is always saying to me   "Get out of my light"
or   "Will you sit down"   Similar
to those whitish flowers   tinged with faintest yellow,
pink, or greenish   I am seldom where others expect me to be.
"Come to bed," he demanded   "What *are* you doing?"
I was on the toilet   madly making plans
to impress him.   Arriving
at the gallery   4 days after the show had closed
I sauntered   nonchalant   among the blank walls
and then quickly took the elevator down   "You Idiot!"
I said to myself   when I reached the street
This is what Nijinsky meant when he wrote   "the maids
have become stupid"   as though some part of himself
had failed him   by their actions.
The tires slid on the ice   I drove continually in wrong lanes.
Lost in wonder   and amazement   I so often forget
The wheels are in my hands!   And we go driving over bumps
and curbs   astonished by the purple glaze on the snow.
Almost at the top of the nearly perpendicular hill
halos of yellow broke over the jeep   "O The Moon"   I
shouted   pointing   stopping in second gear   having to shift
to first   and rolling almost to the bottom   before starting
back up.   Ruth St. Denis created EGYPTA
after receiving inspiration from a cigarette poster
in a drug store.   Did *she* stare open-mouthed   drooling?
or spill her soda   or bump into customers?
Did the man she loved have to say "Turn here!   Turn here!"
or "You're grinding the clutch!"   or "You've left the
lights on . . . again. . . . ."

MAUREEN OWEN

The Confession

Which shall I tell you first
that I finally saw a Yellow-Bellied Sapsucker
drumming on adjacent willows   or that
I ripped the top of the jeep
backing out of the garage   And don't
say anything about it being the "Classic"
little woman wrecks new car
just after my being told I was an insurance
risk   the garage is too low in the first place
& I'm just learning to drive a stick shift anyway
and if a man does something like that   it's just
an accident   but if a woman does
it's because she's a woman   Since it's our car
the roof can be my half now and don't forgive me!
I don't want your forgiveness!

L.R. BERGER

Driving into Rapture

Just south of Castleton Corners
the highway bends and they take over,
mountains circle like gods conferring on you
your real size—one small coin
in the offering plate lined with green felt.
Somehow spared, farmland sprawls
the foothills.

And maybe that's where it begins,
with a man's bare back, hunkered over,
sweating in sun under a sparrow-studded sky.
He's plucking wild blueberries, or
laying the old cranky barncat to rest.
You know him. He's digging up
some treasure he buried as a child
for safekeeping. He wants to hold it now.

Or, maybe it's the figurehead of clouds,
the accompaniment on the radio,
yours now, the dark body of the cello
and wind threading the windows,
when suddenly you're flooded
with all the sweetest moments
of your life, no matter how they turned
or soured later.

That's when it stops short in front of you,
Ford pickup, muffler shot, six
scruffy kids scrapping out back—
when there isn't one jaded hair left
on your disbelieving head, the rusty bumper
plastered in stickers all certain *God Loves You,
Don't Worry, God Loves You.*

ALEXIS QUINLAN

The Length of a State

Driving: We are driving across Texas for the fifty-seventh time, driving on Good Friday and it's good, too: Sunny, clear, cool: We're on our way to a party through fields of bluebonnets but it's illegal to pick them. And speeding: We are twenty miles over the limit to the tune of Lou Reed. (We have always sped to Lou.) We're a little swollen since our last trip—five pounds or so, between us—and then there are the three or four enemies who've cropped up as well as the two new lovers left in their respective beds, sticky, not to mention (but to mention) the several old lovers who have never quite danced away and the two dead fathers who accompany us everywhere. It's a crowded car, but we like the view: We like the endless ranchlands dotted with lonely clapboard houses, sheltering stands of oak; we like the dappled horses wandering behind barbed wire, the many cattle chewing dumbly; we like the broad patches of blue along the highway, the friends waiting at the highway's end; we like it all to the tune of the Velvet Underground (very both).

Yes, our ninety-ninth trip across Texas and we've only stopped once—at the shiny museum, the contemporary, and only to make sure we'd have something to talk about on the way. He tried to steal a Jenny Holzer poster; I tried to pick up a guard half my age; we both failed. Afterward, in the basement gallery, we listened to the prerecorded voice of a male performance artist who said many interesting things on several oddly placed loudspeakers but we especially heard the speaker beneath the floorboards from which he hissed: Sister, how bad is it going to smell when it starts to smell?

The speedometer reads eighty-seven but really we are both pushing thirty, never married, never wanted to, and rather less than more gainfully employed. Freelance, they call it, and we've often agreed that too much free time can sharpen the lance. Now we are speeding but soon we will be stealing, ripping bluebonnets from the hills that slope gently from the road and so we are wondering, idly, if we will be caught. We intend to plead ignorance though we understand that ignorance is no excuse. We practice the word a couple of times, falling hard on the first syllable: *Ignorance.* (We try to be good Texans, always.) Later, as if one of us might have forgotten, he says: We'll tell them we don't know a thing.

But there is something, I say. Isn't there something we know?

No, he says. Nothing.

We were never lovers but we have been jealous like lovers. I in particular have been jealous like a lover, narrowly eyeing his women, hating their silliness, despising their beauty. He likes them silly and beautiful, except for me. And him, he eyes my men from some superior yet supine spot. They're all weirdos, he concluded long ago, over our five hundred and first shot of tequila.

So are we.

Not like them.

The car is crowded (did I say?) but every forty miles or so, in an effort to show what good sports we are, one of us chucks the other on the arm and cracks: Happy Easter, bunny. Once we mention the people we know, old nuns, mothers, who even now are plodding through the stations of the cross, hungry from fasting, eyeing a purple robe draped over a massive crucifix and imagining the last passion of a dead man. We think it's funny.

After we turn up the volume on a song called Heroin—first he turns it, then I turn it—he points to the tape deck and says: That's my next drug. The last one.

But we smoked it, I say, fingering the cassette case while another white clapboard home protected by another stand of oaks, forever, swims past and fast (this our fastest car ever, for this our two hundred and thirty-second road trip).

I have to spike it, he says, adding: Maybe your new guy can get it for me. He pushes the pedal, the bonnets blue on by. I know that my new guy, as he calls him, has not yet become my new guy, will not incarnate into my new guy until the moment I say: Yes, he can get us anything.

Instead: We are a time capsule, I say: encased in this car, listening to Lou Reed and talking about our next fix.

My first fix, he says. I have to spike it.

Okay, okay. It doesn't matter because I can predict the future. I can predict that we will stay later than anyone else at the party, that the weekend will be clear and mild for recovering, and that the bluebonnets will end hanging from the rear-view mirror, dulled green and blue and twisted into the perfect upside-down bouquet I will have formed. I can predict how I'll complain heartfully that, once again, we were not arrested. And on the road back there will be no rift or lull during which we need to mention the museum. We will speed the same speed, play the same tapes, sad Lou will whisper sadly. There will be something we are driving to, too, but how? How bad is it going to smell when it starts to smell?

Oh, we are driving across Texas on the Godforsakenest day of the whole church calendar, but we are lapsed and we don't care. We are driving on Good Friday and it's good enough for us.

JUDY GOLDMAN

Sunday Night, Driving Home

If I close one eye the light from the dial
looks like the tip of a cigarette.
And my mother *is* smoking,
the small fingers of her left hand moving
to her lips, then to the curve of the front seat
close to my father's shoulder.
Her hand is a pigeon
in the shadows that fly in from the road.
My sister and I lie across the back seat,
our shoes touching, each of us resting
on a pillow pressed to the glass.
I think my sister is sleeping.
She is missing the talk from the front seat,
how Aunt Katie seems worse
and maybe should be taken away for awhile.
My mother appears to nod
instead of saying the word yes to my father.
I hear less and less of their low tones
until suddenly the sound of wheels spinning gravel
and I know without opening my eyes
we are home. I also know that my father
will first lift my sister and carry her in,
return for me, placing me lightly
in the narrow bed next to hers,
folding the sheet back over the parrot-colored quilt
and smoothing it flat with the palm of his hand.
Then he will touch my face, listen to me breathe
and reach for the switch on the lamp
that separates our twin beds
like the tall brass branch of a family tree.

DOROTHY BARRESI

Vacation, 1969

Brothers rolling around in the big back seat,
all elbows and skirmishes,
complaints roared across Mt. Rushmore,
that hard family portrait,
across the Badlands purple with heat.
Back home, black children looted fire hydrants
under sinus-gray skies.
Our trailer was a cracker box ready to jackknife
when my sister, good reader,
practiced her phonetics: nā′päm.

I think it was just outside Turlock, California,
that I grew too sullen
for togetherness.
Rocking my new breasts in my arms,
I was conked out by hormones and Mick Jagger,
my face held in acne's blue siege.
So I pulled up oars early that August,
slept while the boys knocked heads
and my iron-eyed parents took turns
lashed to the wheel,
America, by God, filling the car windows.

ALICE NOTLEY

After Tsang Chih

I was brought up in a small town in the Mohave Desert.
The boys wouldn't touch me who was dying to be touched,
    because I was too quote
Smart. Which the truck-drivers didn't think as they
    looked and waved
On their way through town, on the way to my World.

The Silver DeSoto

The first sign came in Miss Hesselbach's Plane Geometry class, when I looked up and saw Mary Jo Keene coming toward me down the aisle, looking straight at me, smiling. It had to mean I had become visible again.

The problem started after Mother died. When I came back to school the Monday after the funeral, everyone managed to be looking the other way when I walked by. I understood. I had become an embarrassment. Someone they didn't know how to deal with.

Now here was Mary Jo, who was about as visible as anyone you'd ever find (can't take my eyes off her, people would say), inviting me to a party.

"Bring a date," she was saying, smiling at me almost the way she smiled at boys. *Some* boys, that is.

"I don't date," I replied. I was only fourteen—two years younger than the others in my class, and Nanna didn't let me have dates yet.

"What about Bob Wyant?" She seemed to be accusing me of something.

"What about him?"

"You think we haven't *seen* you?" She allowed one corner of her pretty mouth to curl ever so slightly.

"Seen what?"

"Forget it." She walked on past me, back to her own seat.

I supposed the invitation was withdrawn. Even so, I was encouraged, knowing they were allowing themselves to see me again. When I was with Bob, anyway. (Bob Wyant, by common consent, was the handsomest boy in Dixter High School.)

The first time Bob had come by for me was the night after Mother's funeral. When the doorbell rang and I went to open the door, I expected to see one of the church ladies who had been so good about bringing us food but so bad about always saying, "Your mother's better off, where she is now," making me feel selfish, as though I were grieving about what happened to me rather than about what happened to her.

But it wasn't a church lady, there at the door. It was Bob Wyant, smiling that brown-eyed smile of his.

"Wanna go for a ride?"

Out behind him, parked at the curb, looking as though it had just landed, was his father's brand new, streamlined, silver DeSoto, the first streamlined car ever to ride the streets of Dixter. All the other cars were the stubby, hit-the-air-head-on kind, with headlights and radiators and windshields that just slammed square up against the wall of the air; but the silver DeSoto was all bulbous and curvy, with billowy fenders and fat balloon tires, like a fat possum that could just nuzzle its way along, as easy as into downy comforts.

Nanna said yes I could go for a ride. *She* understood it wasn't a date, even if no one in school did.

Bob's parents (Russ and Norma Wyant) had been among those friends of Mother's who took turns keeping me, the weeks when she was in the Scott-White Hospital down in Texas. It was while I was staying at their house that the early morning call came from Nanna: the doctors didn't expect Mother to make it through another night. And it was Russ and Norma who decided it wasn't right that I should have to wander around their house all day, waiting, with no one to talk to but this family I scarcely knew.

"Betty Jane," Norma found me in their shade-drawn living room, where I had gone after the call so no one would see me crying. "Russ and I are going to drive you down there. So you run and pack, honey." Then, as she turned to leave, "Need any help?"

"No, ma'am."

I did wish, though, that I had a summer dress. Or a clean skirt. No one I'd stayed with had thought to ask about those same three winter, wool skirts I'd been wearing all these weeks; unlike the blouses—which I kept washed and ironed—the skirts had to go to the dry cleaners, and I had no money. Besides, with the temperature now reaching the nineties every day, they were hot and scratchy.

Within an hour and a half after Nanna's call, Russ had arranged for someone to take his place at the oil rig, Norma had arranged for Bob to stay with a friend, and Russ, Norma, and I, in their big black La Salle, were out on the highway, headed south. Toward that hospital three hundred miles away.

After we got there, Russ and Norma took rooms in the same white frame rooming house with Nanna and me, took turns sitting with Mother while Nanna and I ate. Not until the third day, when Mother was judged to be out of danger, did they speak of returning home. I was to stay a few days longer, then return by bus.

This time, unlike the rushed departure from Dixter, Norma had the landlady make sandwiches to take along, and Russ left the La Salle all day for a check-up—even had it washed and waxed.

Early the following morning, just as the sun slipped loose from the horizon and turned the windows of the hospital into bright pink mirrors, Nanna and I stood on the curb in front of the rooming house and waved good-bye as the big black La Salle, all bright and clean, drove away. Norma, leaning out the window, waving, called, "See you at the bus station!"

But when I got off the bus, I was met by Clara Dotson (another of Mother's friends). Not that I was surprised. Or disappointed. Or even curious. I had grown accustomed to being shunted from one friend to another, one house to another. So, unquestioning, I got into Clara's car, carrying the suitcase containing my three wool skirts and cotton blouses.

Not until three days later did Clara tell me about it. We were sitting together in their wooden swing under the honeysuckle arbor, waiting for an evening breeze. Having had a letter from Nanna saying she and Mother were coming home the next week, I was happy, smelling the heavy sweetness of the honeysuckle, joking with Clara about the noisy locusts.

Then she told me.

I didn't cry. Being alone with my feelings all those weeks, I had lost the knack of showing them.

I remember wanting to scream at the locusts—make them shut up. I even remember thinking the world must be run by locusts. And I remember especially thinking of Mother, lying in that hospital, vulnerable to every vagrant whim of some uncaring power.

"Tell me how it happened," I said.

"A drunk, coming out of a roadhouse," she said, then added, in disbelief that anyone should be getting drunk in a roadhouse in broad daylight, "right in the middle of the day."

The locusts, louder than ever, continued their raucous mocking.

"Just this side of Waco." She told me the story as she had heard it from others and as they had heard it from Russ.

The La Salle, hit from the side, rolled over and over—Russ wasn't sure how many times—into the ditch, out the other side, across a barbed-wire fence, coming to rest upside-down in a field, its front wheels still spinning.

The people who stopped found Russ, pinned by one leg, thrashing about like an animal in a trap, calling out, "Where is my wife? Find my wife."

Because, as he could see, Norma wasn't inside the car. On one of those rolls, as nearly as anyone could piece together, she must have been thrown clear. When they found her, she was lying in a field of Texas bluebonnets, the very bluebonnets, Russ would recall and recount over and over, that only moments before she had called to his attention.

The drunk, staggering from one to another of the people who stopped to help, kept assuring them, "I got insurance, you understand, plenty of insurance."

"When can you take me to see Russ?" I asked.

"That's no place for you; you're too young." The way she said it made it sound like the notion was totally inappropriate. "You'd just be in the way."

As I was inured to being in the way, I insisted. So the next afternoon, she drove me over. "I'll pick you up at the library," she said as I was getting out of the car. (The library had served as one of my surrogate mothers that spring and summer.)

So when I rang the doorbell, I was alone. Wondering how to apologize for being alive and well—and unbereft.

Something I didn't learn until several days later was that the uncle who drove Bob down to Waco didn't tell him until just outside the town that they were not headed for the Waco hospital but for the undertaker's parlor. I tried to imagine what the uncle had talked about, all those five long deceitful hours.

After Norma's funeral Bob had become invisible to everyone but grown-ups. And to me.

The La Salle, crumpled like a discarded letter, ended up in a Texas junk yard. That's how it happened that, right in the middle of the Depression, Russ bought a brand new car. The silver De-Soto. And that's why Bob's taking me for rides in it had nothing to do with his being a boyfriend.

Not that he wouldn't have qualified, with that wide, clear forehead of his and the thick brown hair, and the strong chin. But most of all with those smiling brown eyes. Oh yes, when I would answer the doorbell and see him standing there, grinning that brown-eyed grin, and see the silver DeSoto out at the curb, waiting, and hear him asking, "Wanna go for a ride?" I could easily have cast him as Prince Charming—coach and all. But, fated as he and I were, we had already been cast as Hansel and Gretel.

At school I enjoyed being visible again. Being invited to parties. Though with that invariable proviso, "Bring a date." Prompting my invariable reply, "I don't date," and their "What do you call it then?" and my "Call what?" and their "Running around at night in that fancy car with Bob Wyant."

So it was a standoff—them drawing their own conclusions, me

not knowing how to explain, the girls deciding I was just too jealous to let Bob loose among them, the boys deciding we were just "a couple of spooks."

Either way, the invitations were no longer extended.

Maybe the boys were right, calling us spooks. We were like those ghosts you read about, who no longer belong anywhere, who—unconsolable and invisible—haunt familiar rooms, frighten old friends.

While Bob and I were being initiated into the rites of death, our classmates were being initiated into Dixter's rites of adolescence. They had learned about bunching into booths at Henry's Hot Dogs, about the protocol of grouping and regrouping, like dancers in a pattern, out in front of Coleman's Drug Store, while you waited, double parked, for the carhop to bring your order. They had learned that on a regular date a boy had only a dime to spend, and that for a dime both of you could get a Coke or a Dr. Pepper, or small limeade, cherry Coke, vanilla Coke, lemon Coke, Coke-limeade, frozen malt cone, single-dip cone, or a small chocolate sundae. They also had learned that on a dance date a boy had a quarter and you could suggest going to Henry's for a coney island. And that movie dates, costing more, meant a girl was rather special.

Knowing none of these techniques—and being invisible anyway—Bob and I would ride out on scouting expeditions where, from the security of the DeSoto, we could study the goings-on of our peers.

"Like Marco Polo, ogling the Orientals," Bob said one night as we eased along by the Elks Club, driving so slow the DeSoto stalled. We were watching the silhouettes of couples as they danced by the tall windows, swaying, melding, dividing, like organisms swimming under a microscope.

Rousing myself to answer, I said, "More like Flash Gordon—in his sleek new airship."

Eventually that was the way we thought of ourselves and our nighttime rides—as alien creatures flying in from another planet, hovering low in our silver ship, fascinated by the ways of the natives.

Toward the end of the school year Nanna decided she needed to get away. In Dixter in those days, *away* meant out of the heat. Which meant Colorado Springs.

After driving out as paying passengers with the Howard sisters (who though long since married and even widowed, were still referred to as the Howard sisters), we rented two dark rooms that smelled like the old man who rented them to us—who lived in the rest of the rooms. What this man did with his days I never knew, except that he must have spent a lot of time just standing around in the hallway listening to us, because every came I came out of our door, there he was, and he would come up to me, close and smelly, and start telling me how I should never let myself be a "bad girl"—and all the while that he talked, he would be looking at my breasts.

Through all the endless weeks of that summer neither our routine nor our meals ever varied. For breakfast we ate Rocky Ford cantaloupe and toast, for dinner Rocky Ford cantaloupe and corn on the cob. Every morning we walked to a shopping area that had several antique stores (where Nanna looked but never bought), then we would buy an ice cream cone for our lunch, walk back to our rooms, where Nanna would nap and I would read or walk to the library for a new book. After her nap we would walk to the city park (and always on these walks Nanna's shoelaces would come untied and I would have to squat down on the sidewalk and tie them because she was all girdled up for the day). At the park we would sit on the benches beside the old ladies and the old men, and the old ladies would tell sad tales of fair and flawless daughters, of tall and loving sons—now gone. Or dead. Nanna, in her turn, in her telling, would transform the misery of her life into a golden tale.

And thus the days went by.

But I had secret walks of my own. I walked the moors of *Wuthering Heights* with Heathcliff; I walked the dark passageways of Thornfield Hall, waiting for a Rochester to round the corner. The passionate sufferings of those abandoned children, it seemed to me, were far to be preferred to the blankness of mine.

One night, as I was sitting in our reeking rooms, reading *Tess of the D'Urbervilles*, our landlord knocked on our door.

"A young man to see you," he said, looking down at my breasts.

"Me?" I asked. "You sure?" I didn't know anyone in Colorado Springs—except the Howard sisters.

"Mmm—" he frowned.

Deciding it must be the paper boy, collecting, I got money from Nanna, went down the hall, into the entrance way—and there, in the doorway, stood Bob Wyant, smiling that brown-eyed smile of his. Out behind him at the curb, waiting, was the silver DeSoto—for a minute I almost thought it had flown him here.

"Wanna go for a ride?" he said, proud of himself.

"Yes!" I whirled around, ran back down the hall to tell Nanna where I was going.

Out in the car, we just sat there, grinning, until it occurred to me to ask, "How did you get here?"

"Dad's been going out with a woman who lives here."

"Oh." So Bob was supposed to make himself invisible.

"Been to the Garden of the Gods?" he asked.

"Of course not," I replied.

He started the car, turned on the lights, and off we went. Out to explore the universe.

Not knowing our way, we just followed the broadest streets, checking our direction against the silhouette of the Sangre de Cristo mountains off to the west, a black bulk against the cobwebby clouds of a moon-bright night. We drove past houses with amber windows, houses unlike any in Dixter—steep-roofed, many-gabled houses, turreted and towered houses, houses with stained glass entries that threw their colored pictures out across the porches, houses that had been reaching their pointed roofs into the Colorado sky when Dixter was still a trading settlement in Indian Territory.

Coming to a street lighted up like the midway at the county

fair, where the whole night sky seemed to be spattered with jewels, we turned down it, to investigate. We found three movie houses, an ice cream parlor, and a miniature golf course. Continuing on, we saw again, up ahead of us, our compass—the silhouette of the mountains. Following it, we turned onto a road spangled with neon animals—red rabbits, pink elephants, green cats—and with lots of long-stemmed neon cocktail glasses. And long-stemmed neon waitresses.

"The humanoids here must drink a lot," Bob said.

We hadn't said much, but that was nothing new, for neither to Bob nor to me had words ever been easy. Yet our silences had never been awkward or embarrassing, being always as much a part of our gawking and wondering as were any words we ever spoke.

As the restaurants and roadhouses trailed off, the world grew dim, with only the moth-foggy haze of a single bulb in a few empty gas stations. On a dirt road now, the mountains looming closer and bigger, the dark was broken only by the headlights of the De-Soto and an occasional orange glow from a window, from a few distant houses. The last outposts.

Soon, off in the distance to the left, we saw a great dark blotch, without a single light. Just an emptiness. A black nothingness. At the next crossroad, Bob turned toward it. We passed a last house, with its single, glowing window, went over a rise, and now there was just us and the darkness and the headlights of the DeSoto.

What the headlights revealed was no more than a few unprepossessing foothills.

"Think we should try another planet?" Bob asked.

Before I could say anything, we came to the top of a ridge—and saw the answer.

While Bob and I stared, stunned and silent, the silver DeSoto floated down from the ridge as if coming in for a landing. Bob, reaching out his hand, switched off the headlights, frowned, reached out his hand again, switched off the lights of the instrument panel. As if the gods had spoken, the darkness vanished. And the garden showed itself to us in the same shimmering light as the gods themselves had seen it—the vestigial light of far-off galactic fires.

"What do you think?" Bob whispered.

"I think—" I stopped, shocked by the loudness of my voice. "I think it has," I went on in a whisper, "suffered a visitation."

"Great!" Bob and I were always generous in judging each other's fictions.

"Maybe by a comet's tail . . ." I was warming to the idea. "A hit-and-run comet."

"Sure melted that skyscraper," he pointed to a pinnacle of red rock.

"You suppose they had curb service?" I asked. "Or coney islands?"

"No," he said. Then pointing to a giant formation that resembled an elephant, he added, "But they had a great zoo."

We enjoyed our game. We'd had lots of practice, coloring the empty spaces of our Dixter days.

Lowering my voice to a whisper again, I warned, "Now we've done it."

"Done what?"

I indicated a shadow, wandering disconsolate, from one ridge-top to another. A faint, muzzy shadow. Cast by a gauzy cloud. "Waked the gods."

Bob pulled to the edge of the dirt road, turned off the motor, rolled down his window—a dead and heavy stillness tumbled in on us.

I could even hear Bob's breathing—easy, slow, rhythmic. After listening, there in the silence, I found myself feeling a strange compulsion to match my breathing to his. And I felt something I'd never felt before—an uneasiness with Bob.

"Let's explore," he said, and the sound of his door, opening and slamming, was like a blasphemy.

Softly, I opened my door and stepped out, leaving it ajar.

Out among the ruins of whatever Armageddon the place had suffered, we picked our way, with the shadows from the clouds running ahead of us, giving warning. Scuffing our feet in the astral dust of our imaginings, we christened each ruin, each fossil: a pillar of the temple, the fossil of a mastodon. . . .

Coming to a giant, other-worldly prairie dog, we sat down at its paws. For a while we said nothing, then, "What if it's not a dead planet, after all?" I ventured.

Knowing the game but not the answer, he waited.

"What if it's a brand new one? Trying to get born?" I stopped, embarrassed, having only a tenuous grasp of what I was thinking — or feeling — and the more I understood of it, the less inclined I was to utter it. What I was reaching for was . . . what if the stillness were the kind just before something happens, before something new is conceived? Nothing to do with dying or with an ending, but something to do with a conception, a beginning?

All I could manage to say was, "What if those shapes are just now . . . beginning to become . . . what if they're . . . just groping . . . toward life?"

Bob sat there, saying nothing. Usually, if he didn't take to my fictions, he laughed; he never just left me to feel foolish — like this. Then all at once he jumped up as if an alarm clock had gone off, announcing in a voice loud enough for all of Colorado Springs to hear, "I'd better get you back!"

We started off, up an incline, then I stopped. "Not until we've marked it," I said.

"Marked what?"

"Oh . . . the planet? Like staking our claim to it?" Actually, I was none too sure myself, of just what, or why.

Even though we didn't come up with a good reason for our labors, we worked very hard and for a very long time. All hunched over with the weight, we carried large rocks, placed them on the highest spot around us, stacked them, arranged them, until we achieved something of a puffy, knobby pyramid.

Standing back, admiring it, Bob roared out, "A cairn! That's what it is!"

"Yes!" I shouted.

"All explorers leave a cairn!" Delighted with himself, he picked a twig from a scrubby bush, dubbed it a flag, and wedged it between two of the top rocks. Then, turning suddenly somber, he said, "They also leave them over their dead."

A few days later Bob's father, apparently deciding he had allotted enough time to the business of courtship, drove back to Dixter, taking Bob with him.

When Nanna and I returned, at the end of the summer, I had turned fifteen, and she let me go out on dates. Thus I became qualified for party invitations.

Bob, though two years older and a year ahead of me in school, still did not date and did not accept invitations to parties, for while he had mastered, in the course of our voyages and explorations together, the art of conjuring forth from the unsubstantial air whole histories and towers and domes, he was as yet a novice in the knack of saying nothing, endlessly, in the game of social dalliance.

So it happened that twice that September when he rang our doorbell, I had to tell him I was going out—on a date.

I saw less and less of him.

Soon after the Christmas holidays, the whole high school began to buzz with the news that Bob Wyant was dating Valerie Dobbs. I told myself I was happy for him.

One night when Phil Hanley picked me up for a movie date, I found when we got to the car that Bob and Valerie were in the back seat. Phil hadn't told me we were double-dating. We went to see *Trail of the Lonesome Pine*, and all through the feature Phil held my hand; then after the movie, in the car driving home, he reached out his arm, pulled me over to him.

The next morning the doorbell rang—and there stood Bob. "Wanna go for a ride?" This was the first time he had ever come by in the day.

No sooner had we driven away from the curb than he said, "I was surprised at you last night."

I laughed. "Well, *I* was surprised at Phil!"

Then he laughed too.

But we never double-dated again.

We did, of course, run into each other, on our dates. Out in front of Coleman's Drug Store. At Henry's for a coney island. Like the night Al Moore and I and Mary Jo Keene and Dick Evans were in a booth at Henry's when Bob and Millie Webster walked in together (he had dated several girls since Valerie).

And all at once Mary Jo began to chirp and carry on as if Millie were bringing in the crown jewels. "Over here!" she called, waving and pushing her bottom into Dick's to make room, ordering him, without so much as a glance his way, "Scoot over!"

For the rest of the evening I had to sit there and watch Mary Jo—who for two hours had been pouting about Heaven-knows-what—as she fizzed and bubbled all over the booth. The worst was when she called to Dick, who was putting two nickels into the nickelodeon, telling him to play "When My Dreamboat Comes Home" and then turned to Bob, smiling cow eyes at him. On *Dick's* nickel!

Bob, on his part, never missed a beat—matched joke for joke with Dick, acknowledged every innuendo of Mary Jo's with a non-committal smile. He had schooled himself well in the ceremonies of this once-alien sublunary world.

As I watched him a most extraordinary thing happened. I thought my eyes were playing me false: Bob's features seemed to be melting. I looked over at Dick: *his* were perfectly clear; I looked across to another booth, over to the door—all, perfectly clear. Then I looked back at Bob's face: it was just a confused blur, without out a single distinguishing feature.

It happened again the next Saturday night. Four of us were double parked out in front of Coleman's Drug Store when, seeing a hand wave from the back of Dick Evans's car, I asked my date, "Who's that?"

"Where?"

"There."

He gave me a puzzled look. "Bob Wyant."

Like an insect who acquires the stripes and colors of the leaves he lives among, Bob had acquired at last the stripes and colors of Dixter's natives. But in doing so, he had become, to me at least, invisible. I tried to be happy for him.

As it had been months since Bob had rung my doorbell, I was surprised one night just a few days before he was to leave for college, to go to the door and find him standing there, looking exactly as he had all those months before, his features all clear and distinct again—the wide forehead, the sharp chin, and the brown smiling eyes. Asking the same question, "Wanna go for a ride?"

But everything else was different. Now he opened the door for me as I got in the car. He asked me where I wanted to go. (Always before, the going itself had been enough.)

"Let's just drive," I said.

And so we did. Past Coleman's Drug, waving as we went. Past the Elks Club. But all those marvels and mysteries had given way to the gray certitudes of knowledge, our artless silences to well-rehearsed antiphonies: we had mastered the native patois, were chattering away in it . . . like the earthlings we had become.

But it was a language in which neither of us had anything to say.

"Wanna drop by Jean's?" he asked. She was having an open house for those leaving for college.

"No!" I rejected the idea as if it were castor oil. Then I heard myself saying, "I want to go to another planet."

He didn't answer. He just started some elaborate tinkering with the instrument panel. Good enough for me, I thought.

"Something wrong?" I asked.

"Checking her out," he said, "to make sure she's still up to it." Even in the dim light of the panel, I could see he was smiling.

We drove to Tallisaw, stopped at a root-beer stand, drove down to the train station where a passenger train had just pulled in.

Bob pointed out a strange thing: you couldn't tell—just from the hugging and the crying—who was arriving and who was leaving.

"Take *them*," he pointed to an elderly man and woman, "holding onto each other like the last life boat was pulling off—with only one of them on it."

The man had just stepped off the train.

Driving back to Dixter, we tried to invent a story to go with the scene.

Stripe by stripe we were shedding our protective coloring, settling again into those easy silences we had once known. When we did speak it was in the language of those countries and planets we had left behind, somewhere, last summer, that country where we had seen so much pain and death, those planets of our imaginings—a language all our own, unfolding word by word, like wings.

After one of our long but comfortable silences, Bob said, "We never did decide, you know."

I looked over at him. "Decide what?"

"What the cairn stood for." This was the first time in the intervening months that either of us had mentioned it.

"A Beginning or an Ending . . ." I started, hoping *he* would finish it.

But he said nothing.

Pulling up to the curb in front of my house, switching off the motor, he put his hand over on mine. "We've been so close, you and I."

Bob had never before touched me—so it felt like a beginning. Like in that picture in my church book where God reached out a finger and touched Adam, and Adam awoke. And that had been the beginning of life.

Taking away his hand, he got out of the car, came around for me, took me to the door, said he'd call me when he came home for Christmas.

Call me—that too was a first.

Before Christmas came around, Bob's father, Russ, married the woman from Colorado, sold his Dixter house, and moved to a house he bought in Denver. Bob, of course, had to go to Colorado for Christmas.

The following spring Nanna had a stroke and died; the next fall I went away to college. So neither Bob nor I had a home to come to in Dixter.

I never saw Bob Wyant again.

I went on, as I suppose he did, exploring, marveling at the ways of the peoples just beyond the ridge.

But, as no mere Buick or Boeing 707 could ever go so far or as high as the silver DeSoto, I never again managed such other-worldly flights as when Bob and I flew in low over the streets of Dixter, or as when we landed in the Garden of the Gods and, exploring, scuffed our feet in its astral dust—scaring away its gods.

ROSE MACAULAY

from The Fabled Shore

The road from La Escala to Gerona, via Belcaire and up the Ter valley, is execrable. My front bumper was jerked off, beginning a long series of such decadences. Throughout the nearly four thousand miles of road that I covered in the peninsula, I learnt that cars are not so firmly held together as one had hoped. One piece after another is liable to drop from them; there is a sudden intimidating clatter, and it will be either a bumper or an exhaust pipe or (more perilously, for I was once all but over the edge of a very steep mountain precipice) the steering axle, that, still attached at one end, has broken its bolts at the other and is clattering with a noise of machine guns along the road. If these objects, which I detested, but which were, it seemed, essential to my car's structure, action, and well being, could be fastened on again with straps, I fastened them on with straps, until I reached the next garage. If they could not (like the steering axle) be fastened on with straps, or otherwise replaced by amateur effort, I left the car on the road and walked or got a lift to the next garage, to bring back mechanics with the necessary tools. It was not always quite easy to explain to the mechanics what the necessary tools would be. I had a Spanish motoring phrase book with me, but it said few of the things that I wished to say. It said, 'Have you a really trustworthy man on whom I can rely to clean my car?' and, 'My car has fallen into a ditch. Do me the favour to send an ox (two oxen) to extricate it,' and (more vaguely and pessimistically), 'My car has discomposed itself. I have left it in charge of a peasant — kilometres from here.' (Fortunately I never acquired this peasant, since my car locks.) Once arrived at a garage, even without one's car, one can explain what has gone wrong by indicating similar appliances on other cars and remarking 'Esto no marcha,' 'This part does not go,' or 'This thing has fallen off.' Spaniards are very helpful, kind and intelligent about cars. If they see a woman changing a wheel on the road, they leap from their camions or their cars and offer help; it is, I suppose, one side of their intense and apparently universal astonishment that a woman should be driving a car at all. All over Spain, except in the more sophisticated cities, my driving by was greeted with the same cry—a long, shrill cat-call, reminiscent of a pig having its throat cut, usually wordless, but sometimes accompanied by 'Olé, Olé! Una señora que conduce!' For Spanish women do not drive cars. I was told this many times, and indeed, observation confirmed it; I saw not a single woman driving all the time I was in Spain. Why not, I sometimes asked. 'It is not the custom here. Spanish ladies live very quietly.' One man, more analytic, explained, 'You see, we Spanish do not live in this century at all, nor in the last, but several hundred years back. We hear that in England women do the things men do, but in Spain it has never been the custom.' This is not true: the peasant women work in the fields and drive donkey carts everywhere; what he meant was señoras. And, apparently, so few foreign señoras are seen driving that they are still regarded as prodigies and portents, much like a man suckling a baby. This, together with the intense Spanish interest in people, and particularly in women, makes it impossible for a woman-driven car to be allowed to pass without comment, as a harmless foreign oddity, as we more sophisticated, live-and-let-live English let foreigners and their strange habits go by without turning the head. In Spain, all heads are turned; and there is a disconcerting outcry. If any student of national psychology can analyse and explain this ancient Spanish custom (one gathers from all travellers that it is ancient) it would be an interesting investigation. The demonstrations sound mainly astonished and derisive; some times rather inimical; always excited and inquisitive. Strange ambivalence of the Spanish! If their curiosity is sometimes partly hostile, their helpfulness to foreigners in difficulty, and their flattering compliments to females (even elderly females such as myself) are delightful and admirable; we can never rival or repay them.

But on the Gerona road that evening I needed no help: I tied on my bumper to a headlamp and proceeded to jolt and bound along.

EDITH WHARTON

from A Motor-Flight Through France

The motor-car has restored the romance of travel.

Freeing us from all the compulsions and contacts of the railway, the bondage to fixed hours and the beaten track, the approach to each town through the area of ugliness and desolation created by the railway itself, it has given us back the wonder, the adventure and the novelty which enlivened the way of our posting grandparents. Above all these recovered pleasures must be ranked the delight of taking a town unawares, stealing on it by back ways and unchronicled paths, and surprising in it some intimate aspect of past time, some silhouette hidden for half a century or more by the ugly mask of railway embankments and the iron bulk of a huge station. Then the villages that we missed and yearned for from the window of the train—the unseen villages have been given back to us!

Fontainebleau is charming in May, and at no season do its glades more invitingly detain the wanderer; but it belonged to the familiar, the already-experienced part of our itinerary, and we had to press on to the unexplored. So after a day's roaming of the forest, and a short flight to Moret, mediævally seated in its stout walls on the poplar-edged Loing, we started on our way to the Loire.

Here, too, our wheels were still on beaten tracks; though the morning's flight across country to Orléans was meant to give us a glimpse of a new region. But on that unhappy morning Boreas was up with all his pack, and hunted us savagely across the naked plain, now behind, now on our quarter, now dashing ahead to lie in ambush behind a huddled village, and leap on us as we rounded its last house. The plain stretched on interminably, and the farther it stretched the harder the wind raced us; so that Pithiviers, spite of dulcet associations, appeared to our shrinking eyes only as a wind-break, eagerly striven for and too soon gained and passed;

and when, at luncheon-time, we beat our way, spent and wheezing, into Orléans, even the serried memories of that venerable city endeared it to us less than the fact that it had an inn where we might at last find shelter.

The above wholly inadequate description of an interesting part of France will have convinced any rational being that motoring is no way to see the country. And that morning it certainly was not; but then, what of the afternoon? When we rolled out of Orléans after luncheon, both the day and the scene had changed; and what other form of travel could have brought us into such communion with the spirit of the Loire as our smooth flight along its banks in the bland May air? For, after all, if the motorist sometimes misses details by going too fast, he sometimes has them stamped into his memory by an opportune puncture or a recalcitrant "magneto"; and if, on windy days, he has to rush through nature blindfold, on golden afternoons such as this he can drain every drop of her precious essence.

Certainly we got a great deal of the Loire as we followed its windings that day: a great sense of the steely breadth of its flow, the amenity of its shores, the sweet flatness of the richly gardened and vineyarded landscape, as of a highly cultivated but slightly insipid society; an impression of long white villages and of stout conical towns on little hills; of old brown Beaugency in its cup between two heights, and Madame de Pompadour's Ménars on its bright terraces; of Blois, nobly bestriding the river at a noble bend; and farther south, of yellow cliffs honeycombed with strange dwellings; of Chaumont and Amboise crowning their heaped-up towns; of *manoirs*, walled gardens, rich pastures, willowed islands; and then, toward sunset, of another long bridge, a brace of fretted church-towers, and the widespread roofs of Tours.

Had we visited by rail the principal places named in this itinerary, necessity would have detained us longer in each, and we should have had a fuller store of specific impressions; but we should have missed what is, in one way, the truest initiation of travel, the sense of continuity, of relation between different districts, of familiarity with the unnamed, unhistoried region stretching between successive centres of human history, and exerting, in deep unnoticed ways, so persistent an influence on the turn that history takes. And after all—though some people seem to doubt the fact—it is possible to stop a motor and get out of it; and if, on our way down the Loire, we exercised this privilege infrequently, it was because, here again, we were in a land of old acquaintance, of which the general topography was just the least familiar part.

CAROLYN CASSADY

Cars I Have Known

The very first automobile I'm sure I was ever in—although my
memory only goes back to the age of four or five—was the magnificent Model-T Ford owned by Mr. Penner, the husband of "Penner," my nanny. This would be around 1928 or '29, and I don't think
married women owned anything then. Mr. Penner also owned a
farm about ten miles out of the town of East Lansing, Michigan, home of the "cow college" (now MSU) where my father was a
biochemist.

Although we had a large Dutch Colonial home near the Red
Cedar River on an acre of lawns, trees, orchard, veggie garden, and
even a barn with a Jersey cow named Daisy, we did not own a car.
To this day I can clearly recall the exquisite thrill of being taken to
the farm in that shining black carriage, sparkling with gold and
silver trim. I was boosted into the high leather seat beside Mr.
Penner while Penner spread her bulk on the seat behind. I watched
in awe as Mr. Penner fiddled with the little metal lever beneath the
big black wheel he steered, his Sunday shoes pedaling the pedals
on the spotless floor.

But it's the smells of that magic carpet ride I can conjure up at
any time. The hot sun on metal, canvas and leather, each with its
distinctive aroma. The breeze in my hair through the open sides
carried the scents of summer fields and flowers. This chariot was,
after all, a machine, so the din of its chugs and clatter was consid-
erable, but somehow that made it more impressive still, and even if
possible, I would never have found worthy words for speech. Cin-
derella's coach was not a patch on mine.

When eventually we were forced to get a car, we had two. In 1932
my father accepted a professorship at Vanderbilt University Med-

ical School in Nashville. Since our family consisted of two adults and five children (one abroad), one car would not get us and our baggage there. Number 1 was a handsome sedan in maroon with black trim and the elegant interior fittings cars sported in those days. It was an REO Flying Cloud, made by Ransom E. Olds, whose later cars came to be known as Oldsmobiles. Number 2 was a modest Model-A Ford coupe. My eldest brother, who had just turned sixteen, drove the Reo, my father the Ford.

My lifelong fear of wet roads, mountain roads, and cars in general probably started from this, my first long drive in a car. On a wet Kentucky mountain road, the Reo skidded into a ditch, catapulting my mother from the right rear seat, through the left (fortunately open) window, traversing a large trunk and my lap, and straight into the mountain's rocky side. She had automatically raised her right arm to protect her face, which caused her hand to telescope into her wrist. I'll skip the intricate machinations of finding doctors in rural Kentucky, but the whole process traumatized me—even though we repeated that trip every summer to go to our cottage in upper Michigan, and never again did we encounter wet mountain roads. I often wonder what became of those two cars.

"Of all the words of tongue or pen, the saddest are these: It might have been."

I must be brief with this one. The pain, oh, the pain. . . .

In my last year of college, in Vermont, I would sit and study on a grassy knoll near the edge of campus. Nearby were the garages for faculty cars and college vehicles. Several times that spring, I noticed the college mechanic working on or polishing a huge lemon-yellow car, and one day I walked over and asked him about it. He invited my inspection with enthusiasm. It was six years old. He had completely restored the engine, brakes, etc., so all mechanical parts were "as new." The black leather seats, canvas roof, Isinglass "curtains" with windows, the paint and tires, were all in mint condition. The best part was its size. It could seat nine people, and he said it had been used in a number of capacities, the latest that of a hearse. The more I looked at it in the succeeding days, the more I fell in love with it. To ease this yearning, I asked if he'd consider selling it and for how much, sure that the impossible price would cure my ache. When he said $100, I lost control.

I'd had to earn my own spending money while at college, which I did by working the switchboard and manning one of the snack bars. Also, from time to time I painted pastel portraits of any girl so inclined for $25. Now I did a whirlwind tour and solicited four subjects. By the end of one day I had my $100, and in no time I was the proud owner of "Yellow Fever." I was thrilled—and scared. I could think of no way to tell my father what I'd done, nor how to get this beast home to Tennessee when I graduated in two or three months time. He'd never see the sense in my buying any car, let alone this one.

I shelved my doubts and fears for the next month and wallowed in my treasure. Piled high with giggling schoolgirls it cruised the town to dinner or the movies. Going downhill was a bit tricky, since the weight of the car increased the momentum, but she held up and performed like the angel she was. Once a girl persuaded me to hunt lost friends of hers somewhere in Vermont. We got thoroughly lost, drove straight over fields, stopped to join a barn dance, spent a night with someone she'd heard about from someone in a house where garages were provided for at least ten cars. We never found her friends, but we had a helluva time.

Now then. The showdown. A girl from the class below me came forth and offered to look after Yellow Fever the next term at college, which would give me time to soften up my dad and maybe find a brother to come drive it home. Sounded OK, and I went merrily off to Tennessee.

Well, the painful ending is that my friend wrote and said she had "rented" the car to some presumed college boys and never saw it or a check again. She, being a terminally wealthy girl, wasn't bothered. She's never known what it did to me. How often I've thought of how my husband and son would have flipped over that car—and what it might be worth now! If anyone sees a yellow 1937 LaSalle touring car, give it my love (sob).

I'm a one-man woman, and, it would appear, a one-car woman too. Cars became the bane of my existence when I married Neal Cassady—the "fastest man alive," legendary for his driving skills. He, fickle in his affections for both women and cars, was possessed by the desire for them both, and he loved them all. *Cars* are our subject here. . . . When you took on Neal, you took on cars, and the racing of, from midgets to Monaco. There was no letup. We ourselves either had no cars, none that ran, or no fewer than five at a time. Usually one could be persuaded to run, if fitfully. This aspect made them more interesting for him, but unreliable transport is a nightmare for me. It took many years and dozens of cars of all makes and descriptions for me to reach the limit of my endurance. I vowed never again to push a car to start it, and went out and bought a new and guaranteed one of my own, forbidding him to drive it. I had already stopped riding in his. It isn't that he was a bad driver—quite the contrary. His perception was so much more acute than anyone else's, the close shaves turned your hair white, but he never dented a fender, never even scratched the paint. It was the interior and the works he seemed to destroy, probably because of his tremendous energy and enthusiasm, especially in a car.

In the thirties and forties cars had some "class," some eye-catching design. Now they all look alike to me, and I've no idea which is which, except of course the rare and costly ones. My son seems to have inherited his father's talent for collecting broken cars; his driveway, too, sports five car patients awaiting treatment. One is my own old 1970 Ford Torino station wagon—"tuna boat" to the family. I've begged him to dispose of it, since it costs too much to insure and register for my short visits, but sentiment keeps getting in the way of his saying goodbye to Bessie, such a long-time family friend. She's still the best-lookin' of the lot.

I have at last reached freedom from the large price to pay and larger, constant cost of maintenance and repair of The Car. Better still, I am privileged to have free transport of several kinds. I moved to London. All that money saved goes to more rewarding adventures. I'm happy to let "them" do the driving. Drive on!

KALIA DONER

Car Pastures: Indiana 1963

In my hometown, cars were more important than houses—they seemed to withstand tornados better, and they made it possible to stop hanging out and doing nothing and start driving around and doing nothing. Remember, this is the state where the most exciting event of the year is watching a bunch of guys race in circles for 500 miles.

My father bought a Mercedes Benz in 1963. It was a dream of his to own one even though it cost as much as the down payment he'd borrowed from his folks to buy the house we lived in. I was fourteen, the tallest girl in my class and the only person in town who had to ride around in a stolid, navy blue German car, square and shiny, with four forward gears on the shaft and red leather interior. Like being the tallest, it was a distinction that publicly humiliated me, but privately I felt both misunderstood and superior. After all, I lived in a world where you were accused of being a Communist for supporting Lyndon Johnson over Barry Goldwater. I wanted to fit in but if I couldn't, I wanted to cause some degree of irritation. Little wonder I walked around school with a copy of the Communist Manifesto pasted to the outside of my three-ring notebook.

That same year I went steady with a junior named Steve who peroxided his hair and played on the football team. I couldn't stand him but he had a white Rambler convertible with white vinyl interior. My father forbade me to ride in it, so every day after school Steve would drive slowly the five blocks to my house as I walked alongside on the curb.

When I finally got my license at sixteen my folks changed their tune about moving vehicles. They were overjoyed to have me in a car—preferably running errands. I took my nine-year-old sister to Indianapolis once a week for ballet lessons. We raced one-hundred miles an hour down old Highway 52. Cornfields would flicker by, the long rows perpendicular to the two-lane asphalt. Sometimes we wouldn't see another car the whole way.

Once, when my parents had a party, they asked me to take the car and pick up an extra fifth of Jim Beam. It never occurred to them that I was breaking the law. They thought of themselves as too European for such silliness—an attitude I attributed to the arrival of the Mercedes, since they were both from South Dakota.

Every adventure I ever had took place in a car. That summer I was on a blind date with a guy named Tom who went to the Catholic high school across the river. It was a double date with Karen Sue and her boyfriend Clyde—we'd seen the movie *Tom Jones*—when the cops pulled us over because Clyde had stolen hubcaps on his '56 Chevy. They also found a case of beer in the trunk. All four of us had to go down to the police station, which was housed in a tiny two-story carriage house that used to be the public library. After about a half hour I went up to the desk sergeant and said, "It's almost eleven and if I'm not back on time my Mom will kill me." So he let Tom take me home if he promised to come back to the station.

After I'd been running errands for a while, my Dad decided he could trust me with the car. "Going out, taking the car, be back later," I'd yell over my shoulder as I headed out to pick up my girlfriends. We always drove down to the levee, through the parking lot of the Park 'n' Eat on the way to the XXX Drive-In and Frisch's Big Boy, before hitting the courthouse square. Driving the Mercedes made it hard to get the right cruising attitude: Everyone else was slouched down in the comfy seats of a Detroit special. We were perched in the air on the Mercedes's tightly stuffed red leather seats like some harem riding on an elephant's back.

Still, I couldn't help myself—I fell into the great circling pattern from drive-in to Courthouse Square and back, the gasoline-fueled mating dance of the children of Indiana. It was like being in a slot car race—the path is so worn you can't make a turn in another direction even if you want to, and it never occurs to you to want to.

Later I told my mom I felt like some old fuddyduddy driving

around in that car. She tried to make it up to me by drag racing—and beating—a car full of hoods from the eastside, across the Wabash River Bridge. It didn't do much for my attitude toward the car—but it did make a big difference in my attitude toward Mom.

Six months after I got my license I hooked up with a college guy who drove a Chevy and I stopped having to cruise through drive-ins in the Mercedes. I was ready to discover the second most important use for a car.

I know you think I'm going to tell you about the time I lost my virginity in the front seat of that Chevy. But I didn't. Girls that had sex in cars never made it off the front seat. They went from driving through the parking lots of drive-ins, to parking in the corn fields, to driving through the parking lots of grocery stores with a car full of little brats all waiting impatiently for the day they could drive too.

What my boyfriend and I would do was drive through the drive-ins—stopping to eat a fried tenderloin sandwich and fries in the car—and then take about a hundred paper napkins and head to the cornfields where we'd do our almost sex, which left me free from worry about having to stay in the front seat of a Chevy for the rest of my life (and oblivious to how it made him feel one way or the other).

Eventually, I moved to New York. I gave up both cars and the boys who liked them and took up real sex. It was a smart tradeoff. I let my driver's license lapse for five years and barely noticed.

But you don't ever quite escape where you come from and after years of playing around with city boys, I married a guy from Ohio whose dream is to put a GTO up on blocks in a driveway. He insisted I get my license again.

And that's got me thinking. It's been thirty years since I was in Indiana. But it might be time to take a road trip. To see what it's like to go all the way in the front seat of an American car with an all-American boy.

ELINOR NAUEN

Trojan

And then that summer my boyfriend gave me a car.
This was amazing as I was not that kind of girl
boys made grand gestures toward, my boyfriends
were the kind of morons who liked
smart girls.

Dave hung his arm over my shoulder—
his stiff Swedish version of a hug—& laid me up
against the last elm on the block that hadn't succumbed to
    disease.
"My Mustang," he said.
"Yeah," I said.
"I'm getting a Firebird," he said.
My other boyfriend Ken had a black Firebird.
We cruised up Main & down Dakota
for rubbery burgers at Teddy the Greek's drive-in
or to sneak in to the Dew Drop Inn.

"You can have the Mustang," Dave said.
"OK, cool," I said.
My parents would kill me so I figured he didn't mean it.

I called my friend Debbie whose dad let me park it
in their field where nothing but horseradish grew

till I thought to tell my folks
Dave was letting me drive it
that one last summer before we blasted off to college
or the army or the moronic jobs
my boyfriends would have for the rest of their lives.

Gas was 20¢ a gallon
a dollar's worth could gallop us halfway across the prairie,
a nighttime ride to wherever we weren't supposed to go.

Alas the hidden treacheries—the shocks, the sparks,
the struts & clutch I was heir to, what Dave wanted.

GAIL MAZUR

Desire

It was a kind of torture—waiting
to be kissed. A dark car parked away
from the street lamp, away from our house
where my tall father would wait, his face
visible at a pane high in the front door.
Was my mother always asleep? A boy
reached for me, I leaned eagerly into him,
soon the windshield was steaming.

Midnight. A neighbor's bedroom light
goes on, then off. The street is quiet. . . .

Until I married, I didn't have my own key,
that wasn't how it worked, not at our house.
You had to wake someone with the bell,
or he was there, waiting. Someone let you in.
These pleasures on the front seat of a boy's
father's car were "guilty," yet my body knew
they were the only right thing to do,

my body hated the cage it had become. . . .

One of those boys died in a car crash;
one is a mechanic; one's a musician.
They were young and soft and, mostly, dumb.
I loved their lips, their eyebrows, the bones
of their cheeks, cheeks that scraped mine raw,
so I'd turn away from the parent who let me
angrily in. And always, the next day,

no one at home could penetrate the fog
around me. I'd re-live the precious night
as if it were a bridge to my new state
from the old world I'd been imprisoned by,
and I've been allowed to walk on it, to cross
a border—there's an invisible line
in the middle of the bridge, in the fog,
where I'm released, where I think I'm free.

PANSY MAURER-ALVAREZ

This Sure Isn't the Pennsylvania Turnpike

You're doing the driving and it's real smooth the way we're
   zipping along
at 150 km/hr, way past a clear midnight.
But nothing's actually clear

   BECAUSE

it hasn't happened yet and how would I know
it's coming? The only thing that keeps coming
is the passing line of white staccatos. More regular than
   breathing
and much faster.
The only reason that I'm not talking is

   BECAUSE

I'm too tired to.
I put my feet up on the dashboard

   BECAUSE

they're swollen and burn from walking all over the place in the
   heat.
The passing line's perfectly insistent,
like it can't believe the way we keep eating it up
in front and shitting it out the back. It keeps coming
like it doesn't know what's happening. And yet, by now it must

BECAUSE

we've been doing this for over an hour already.
I've got this indecisive feeling poking
around in my intestines looking for a place to snuggle up in,
you know like to prepare for the great combust.
You were hungry and wanted a man-pleasing meal. And
you drank a lot
beer

BECAUSE

you were thirsty

BECAUSE

of the heat.
I'm getting horny with my feet
up on the dashboard like this. My legs
look kind of nice in the dark. But it's like you're not even here

BECAUSE

you're not saying anything and I can't hear
your breathing

BECAUSE

of the way the car's rumbling.
We can't stop until the highway stops. I bet
you wouldn't even stop if I had to go to the bathroom.
At customs we stopped; you turned up the radio,
so we listened to "Midnight Reveries"

BECAUSE

that's about the time it was.
We had to wait a while in line

BECAUSE

there were all these vacationers with trailers,
traveling at night to avoid the heat and the traffic. And there we
    were,
no luggage,
just the clothes on our backs and a tank of gas

BECAUSE

you came in yesterday afternoon late and said,
"Hey, get in the car. Let's cross some borders." So hey, wow, off we
    went
just driving, driving and driving and then we were in France.
That's where we came across that church. Eleventh century.
You weren't about to go in and have a look

BECAUSE

Hell, I'm not religious either, but just a look?
You were in a bad mood

ON ACCOUNT OF

my going in anyway.
It was special in there. Heavy with cool, like the air outside was
    heavy with heat.
You could walk around, round and around

BECAUSE

it was octagonal. So I did.
There were galleries way up high

that went round, round and around. With pale turquoise frescoes.
It reminded me of some place we'd been, some place in Salzburg.
I ran my hands over the columns

BECAUSE

no one was in there praying or anything.
I held the inside of my thigh against a column

BECAUSE

I was alone.
It felt good, cool and massive.
"Man! This place wouldn't fall down in a hurry," is what I was
    thinking.
Then I thought I'd better get back outside

BECAUSE

you'd be waiting. But you weren't there.
I walked around the parking lot and all around the church,
    poking
in the bushes

BECAUSE

you might think it'd be fun to hide
and jump out at me. Apparently, you weren't thinking
along those lines. So I walked into the village. Walked
all up and down the side streets, too. And the whole
way back to the church. You said you went for a beer

BECAUSE

it was so hot and you got talking to this guy. Long talk!
But I didn't say that so as not to spoil the day.

Then you wanted to go for a walk. A what?
Through pre-harvest fields

BECAUSE

of the sunset and

BECAUSE

we live in the gray heart of a city. Okay, so
this is supposed to be romantic, like bucolic. Like bull!
A haystack, exciting? Just plain prickly,
if you ask me, except that you didn't.
You felt real good afterwards and wanted a man-pleasing meal.
Alsatian Sauerkraut. In summer?
Menu touristique: big helping, cheap. So, okay.
We drank a lot

BECAUSE

you were still thirsty.
Around midnight we crossed back into Switzerland
with nothing to declare.
That was before you said it.
That there was no point. No point in going on.
We're going on all right, on, on and on

BECAUSE

that's where the road's going and we haven't eaten up all the
    staccatos yet.
No point.

BECAUSE

you can't stand it anymore.
I don't get that. It's what I've been doing all along, but I don't
  say this

BECAUSE

I see there's no point. It has happened.

JOY WILLIAMS

Rot

Lucy was watching the street when an old Ford Thunderbird turned into their driveway. She had never seen the car before and her husband, Dwight, was driving it. One of Dwight's old girlfriends leapt from the passenger seat and ran toward the house. Her name was Caroline, she had curly hair and big white teeth, more than seemed normal, and Lucy liked her the least of all of Dwight's old girlfriends. Nevertheless, when she came inside, Lucy said, "Would you like a glass of water or something?"

"I was the horn," Caroline said. "That car doesn't have one so I was it. I'd yell out the window, 'Watch out!'"

"Were you the brakes too or just the horn?" Lucy asked.

"It has brakes," Caroline said, showing her startling teeth. She went into the living room and said, "Hello, rug." She always spoke to the rug lying there. The rug was from Mexico with birds of different colors flying across it. All of the birds had long, white eyes. Dwight and Caroline had brought the rug back from the Yucatán when they had gone snorkeling there years before. Some of the coves were so popular that the fish could scarcely be seen for all the suntan oil floating in the water. At Garrafon in Isla Mujeres, Dwight told Lucy, he had raised his head and seen a hundred people bobbing facedown over the rocks of the reef and a clean white tampon bobbing there among them. Caroline had said at the time, "It's disgusting, but it's obviously some joke."

Caroline muttered little things to the rug, showing off, Lucy thought, although she wasn't speaking Spanish to it, she didn't know Spanish. Lucy looked out the window at Dwight sitting in the Thunderbird. It was old with new paint, black, with a white top and portholes and skirts. He looked a little big for it. He got out abruptly and ran to the house as though through rain, but there was no rain. It was a gray, still day in spring, just before Easter, with an odious weight to the air. Recently, when they had been coming inside, synthetic stuff from Easter baskets had been traveling in with them, the fake nesting matter, the pastel and crinkly stuff of Easter baskets. Lucy couldn't imagine where they kept picking it up from, but no festive detritus came in this time.

Dwight gave her a hard, wandering kiss on the mouth. Lately, it was as though he were trying out kisses, trying to adjust them.

"You'll tell me all about this, I guess," Lucy said.

"Lucy," Dwight said solemnly.

Caroline joined them and said, "I've got to be off. I don't know the time, but I bet I can guess it to within a minute. I can do that," she assured Lucy. Caroline closed her eyes. Her teeth seemed still to be looking out at them, however. "Five ten," she said after a while. Lucy looked at the clock on the wall which showed ten minutes past five. She shrugged.

"That car is some cute," Caroline said, giving Dwight a little squeeze. "Isn't it some cute?" she said to Lucy. "Your Dwight's been tracking this car for days."

"I bought it from the next of kin," Dwight said.

Lucy looked at him impassively. She was not a girl who was quick to alarm.

"I was down at the Aquarium last week looking at the fish," Dwight began.

"Oh, that Aquarium," Lucy said.

The Aquarium was where a baby seal had been put to sleep because he was born too ugly to be viewed by children. He had not been considered viewable so off he went. The Aquarium offended Lucy. "I like fish," Dwight had told Lucy when she asked why he spent so much of his free time at the Aquarium. "Men like fish."

"And when I came out into the parking lot, next to our car was this little Thunderbird and there was a dead man sitting behind the wheel."

"Isn't that something!" Caroline exclaimed.

"I was the first to find him," Dwight said. "I'm no expert but that man was gone."

"What did this dead man look like?" Lucy asked Dwight.

He thought for a moment, then said, "He looked like someone in the movies. He had a large head."

"He didn't resemble you, did he?" she asked.

"Oh no, darling, not in the slightest."

"In any case," Lucy said a little impatiently.

"In any case," Dwight said, "this car just jumped at me, you know the way some things do. I knew I just had to have this car, it was just so pretty. It's the same age as you are, darling. That was the year the good things came out."

Lucy made a face for she wearied of references to her youth. She was almost twenty-five years younger than Dwight. Actually, theirs was rather a peculiar story.

"This car is almost cherry," Dwight said, gesturing out at it, "and now it's ours."

"That car is not almost cherry," Lucy said. "A man died in it. I would say that this car was about as un-cherry as you can get." She went on vehemently in this way for awhile.

Caroline gazed at her, her lips parted, her teeth making no judgment. Then she said, "I've got to get back to my lonely home." She did not live far away. Almost everybody they knew, and a lot of people they didn't, lived close by. "Now you two have fun in that car, it's a sweet little car." She kissed Dwight and he patted her back in an avuncular fashion as he walked her to the door. The air outside had a faint, thin smell of fruit and rubber. A siren screamed through it.

When Dwight returned, Lucy said, "I don't want a car a man died in for my birthday."

"It's not your birthday coming up, is it?"

Lucy admitted it was not, although Dwight often planned for her birthday months in advance. She blushed.

"It's funny how some people live longer than others, isn't it," she finally said.

❖

Lucy and Dwight had been married for five years. When Dwight had first seen her, he was twenty-five years old and she was a four-month-old baby.

"I'm gonna marry you," Dwight said to the baby. People heard him. He was tall and had black hair, and was wearing a leather jacket that a girlfriend had sewed a violet silk liner into. It was a New Year's Eve party at this girlfriend's house and the girl was standing beside him. "Oh, right," she said. She didn't see anything particularly intriguing about this baby. They could make better babies than this, she thought. Lucy lay in a white wicker basket on a sofa. Her hair was sparse and her expression solemn. "You're gonna be my wife," Dwight said. He was very good with babies and good with children too. When Lucy was five, her favorite things were pop-up books in which one found what was missing by pushing or pulling or turning a tab, and for her birthday Dwight bought her fifteen of these, surely as many as had ever been produced. When she was ten he bought her a playhouse and filled it with balloons. Dwight was good with adolescents as well. When she was fourteen, he rented her a horse for a year. As for women, he had a special touch with them, as all his girlfriends would attest. Dwight wasn't faithful to Lucy as she was growing up, but he was attentive and devoted. Dwight kept up the pace nicely. And all the time Lucy was stoically growing up, learning how to dress herself and read, letting her hair grow, then cutting it all off, joining clubs and playing records, doing her algebra, going on dates, Dwight was out in the world. He always sent her little stones from the places he visited and she ordered them by size or color and put them in and out of boxes and jars until there came to be so many she grew confused as to where each had come from. This alarmed her at first, and then it annoyed her. At about the time Lucy didn't care if she saw another little stone in her life, they got married. They bought a house and settled in. The house was a large, comfortable one, large enough, was the inference, to accommodate growth of various sorts. Things were all right. Dwight was like a big strange

book where Lucy just needed to turn the pages and there everything was already.

They went out and looked at the Thunderbird in the waning light.

"It's a beauty, isn't it," Dwight said. "Wide whites, complete engine dress." He opened the hood, exposing the gleaming motor.
Dwight was happy, his inky eyes shone. When he slammed the
hood shut there was a soft rattling as of pebbles being thrown.

"What's that?" Lucy asked.

"What's what, my sweet?"

"That," Lucy said, "on the ground." She picked up a piece of
rust, as big as her small hand and very light. Dwight peered at it.
As she was trying to hand it to him, it dropped and crumbled.

"It looked so solid, I didn't check underneath," Dwight said. "I'll
have some body men come over tomorrow and look at it. I'm sure
it's no problem, just superficial stuff."

She ran her fingers behind the rocker panel of the door and
came up with a handful of flakes.

"I don't know why you'd want to make it worse," Dwight said.

The next morning, two men were scooting around on their
backs beneath the T-Bird, poking here and there with screwdrivers
and squinting at the undercarriage. Lucy, who enjoyed a leisurely
breakfast, was still in the kitchen, finishing it. As she ate her ce-
real, she studied the milk carton, a panel of which made a request
for organs. Lucy was aware of a new determination in the world to
keep things going. She rinsed her bowl and went outside just as
the two men had slipped from beneath the car and were standing
up, staring at Dwight. Gouts and clots of rust littered the drive.

"This for your daughter here?" one of them said.

"No," Dwight said irritably.

"I wouldn't give this to my daughter."

"It's not for anyone like that!" Dwight said.

"Bottom's just about to go," the other one said. "Riding along, these plates give, floor falls out, your butt's on the road. You need new pans at least. Pans are no problem." He chewed on his thumbnail. "It's rusted out too where the leaf springs meet the frame. Needs some work, no doubt about that. Somebody's done a lot of work but it needs a lot more work for sure. Donny, get me the Hemmings out of the truck."

The other man ambled off and returned with a thick brown catalogue.

"Maybe you should trade up," the first man said. "Get a car with a solid frame."

Dwight shook his head. "You can't repair it?"

"Why sure we can repair it!" Donny said. "You can get everything for these cars, all the parts, you got yourself a classic here!" He thumbed through the catalogue until he came to a page which offered the services of something called *The T-Bird Sanctuary.* The Sanctuary seemed to be a wrecking yard. A grainy photograph showed a jumble of cannibalized cars scattered among trees. It was the kind of picture that looked as though it had been taken furtively with a concealed camera.

"I'd trade up," the other man said. "Lookit over here, this page here, *Fifty-seven F-Bird supercharged, torch red, total body-off restoration, nothing left undone, ready to show . . .*"

"Be still, my heart," Donny said.

"You know if you are going to stick with this car you got," the other man said, "and I'm not advising you to, you should paint it the original color. This black ain't original." He opened the door and pointed at a smudge near the hinges. "See here, Powderblue."

"Starmist blue," Donny said, looking at him furiously.

The men glared at each other and when it appeared that they were about to come to blows, Lucy returned to the house. She stood inside, thinking, looking out at the street. When she had been a little girl on her way to school, she had once found an envelope on the street with her name on it, but there hadn't been anything in the envelope.

"We're getting another opinion," Dwight said when he came in. "We're taking it over to Boris, the best in the business."

They drove to the edge of town, to where another town began, to a big brown building there. Lucy enjoyed the car. It handled very well, she thought. They hurtled along, even though bigger cars passed them.

Boris was small, bald and stern. The German shepherd that stood beside him seemed remarkably large. His paws were delicately rounded but each was the size of a football. There was room, easily, for another German shepherd inside him, Lucy thought. Boris drove the Thunderbird onto a lift and elevated it. He walked slowly beneath it, his hands on his hips. Not a hair grew from his head. He lowered the car down and said, "Hopeless." When neither Lucy nor Dwight spoke, he shouted, "Worthless. Useless." The German shepherd sighed as though he had heard this prognosis many times.

"What about where the leaf springs meet the frame?" Lucy said. The phrase enchanted her.

Boris moved his hands around and then clutched and twisted them together in a pleading fashion.

"How can I make you nice people understand that it is hopeless? What can I say so that you will hear me, so that you will believe me? Do you like ripping up one-hundred-dollar bills? Is this what you want to do with the rest of your life? What kind of masochists are you? It would be wicked of me to give you hope. This car is unrestorable. It is full of rust and rot. Rust is a living thing, it breathes, it eats and it is swallowing up your car. These quarters and rockers have already been replaced, once, twice, who knows how many times. You will replace them again. It is nothing to replace quarters and rockers! How can I save you from your innocence and foolishness and delusions. You take out a bad part, say, you solder in new metal, you line-weld it tight, you replace the whole rear end, say, and what have you accomplished, you have accomplished only a small part of what is necessary, you have accomplished hardly anything! I can see you feel dread and nausea at what I'm saying but it is nothing compared to the dread and nausea you will feel if you continue in this unfortunate project. Stop wasting your thoughts! Rot like this cannot be stayed. This brings us to the question, What is man? with its three subdivisions, What can he know? What ought he do? What may he hope? Questions which concern us all, even you, little lady."

"What!" Dwight said.

"My suggestion is to drive this car," Boris said in a calmer tone, "enjoy it, but for the spring and summer only, then dump it, part it out. Otherwise, you'll be putting in new welds, more and more new welds, but always the collapse will be just ahead of you. Years will pass and then will come the day when there is nothing to weld the weld to, there is no frame, nothing. Once rot, then nothing." He bowed, then retired to his office, which was sheeted with one-way glass.

Driving home, Dwight said, "You never used to hear about rust and rot all the time. It's new, this rust and rot business. You don't know what's around you any more."

Lucy knew Dwight was depressed and tried to look concerned, though in truth she didn't care much about the T-Bird. She was distracted by a tune that was going through her head. It was a song she remembered hearing when she was a little baby, about a tiny ant being at his doorway. She finally told Dwight about it and hummed the tune.

"Do you remember that little song?" she asked.

"Almost," Dwight said.

"What was that about anyway," Lucy asked. "The tiny ant didn't do anything, he was just waiting at his doorway."

"It was just nonsense stuff you'd sing to a little baby," Dwight said. He looked at her vaguely and said, "My sweet . . ."

Lucy called up her friend Daisy and told her about the black Thunderbird. She did not mention rot. Daisy was ten years older than Lucy and was one of the last of Dwight's girlfriends. Daisy had recently had one of her legs amputated. There had been a climbing accident and then she had just let things go on for too long. She was a tall, boyish-looking woman who before the amputation had always worn jeans. Now she slung herself about in skirts, for she found it disturbed people less when she wore a skirt, but when she went to the beach she wore a bathing suit, and she didn't care if she disturbed people or not because she loved the beach, the water, so still and so heavy, hiding so much.

"I didn't read in the paper about a dead man just sitting in his car like that," Daisy said. "Don't they usually report such things? It's unusual, isn't it?"

Lucy had fostered Daisy's friendship because she knew Daisy was still in love with Dwight. If someone, God, for example, had asked Daisy if she'd rather have her leg back or Dwight, she would have said, "Dwight." Lucy felt excited about this and at the same time mystified and pitying. Knowing it always cheered Lucy up when she felt out of sorts.

"Did I tell you about the man in the supermarket with only one leg?" Daisy asked. "I had never seen him before. He was with his wife and baby and instead of being in the mother's arms the baby was in a stroller so the three of them took up a great deal of room in the aisle, and when I turned down the aisle I became entangled with this little family. I felt that I had known this man all my life, of course. People were smiling at us. Even the wife was smiling. It was dreadful."

"You should find someone," Lucy said without much interest.

Daisy's leg was in ashes in a drawer in a church garden, waiting for the rest of her.

"Oh no, no," Daisy said modestly. "So!" she said, "You're going to have another car!"

It was almost suppertime and there was the smell of meat on the air. Two small, brown birds hopped across the patchy grass and Lucy watched them with interest for birds seldom frequented their neighborhood. Whenever there were more than three birds in a given place, it was considered an infestation and a variety of measures were taken which reduced their numbers to an acceptable level. Lucy remembered that when she was little, the birds that flew overhead sometimes cast shadows on the ground. There were flocks of them at times and she remembered hearing the creaking of their wings, but she supposed that was just the sort of thing a child might remember, having seen or heard it only once.

She set the dining-room table for three as this was the night each spring when Rosette would come for dinner, bringing shad and shad roe, Dwight's favorite meal. Rosette had been the most elegant of Dwight's girlfriends, and the one with the smallest waist. She was now married to a man named Bob. When Rosette had been Dwight's girlfriend, she had been called Muffin. For the last five springs, ever since Lucy and Dwight had been married, she would have the shad flown down from the North and she would bring it to their house and cook it. Yet even though shad was his favorite fish and he only got it once a year, Dwight would be coming home a little late this night because he was getting another opinion on the T-Bird. Lucy no longer accompanied him on these discouraging expeditions.

Rosette appeared in a scant, white cocktail dress and red high-heeled shoes. She had brought her own china, silver, candles and wine. She reset the table, dimmed the lights and made Lucy and herself large martinis. They sat, waiting for Dwight, speaking in an aimless way about things. Rosette and Bob were providing a foster home for two delinquents whose names were Jerry and Jackie.

"What awful children," Rosette said. "They're so homely too. They were cuter when they were younger, now their noses are really long and their jaws are odd-looking too. I gave them bunny baskets this year and Jackie wrote me a note saying that what she really needed was a prescription for birth-control pills."

When Dwight arrived, Rosette was saying, "Guilt's not a bad thing to have. There are worse things to have than guilt." She looked admiringly at Dwight and said, "You're a handsome eyeful." She made him a martini which he drank quickly, then she made them all another one. Drinking hers, Lucy stood and watched the T-Bird in the driveway. It was a dainty car, and the paint was so black it looked wet. Rosette prepared the fish with great solemnity, bending over Lucy's somewhat dirty broiler. They all ate in a measured way. Lucy tried to eat the roe one small egg at a time but found that this was impossible.

"I saw Jerry this afternoon walking down the street carrying a Weedwacker," Dwight said. "Does he do yard work now? Yard work's a good occupation for a boy."

"Delinquents aren't always culprits," Rosette said. "That's what many people don't understand, but no, Jerry is not doing yard work, he probably stole that thing off someone's lawn. Bob tries to talk to him but Jerry doesn't heed a word he says. Bob's not very convincing."

"How is Bob?" Lucy asked.

"Husband Bob is a call I never should have answered," Rosette said.

Lucy crossed her arms over her stomach and squeezed herself with delight because Rosette said the same thing each year when she was asked about Bob.

"Life with Husband Bob is a long twilight of drinking and listless anecdote," Rosette said.

Lucy giggled, because Rosette always said this, too.

The next day, Dwight told Lucy of his intentions to bring the T-Bird into the house. "She won't last long on the street," he said. "She's a honey but she's tired. Elements are hard on a car and it's the elements that have done this sweet little car in. We'll put her in the living room which is under-furnished anyway and it will be like living with a work of art right in our living room. We'll keep her shined up and sit inside her and talk. It's very peaceful inside that little car, you know."

The T-Bird looked alert and coquettish as they spoke around it.

"That car was meant to know the open road," Lucy said. "I think we should drive it till it drops." Dwight looked at her sorrowfully and she widened her eyes, not believing she had said such a thing. "Well," she said, "I don't think a car should be in a house, but maybe we could bring it in for a little while and then if we don't like it we could take it out again."

He put his arms around her and embraced her and she could hear his heart pounding away in his chest with gratitude and excitement.

Lucy called Daisy on the telephone. The banging and sawing had already begun. "Men go odd in different ways than women," Daisy said. "That's always been the case. For example, I read that men are exploring ways of turning the earth around toxic waste dumps into glass by the insertion of high-temperature electric probes. A woman would never think of something like that."

Dwight worked feverishly for days. He removed the picture window, took down the wall, shored up the floor, built a ramp, drained the car of all its fluids so it wouldn't leak on the rug, pushed it into the house, replaced the studs, put back the window, erected fresh Sheetrock and repainted the entire room. Lucy was amazed that it was so easy to tear a wall down and put it back up again. In the room, the car looked like a big doll's car. But it didn't look bad inside the house at all and Lucy didn't mind it being there, although she didn't like it when Dwight raised the hood. She didn't care for the hood being raised one bit and always lowered it when she saw it was up. She thought about the Thunderbird most often at night when she was in bed lying beside Dwight and then she would marvel at its silent, unseen presence in the room beside them, taking up space, so strange and shining and full of rot.

They would sit frequently in the car, in their house, not going anywhere, looking through the windshield out at the window and through the window to the street. They didn't invite anyone over for this. Soon, Dwight took to sitting in the car by himself. Dwight was tired. It was taking him a while to bounce back from the carpentry. Lucy saw him there one day behind the wheel, one arm bent and dangling over the glossy door, his eyes shut, his mouth slightly open, his hair as black as she had ever seen it. She couldn't remember the first time she had noticed him, really noticed him, the way he must have first noticed her when she'd been a baby.

"I wish you'd stop that, Dwight," she said, "sitting there pale like that."

He opened his eyes. "You should try this by yourself," he said. "Just try it and tell me what you think."

She sat for some time in the car alone, then went into the kitchen where Dwight stood, drinking water. It was a gray day, with a gray careless light falling everywhere.

"I had the tiniest feeling in there that the point being made was that something has robbed this world of its promise," Lucy said. She did not have a sentimental nature.

Dwight was holding a glass of water in one of his large hands, frowning a little at it. Water poured into the sink and down the drain, part of the same water he was drinking. On the counter was a television set with a picture but no sound. Men were wheeling two stretchers out of a house and across a lawn and on each stretcher was a long still thing covered in a green cloth. The house was a cement-block house with two metal chairs on the porch with little cushions on them, and under the roof's overhang a basket of flowers swung.

"Is this the only channel we ever get?" Lucy said. She turned the water faucet off.

"It's the news, Lucy."

"I've seen this news a hundred times before. It's always this kind of news."

"This is the Sun Belt, Lucy."

The way he kept saying her name began to irritate her. "Well, Dwight," she said. "Dwight, Dwight, Dwight."

Dwight looked at her mildly and went back to the living room. Lucy trailed after him. They both looked at the car and Lucy said to it, "I'd like an emerald ring. I'd like a baby boy."

"You don't ask it for things, Lucy," Dwight said.

"I'd like a Porsche Carrera," Lucy said to it.

"Are you crazy or what!" Dwight demanded.

"I would like a little baby," she mused.

"You were a little baby once," Dwight said.

"Well, I know that."

"So isn't that enough?"

She looked at him uneasily, then said, "Do you know what I used to like that you did? You'd say, 'That's my wife's favorite color...' or 'That's just what my wife says...'" Dwight gazed at her from his big, inky eyes. "And of course your wife was me!" she exclaimed. "I always thought that was kind of sexy."

"We're not talking sex any more, Lucy," he said. She blushed.

Dwight got into the Thunderbird and rested his hands on the wheel. She saw his fingers pressing against the horn rim which made no sound.

"I don't think this car should be in the house," Lucy said, still fiercely blushing.

"It's a place where I can think, Lucy."

"But it's in the middle of the living room! It takes up practically the whole living room!"

"A man's got to think, Lucy. A man's got to prepare for things."

"Where did you think before we got married," she said crossly.

"All over, Lucy. I thought of you everywhere. You were part of everything."

Lucy did not want to be part of everything. She did not want to be part of another woman's kissing, for example. She did not want to be part of Daisy's leg which she was certain, in their time, had played its part and been something Dwight had paid attention to. She did not want to be part of a great many things that she could mention.

"I don't want to be part of everything," she said.

"Life is different from when I was young and you were a little baby," Dwight said.

"I never did want to be part of everything," she said excitedly.

Dwight worked his shoulders back into the seat and stared out the window.

"Maybe the man who had this car before died of a broken heart, did you ever think of that?" Lucy said. When he said nothing, she said, "I don't want to start waiting on you again, Dwight." Her face had cooled off now.

"You wait the way you want to wait," Dwight said. "You've got to know what you want while you're waiting." He patted the seat beside him and smiled at her. It wasn't just a question of moving this used-up thing out again, she knew that. Time wasn't moving sideways the way it had always seemed to her to move but was climbing upward, then falling back, then lurching in a circle like some poisoned, damaged thing. Eventually, she sat down next to him. She looked through the glass at the other glass, then past that.

"It's raining," Lucy said.

There was a light rain falling, a warm spring rain. As she watched, it fell more quickly. It was silverish, but as it fell faster it appeared less and less like rain and she could almost hear it rattling as it struck the street.

Contributor Notes

British-born JILL AMADIO is an author and journalist. She has covered auto racing in America for twenty years and writes a syndicated car column. Her latest book, *My Vagabond Lover* (Taylor Publishing, 1996), is an intimate biography of crooner Rudy Vallee, written in collaboration with his widow.

DOROTHY BARRESI is the author of two books of poetry, *The Post-Rapture Diner* (University of Pittsburgh Press, 1996) and *All of the Above* (Beacon Press, 1991), which won the 1990 Barnard College New Women Poets Prize. Her essays and poems have been published in numerous journals, including *Poetry, Parnassus,* the *Gettysburg Review,* and *Harvard Review.* She is currently an associate professor in the English Department of California State University, Northridge.

LISA BERNSTEIN (LISA B)'s books of poetry include *The Transparent Body* and *Anorexia.* Her poetry has appeared in many magazines and anthologies, including the *Kenyon Review, Tikkun, Yellow Silk, Antaeus, Ploughshares,* and *Feminist Studies,* and she is the recipient of a creative writing fellowship from the National Endowment for the Arts. She performs throughout the San Francisco Bay Area with her band as the singer and spoken word artist Lisa B. Her CD/cassette *Be the Word* has received nationwide radio play.

L. R. BERGER's poems have appeared recently in the *American Literary Review,* the *American Voice,* the *Beloit Poetry Journal, Descant,* and *Gulf Coast.* She lives in rural New Hampshire, teaches in Boston, and spends a good deal of time driving.

DEBRA BRUCE is the author of *Pure Daughter* and *Sudden Hunger,* both published by the University of Arkansas Press. Her work has appeared most recently in *Poetry,* the *North American Review,* and *A*

Formal Feeling Comes, an anthology of formal poetry by women. She teaches at Northeastern Illinois University and lives in Chicago.

CAROLYN CASSADY studied at Bennington College and the University of Denver, where she met and married legendary driver Neal Cassady, Dean Moriarty of Jack Kerouac's *On the Road*. She is the author of *Heart Beat: My Life with Jack & Neal* and *Off the Road: My Years with Cassady, Kerouac and Ginsberg*. She now lives in London, where she writes and paints.

MARTHA COLLINS's third collection of poems, *A History of Small Life on a Windy Planet*, won the Alice Fay Di Castagnola Award and was published by the University of Georgia in 1993. She teaches at the University of Massachusetts-Boston, where she founded and co-directs the Creative Writing Program.

KATE CULKIN grew up in Denver, went to college in Vermont, and currently lives in New York City. She loves cars, lipstick, and shoes, not necessarily in that order.

EMILY DICKINSON (1831–1886) wrote 1,775 poems and fragments that have had an enormous influence on twentieth-century poetry.

KALIA DONER is a New York-based writer of nonfiction books and slightly fictionalized recollections of her misspent Midwestern youth.

MAGGIE DUBRIS is a poet, novelist, musician, and paramedic. She received the 1994 Margolis Award for poetry and was co-recipient of a 1994 NEA grant for Opera/Musical Theater. She is currently finishing a novel, *Skels*, and works full time as a medic in New York City's 911 system.

LYNN EMANUEL is the author of two books of poetry, *Hotel Fiesta* and *The Dig*. She has been the recipient of two NEA Fellowships, the National Poetry Series Award, and two Pushcart Prizes. With

David St. John she was poetry editor for the 1994–95 *Pushcart Prize Anthology*. Her work appears in the 1995 edition of *The Best American Poetry*, edited by Richard Howard. She is currently a professor at the University of Pittsburgh.

EDNA FERBER (1887–1968) won the Pulitzer Prize for *So Big* in 1924. Other novels include *Show Boat, Giant,* and *Cimarron.* Among the plays she wrote with George S. Kaufman are *Stage Door* and *Dinner at Eight.*

SUSAN FIRER's most recent book of poems, *The Lives of the Saints and Everything,* won the 1993 Cleveland State University Poetry Center Prize and the Posner Award. She has new work forthcoming in the *Iowa Review* and *Prairie Schooner.*

CHERYL FISH has published poems in journals and anthologies and is the author of *Wing Span* and *My City Flies By.* She is currently co-editing a book of African-American travel narratives for Beacon Press and teaching at Nassau Community College.

PATTY LOU FLOYD grew up in Duncan, Oklahoma, with a five-year hiatus in San Diego. Returning from the land of bays and beaches and mountains to the Oklahoma of the Dust Bowl, followed by her mother's illness and death, Duncan became for her the very symbol of loss, of her own and of all the lost, wasted lives around her in that blighted land.

JUDY GOLDMAN's poems have appeared in *Kenyon Review, Prairie Schooner,* the *Gettysburg Review, Southern Review,* and elsewhere. Her books are *Holding Back Winter* and *Wanting to Know the End.* She lives in Charlotte, North Carolina.

KATHARINE HARER ran Small Press Traffic Literary Arts Center in San Francisco and has worked with the California Poets in the Schools Program. Her poetry has been published in magazines, anthologies, and the small press collections *Spring Cycle, In These Bodies, The Border,* and *Hubba Hubba.*

NORMA HARRS was born and raised in Ireland. She came to Canada as a young woman, where she married and raised two sons. She has performed on the professional stage, been a free-lance broadcaster and writer working for the CBC and various newspapers, written four plays, published in literary journals in Canada and the U.S., and been a winner twice in the *Toronto Star* short-story contest and a finalist four times in the CBC literary contest. She is currently working on a new play and a collection of short stories.

British-born LESLEY HAZLETON drives fast cars, flies slow planes, and writes on a houseboat in Seattle. Her books include *Jerusalem, Jerusalem* (1986), *Confessions of a Fast Woman* (1992), and *Everything Women Always Wanted to Know about Cars* (1995).

ELOISE KLEIN HEALY has published four books of poetry: *Building Some Changes, A Pacet Beating Like a Heart, Ordinary Wisdom,* and *Artemis in Echo Park,* which was nominated for a Lambda Literary Award. She is the director of the MFA in Writing Program at Anti-och University Los Angeles.

JOSEPHINE JACOBSEN served two years as Poetry Consultant to the Library of Congress. Her collected poems, *In the Crevice of Time* (The Johns Hopkins Press, 1996), won the William Carlos Williams Award.

HETTIE JONES is the author of *How I Became Hettie Jones* (Viking Penguin), a memoir of the "beat" 1950s and 1960s, as well as numerous books for children and young adults, including an ALA Notable, *The Trees Stand Shining* (Dial), and the award-winning *Big Star Fallin' Mama (Five Women in Black Music)* (Viking). Her poems have appeared most recently in *Hanging Loose* and *Long Shot* and her stories in *Frontiers*. She teaches writing at Parsons School of Design, the 92nd Street Y, and the New York State Correctional Facility for Women at Bedford Hills.

VIVETTE J. KADY was born in South Africa and has lived in Toronto since 1976. Her fiction has appeared in numerous journals and magazines and in the anthology *Best Canadian Stories*.

ANNA KAVAN (1904–1968) was the author of *Asylum Piece & Other Stories, Ice, Julia & the Bazooka, A Scarcity of Love*.

LINDA KITTELL has been a part-time temporary instructor at Washington State University for twelve years, giving new meaning to the term "temporary." She lives in Troy, Idaho, with her husband, Ron Goble, and their daughter, Jessi Linder.

MARY A. KONCEL is a writing instructor and freelance writer. Her prose poems have appeared in several journals, including the *Massachusetts Review*, the *Denver Quarterly*, and the *Prose Poem: An International Journal*. She lives in Worthington, Massachusetts.

KAREN LATUCHIE has published stories in the *Paris Review, Southwest Review, Other Voices, Gulf Coast, Confrontation*, and *Street Songs 1: New Voices in Fiction*. She received a New York Foundation for the Arts fellowship in fiction in 1991. She lives, works, and drives in New York City.

MARCIA LAWTHER lives in New York City and is an editor at *In Style* magazine. Her poems have appeared in *Blueline, Caliban, Margin, Wesleyan*, and other publications.

Dame ROSE MACAULAY (1881–1958) was one of the most popular novelists of her day, author of some thirty-nine books of fiction, poetry, essays and criticism, including *The Towers of Trebizond, Told by an Idiot, The World My Wilderness*, and *The Shadow Flies*. *The Fabled Shore* was written after a solo trip taken when she was in her late sixties.

CAROL MASTERS is a poet and fiction writer. Her first collection of short stories, *The Peace Terrorist*, (New Rivers Press, 1994), was a

Minnesota Voices winner. She and her husband and sons (two, tall) and dog (now deceased) have loved car camping in Volkswagens (Rabbit, Golf). Well, maybe the dog didn't.

PANSY MAURER-ALVAREZ was born in Puerto Rico, grew up and was educated in Pennsylvania, and has lived in Europe since 1973. Her poetry has appeared in numerous publications in France, the U.K., and the U.S. *Dolores: The Alpine Years,* which includes "This Sure Isn't the Pennsylvania Turnpike," is her first full-length collection. She lives in Paris and Zurich and writes full-time.

FREYA MANFRED has taught at the University of South Dakota and on the Rosebud Indian Reservation, been a poet in the schools in New England, the Midwest, and California, and a poetry consultant for National Public Radio's "Good Evening" with Noah Adams, and received a National Endowment for the Arts fellowship and residencies at Yaddo and MacDowell. Her books include *A Goldenrod Will Grow, Yellow Squash Woman,* and *American Roads.*

GAIL MAZUR is author of three books of poetry, *Nightfire, The Pose of Happiness,* and *The Common* (University of Chicago Press, 1995). She lives in Cambridge, Massachusetts, where she teaches and is the founding director of the Blacksmith House Poetry Center.

DENISE McCLUGGAGE has spent four decades with cars as a racer, writer, and photographer. She began writing about them as a sports reporter for the *New York Herald Tribune,* and has also written for *Road & Track, Car and Driver,* and *Motor Trend.* She is the only woman to have ever won the prestigious Ken Purdy Award for Excellence in Automotive Journalism.

LOUISE McNEILL (1911–1993) was the prize-winning author of many books including *Paradox Hill: From Appalachia to Lunar Shore, The Milkweed Ladies, Fermi Buffalo, Time Is Our House, Gauley Mountain,* and *Hill Daughter: New & Selected Poems.*

JEREDITH MERRIN teaches literature and creative writing at Ohio State University and is the author of *An Enabling Humility: Marianne Moore, Elizabeth Bishop and the Uses of Tradition* (Rutgers University Press, 1990), and *Shift*, a book of lyric poetry in the Phoenix Poets Series of the University of Chicago Press, 1996.

LINDA MIZEJEWSKI is an associate professor of English at Ohio State University.

EILEEN MYLES's most recent book is *Maxfield Parrish: early & new poems* (Black Sparrow, 1995). A collection of stories, *Chelsea Girls* (Black Sparrow), came out the year before. She is the co-editor (with Liz Kotz) of *The New Fuck You/adventures in lesbian reading* (Semiotext(e) 1995), which won a Lambda Literary Award in 1996. She lives in New York and is currently writing a novel.

ELINOR NAUEN's books include *Cars and other poems, Diamonds Are a Girl's Best Friend: Women Writers on Baseball* (Faber and Faber, 1994), and *American Guys* (Hanging Loose, 1996). She has published poetry and fiction in many literary magazines. She often has crushes on mechanics and once did a valve job on a '54 Ford pickup named Leroy.

LESLEÁ NEWMAN is the author of twenty books and the editor of five anthologies. Her titles include *Writing from the Heart, Every Woman's Dream, The Femme Mystique,* and *Heather Has Two Mommies.* "Have Femme Will Travel" is from a forthcoming book of humor entitled *Out of the Closet and Nothing to Wear* (Alyson Publications).

ALICE NOTLEY is the author of more than twenty books of poetry, including *At Night the States*, the double volume *Close to Me and Closer . . . (The Language of Heaven)* and *Désamère*, and *How Spring Comes*, a winner of the San Francisco Poetry Award. Her *Selected Poems* was published in 1993. She is the recipient of grants from the National Endowment for the Arts, the General Electric Foundation, and New York Foundation for the Arts. She lives in Paris.

FLANNERY O'CONNOR (1925–1964), winner of the 1971 National Book Award for *The Complete Stories*, also wrote *Everything That Rises Must Converge, The Violent Bear It Away, Wise Blood*, and *Mystery and Manners*.

MAUREEN OWEN hails from Graceville, Minnesota, and has lived for significant periods in California, Washington, Japan, New York, and, in recent years, Connecticut. Much of her time in those places has been taken up with writing poems in which, as Paul Hoover has written, "astonishing things quietly occur." Among her books are *No Travels Journal, Imaginary Income*, and *Zombie Notes*.

LINDA PASTAN's ninth book of poems, *An Early Afterlife*, has recently been issued in paperback by Norton.

JAYNE ANNE PHILLIPS is the author of two widely anthologized collections of short stories, *Black Tickets* and *Fast Lanes*, and two novels, *Machine Dreams* and *Shelter*. Her work has been translated into twelve languages.

MELISSA HOLBROOK PIERSON is the author of *The Perfect Vehicle: What It Is About Motorcycles* (forthcoming 1997 from W. W. Norton). She currently lives in Brooklyn with her husband, writer Luc Sante, and their border collie, Mercy.

EMILY POST (1873–1960) is best known for her books of advice on weddings, entertaining, guests and hosts, and other issues of etiquette.

ALEXIS QUINLAN is a freelance writer living in Santa Monica, California.

JOSEPHINE REDLIN was born and raised on a small farm in southeastern South Dakota, and in 1961 migrated to California. After raising a family, she returned to college, receiving an M.A. in English-Creative Writing from Fresno State in 1994. She won the

1992 Ernesto Trejo Prize (from the Academy of American Poets) at CSU-Fresno and a 1993 AWP Intro Award. Her poems have been published in *New England Review, Antioch Review,* the *Journal, Ploughshares, North Dakota Quarterly,* and the *Sun.*

ADRIENNE RICH is the author of more than fifteen books of poetry and four prose works, including *Blood, Bread, and Poetry, Collected Early Poems: 1950–1970, An Atlas of the Difficult World: Poems 1988–1991,* and most recently, *Dark Fields of the Republic, Poems 1991–95.* She is the co-winner of the National Book Award and the recipient of a MacArthur Fellowship.

ELISAVIETTA RITCHIE's *Flying Time: Stories & Half-Stories* contains four PEN Syndicated Fiction winners. Her poetry collections include *The Arc of the Storm, Elegy for the Other Woman: New & Collected Terribly Female Poems,* and *Wild Garlic: The Journal of Maria X.* She also edited *The Dolphin's Arc: Poems on Endangered Creatures of the Sea.* Her poems have appeared in *Poetry, American Scholar,* the *New York Times, Christian Science Monitor,* and other publications.

PAULA SHARP is the author of *The Woman Who Was Not All There, The Imposter, Lost in Jersey City,* and *Crows Over a Wheatfield.*

OONA SHORT writes for television, theater, and magazines, and is currently at work on a novel. Her learner's permit expires in July, 1999.

PATTI SMITH is a poet and musician, with several important albums to her credit, including *Horses, Radio Ethiopa,* and *Easter,* and the recent books *The Coral Sea* and *Early Work: 1970–1979.* She lives in Michigan with her two children, Jackson and Jesse.

DEANNE STILLMAN is a contributing writer at *Los Angeles Magazine.* She has written for the *Los Angeles Times Magazine,* the *New York Times Magazine,* the *Village Voice,* and many other publications, as well as for television. Her recent adaptation of *Antigone* for the

Hudson Guild Theater in Los Angeles won a 1995 Dramalogue Award for best production. She is currently writing a book for Avon called *The Murders in Twentynine Palms.*

MARGARET C. SZUMOWSKI was a Peace Corps volunteer in Africa and has taught English and theater in Zaire, Ethiopia, the Rio Grande Valley of Texas, Wisconsin, and, currently, Massachusetts. She is the author of the chapbook *Ruby's Café* (Devil's Milhopper Press at the University of South Carolina, 1993) and *The Paradise Stamp.* Her poems have appeared in *American Poetry Review, River Styx, Calyx,* the *Agni Review, Poetry East,* and other publications.

ANNE WALDMAN is the author of more than thirty books of poetry, including, most recently, *Kill or Cure* (Penguin), *Iovis* (Coffee House), *Songs of the Sons and Daughters of Buddha* (translations with Andrew Schelling, Shambhala Publications), and *Fast-Speaking Woman* (twentieth anniversary edition, City Lights). She edited *The Beat Book* and *Disembodied Poetics: Annals of the Jack Kerouac School,* is a co-winner of the 1996 Shelley Memorial Award, directed the Poetry Project at St. Mark's Church-in-the-Bowery, and co-founded (with Allen Ginsberg) the Jack Kerouac School of Disembodied Poetics at the Naropa Institute, where she still teaches.

VIOLA WEINBERG lives in Sacramento, California, where she is producer of a weeknight PBS news magazine. She has written three books of poetry and recently won the Mayor's Award for lifetime achievement in the literary arts. She is at work on a collection of short stories, *The No Bull Ranch.*

EUDORA WELTY was born in Jackson, Mississippi, which is still her home. Her books include *The Optimist's Daughter* (awarded a Pulitzer Prize in 1972), *Delta Wedding, The Eye of the Story, Collected Stories,* and *One Writer's Beginning.*

EDITH WHARTON (1862–1937) was born into an old, wealthy New York family. The recipient of the Cross of the Legion of Honor, she lived in Paris from 1913 to her death. Among her forty-plus books of fiction, war reportage, and travel are the novels *The Age of Innocence, House of Mirth,* and *Ethan Frome. A Motor-Flight Through France* was published in 1908.

JOY WILLIAMS has written three novels and two collections of short stories and is the recipient of the Strauss Living Award from the American Academy.

Acknowledgments

THANK YOU, THANK YOU: Jill Amadio, Jean Hastings Ardell, Steve Baal, Harriet Barlow (and the Saab), Blue Mountain Center and staff, Mary Bisbee-Beek, Anselm Berrigan, Sarah Chalfant, Valerie Cimino, Tom Coppock, Kate Culkin, Kalia Doner, Maggie Dubris, Ed Friedman, Bonnie Goldman, Jim Gorzelany, Lesley Hazleton, Richard Hell, Eloise Klein Healy, Sheila Kinney, Linda Kittel, Jimmy "Beau" Kousar, Jack LeVert, Greg Masters, Denise McCluggage, Peter Miller, Charlie Nauen, Lindsay Nauen, Murat Nemet-Nejat, Alexandra Neil, Jeff Posternak, Joanna Rakoff, the indefatigable Elisavietta Ritchie, Annie Silverman, Dan Simon, Johnny "Jsen" Stanton, Ben Strader for the title, Steve Willis for letting me learn to drive a stick on his car, Betsy Uhrig, Diane Umansky, Chuck Wachtel, and the inspector at South Dakota Motor Vehicles who passed me even though I (age sixteen) ran ("rolled") a stop sign.

In addition, grateful acknowledgment is made to the following for permission to reprint material copyrighted or controlled by them:

Jill Amadio for "Run, Rabbit, Run" first published in slightly different form in Gannett Newspapers' Westchester Rockland group including the *White Plains Reporter Dispatch*, October 11, 1975 © 1996 by Jill Amadio. By permission of the author.

Dorothy Barresi for "Vacation, 1969" from *All of the Above*, 1991 (Beacon Press) © 1991 by Dorothy Barresi. By permission of Beacon Press, Boston.

L. R. Berger for "Driving into Rapture" from the *American Literary Review* Vol. vi Number 1 Spring 95 © 1995 by L. R. Berger. By permission of the author.

Lisa Bernstein for "Apricots" from *Bastard Review* 1990 No. 3/4 © 1990 by Lisa Bernstein (Lisa B). By permission of the author.

Debra Bruce-Kinnebrew for "First Ticket" from *Pure Daughter* (University of Arkansas Press) © 1983 by Debra Bruce-Kinnebrew. By permission of the author.

Carolyn Cassady for "Cars I Have Known" © 1996 by Carolyn Cassady. By permission of the author.

ing the Oil" from *Artemis in Echo Park* (Firebrand Books, 1991) © 1991 by Eloise Klein Healy. By permission of the author.

Josephine Jacobsen for "Country Drive-in" from *The Chinese Insomniacs* (University of Pennsylvania Press, 1981) © 1981 by Josephine Jacobsen. By permission of the author.

Hettie Jones for "Paleface" and "Ode to My Car" © 1996 by Hettie Jones. By permission of the author.

Vivette J. Kady for "Lessons in Steering" © 1996 by Vivette J. Kady. By permission of the author.

Anna Kavan, "World of Heroes" from *Julia and the Bazooka* (Peter Owen) © 1970 by Anna Kavan. By permission of Harold Ober Associates.

Linda Kittell for "Michael" © 1996 by Linda Kittell. By permission of the author.

Mary A. Koncel for "The Big Deep Voice of God" from *The Prose Poem: An International Journal*, 1994 © 1994 by Mary A. Koncel. By permission of the author.

Karen Latuchie for a section of "Counting Backward" © 1996 by Karen Latuchie. By permission of the author.

Marcia Lawther for "Driving the Central Valley" from *South Coast Poetry Journal* Spring/Fall No. 7, 1989 © 1989 by Marcia Lawther. By permission of the author.

From *Fabled Shore: From the Pyrenees to Portugal* by Rose Macaulay © 1949 by Rose Macaulay. First published 1949 by Hamish Hamilton; issued as an Oxford University Press paperback 1986. Reprinted by permission of the Peters Fraser & Dunlop Group Ltd.

Freya Manfred for "American Roads" from *American Roads*, The Overlook Press, Inc. © 1979 by The Overlook Press. By permission of the author.

Carol Masters for "hwy 30" © 1996 by Carol Masters. By permission of the author.

Pansy Maurer-Alvarez for "This Sure Isn't the Pennsylvania Turnpike" from *Dolores: The Alpine Years* (Hanging Loose Press, 1996) © 1996 by Pansy Maurer-Alvarez. By permission of the author.

Jayne Anne Phillips for "Fast Lanes" from *Fast Lanes* (Dutton; Washington Square Press) © 1987 by Jayne Anne Phillips. By permission of the author.

Melissa Holbrook Pierson for "On Two Wheels" © 1996 by Melissa Holbrook Pierson. By permission of the author.

Alexis Quinlan for "The Length of a State" © 1996 by Alexis Quinlan.

Josephine Redlin for "All the Carefully Measured Seconds" from *Ploughshares* Vol. 21 No. 1 © 1995 by Josephine Redlin. By permission of the author.

"Song" from *Diving into the Wreck: Poems 1971–1972* by Adrienne Rich. Copyright © 1973 by W. W. Norton & Company, Inc. Reprinted by permission of the author and W. W. Norton & Company, Inc.

Elisavietta Ritchie for "Why some nights I go to bed without undressing" from *Full Moon, Empty Window Review* 1984, the anthology *Out of Season*, 1993 and the collection *The Arc of the Storm* (Signal Books, 1996) © 1996 by Elisavietta Ritchie. By permission of the author.

Paula Sharp for "A Meeting on the Highway" from *The Imposter* (HarperCollins) © 1991 by Paula Sharp. By permission of Gina Mccoby Literary Agency. Originally published in *The Threepenny Review*.

Oona Short for "One of Life's Passengers" © 1996 by Oona Short. By permission of the author.

"ballad of a bad boy" from *Early Work: 1970–1979* by Patti Smith. Copyright © 1994 by Patti Smith. Reprinted by permission of W. W. Norton & Company, Inc.

Deanne Stillman for "You Should Have Been Here an Hour Ago" as it appeared onstage in the National Lampoon Revue at the Williamstown Theater Festival, July 1990 © by Deanne Stillman. By permission of the author.

Margaret C. Szumowski for "Born Again at the Golden Nozzle" from the *Massachusetts Review*, 1989, and *Ruby's Café* (Devil's Milhopper Press, USC, 1991) © 1989 by Margaret C. Szumowski, and "Wild Women on Motorcycles" from *Earth's Daughters* Vol. No. 37, 1991, and *Ruby's Café* (Devil's Milhopper Press, USC, 1991) © 1991 by Margaret C. Szumowski. By permission of the author.